M.E.S. School Readiness Curriculum
Edition 1

Marvin Dutton

Marvin's Education Services LLC.

www.marvinseducationservices.com

Copyright 2016

All rights reserved. No part of this work may be reproduced or transmitted in any form or by any means, electronic or mechanical, including, photocopying, or by any information storage or retrieval system, except as is explicitly permitted by the Copyright Art or in writing by the author.

ISBN-13:
978-0997517309

ISBN-10:
0997517301

www.marvinseducationservices.com

The M.E.S. Readiness Curriculum Edition 1 is a valuable resource for parents and education providers. It is a 34 week intervention plan for students in grades Pre-K through 3rd grade that equips students with important foundational skills. Students learn various skills including letter identification, letter sounds, print concepts, phonemic awareness, rote counting, rational counting and much more. The curriculum was created for our target population to address educational gaps that exist in the community and their specific needs in producing better outcomes.

Dear Guardian/Educational Provider,

Thank you for your decision to invest in to our children. This book contains guides and lesson plans that will help guide your instruction and your daily schedule. The School Readiness Curriculum was launched in an effort to provide you with an educational resource for your child/children. M.E.S. is here to provide any necessary training as it relates to the usage of this curriculum guide. We are partners now and together we will change the world.

Suggestions for using this book

- Remember to use this book as a resource for your daily lesson planning. Continue to write your own lesson plans

- This edition has 34 lessons that could be used on a weekly basis. Please look forward to the upcoming editions that will contain daily lesson plans

- Please call M.E.S. with any follow up questions. We can be reached at 267-575-3547 or 267-475-0658

Week 1

Time: 9:00- 12:00

Focus: To establish a baseline for all students in ELA and Math. To welcome & get to know students.

Objective: Student will be able to:
- complete assessment to their academic level and establish baseline to begin tutoring from.
- identify each other by name & get to know a fact about peers.

Materials:
Assessment: Concepts about Print
Website:
http://readingandwritingproject.com/public/resources/assessments/reading/concepts_about_print/concepts_about_print_directions.pdf
rules & procedures & schedule must be displayed in the room, name tags pre-written with student names (be sure there is blank space around the name for students to decorate), construction paper or story paper (based on the read aloud that you choose to do= see options below), read aloud book (see options below), a teacher All About Me pre-made bag, timer, inflatable ball or some other object to pass

ELA Lessons:
I do: Teacher will read the directions for the Concepts about Print Assessment that will be administered to students on the first day.
The teacher will gather students together in one large circle. Explain that we will play the Name Game so that everyone, including the teacher can become familiar with everyone's name. Here are the rules: I will say the letters in the alphabet, when I say the letter that your name begins with you will stand up and tell us your name. For example, if you name is Dominique, when I say the letter D, you will stand up and say Dominique. If more than one person stands up, then we'll start with one person and the next will go. Ready!? Let's begin. The teacher will begin saying the ABC's. Be sure to stop when your letter is said too.

We do: Students will play the Name Game. If time permits and the teacher feel the class is still attentive and ready play again but this time when a student stands up have the class say the students name instead of the student telling the class.

I do: The teacher must go over the rules (protocols) and procedures (routine) of the class with students. Be sure that the rules are clear, concise and no more than 5 written down. That is realistically what students will remember. This should not take more than 10-15 mins!! This will set a positive, structured tone in your room & is very important. Or break into two sessions. Talk about rules now and procedures after the read aloud.

We/You do: Decorate a name tag. Teacher will provide students with name tags that have their name pre-written on them. Students will have 10 minutes to decorate the name tags however they want. Be sure to tell students that we must still be able to read the name so don't color over it.

Read Aloud: Choices based on library selection: The Kissing Hand by: Audrey Penn, A Bad Case of Stripes by: David Shannon, No David by: David Shannon, Wemberly Worried by: Kevin Henkes or How I Spent My Summer Vacation by: Mark Teague

Based on read aloud selection: *The Kissing Hand* or *Wemberly Worried*: Once finished reading the teacher will ask how many students felt nervous/worried about coming here today or miss their family right now? Have 1-2 students express how they are feeling. Activity: Teacher will have students create a card for the person or for their family simply saying "I Love You" and address it to the person.
A Bad Case of Stripes: Once finished reading the teacher will ask students to describe how Camilla was feeling throughout the story. Allow students to connect to the feeling as they think of a time someone laughed at them or bullied/hurt them. The teacher will then explain that each person is different, it can be based on how we look, talk, eat, wear, act, like, etc. But it's important to respect each person's differences and not hurt them because of it.
Activity: Have students think of something that they like. Then on construction paper, students will draw themselves doing, eating, wearing, something that they like. At the top of the paper students will write the word RESPECT in uppercase letters and write their names at the bottom. Display in the room under a title/heading of We Respect Our Differences.
No David: Once finished reading the teacher will ask students how many of them have gotten in trouble at home for something that they did. How did it you feel after or while you were in trouble? Have 1-2 students express how they were feeling. The teacher will explain that even though we get in trouble its important to know that while that person may be upset with you at the moment, they will care about you.
Activity: Have students draw a time they were doing something that got them in trouble. At the top of the paper students will write No _____ and their name.
How I Spent My Summer Vacation: Once finished reading the teacher will ask students what is one thing they did over summer vacation? Have 2-3 students share aloud ONE thing they did.
Activity: Have students pick one thing that they did over summer vacation and on story paper students will illustrate the one thing they did. For younger students (pre-k & early Kinder) have students tell you about the picture in one sentence starting with This summer I ___. Write the sentence down on the lines that they told you. Visually seeing what they said in writing helps promote writing for them!! Extension for older students: On the lines have students write a sentence or two telling what they did. Inventive spelling (sound out) is highly encouraged! Teachers: don't spell every single word for students!

I do: The teacher must go over the procedures (routine) of the class with students. Be sure that the procedures are clear & concise. Model them, especially if its where you want students to place their belongings when they walk in the room. How we get materials, where things go, how to pack-up and line up to go somewhere, etc. This should not take more than 10-15 mins!! This will set a positive, structured tone in your room & is very important.

Bathroom Break!

I do: All About the teacher: It is important that students know a little about you as well. In a bag place a few items that you can share with students so that they know a little of who you are. Possible ideas: pic of fav food, fav color, family pic, a book, toy, memorabilia from somewhere, etc. As you take an item from a bag share with students what it means. Some students may relate to what you are sharing.

Math: 11:00-11:30

I do: Teacher will gather students together to play a game (this is also a pre-assessment to check how many students know their numbers). Take an inflatable ball or some other object. Explain to students that we're going to play a number game and we're going to try to beat the timer! The game works like this, the person who starts off with the ball (object) will say the number 1 and then pass (not throw) the object to the next person & they will say 2 and pass the obj. That person will say 3 and so on and so on. When the obj gets back to the person it started they will keep counting & say the next number. We keep going around until someone says the wrong number. Once that happens we have start over. The idea is to see how far we get counting each time & if we do it faster each time to beat the timer. The timer will be set on 3 mins. But we'll do one practice round first to make sure everyone knows how to play. You have to pay attention so you know when it's your turn & what number to say!

We/You do: Begin the practice round. Once the teacher feel as though students understand, set the timer to 3 minutes and begin.

Match Back to School Activity Sheet pgs 7 & 8 (see Appendix.) Have students work on completing the tracing and sorting numbers from letters activity sheets.

Closing Activity: (11:35-11:45)
1. Gather students together for a closing activity game on the projector & computer. Choices include Reading Eggs (if accessible) or an ABC game on Starfall.com

DEAR (Drop Everything And Read) (11:45-11:57)

Week 2 (9:00-12:00)

ELA Focus/Skill: Alphabet (both lower & upper cases) & Title of books
Sound Words: Africa
Sight Words: Student's names, the, no, is, can
Big Book: ABC Flip Chart (Poems & Songs) or "Alphabet Rescue" by Audrey Wood
Writing Focus: What's an Author?
Math Focus: Numbers 1-5

Objectives: Students will be able to:
- repeat and identify the day, weather and season
- repeat the letters of the alphabet sequentially
- identify the letters of the alphabet in both upper & lower case forms
- locate and identify the title in a text
- identify sight words & use in context
- participate and repeat the songs and/or poems from shared read focused on the alphabet
- describe the author's role in texts
- repeat, identify, represent and write the numbers 1-5 using manipulative

Materials:
"All About Today" pocket chart, ABC Flip Chart or "Alphabet Rescue", white lap boards, dry erase markers, board erasers, magnetic alphabet letters, play doh, chart paper with sight words pre-written, index cards with (the, no, is can pre-written on them), handwriting sheets with sight words pre-written once (www.handwritingworksheets.com), handwriting sheets with the numbers 1-5 written twice numerically, post-its, Instant Learning Centers: Letter Recognition and Beginning Sounds, hand writing paper with picture space and the pre-written sentence frame: This summer I __., crayons, pencils, erasers, bear & circle counters, projector & computer

ELA
Whole Group: Morning Meeting/Shared Read: (9:00- 9:15)
1. Students will gather together for Morning Meeting where the teacher will model how to use the "All About Today" pocket chart. The teacher will read the information on the pocket chart, using a pointer, starting with the month, date and year using the sentence frame "Today is __." Next have the students repeat the sentence. After that the teacher will continue on with the pocket chart moving to "Yesterday was __." Students will repeat each section after the teacher has pointed and read it aloud. Then teacher will read aloud the objectives for the day, briefly explaining that this is what the goal is by the end of their time together (Use academic language). If extra time, have 1-2 students share something exciting or important news about themselves.

2. (9:15-9:45) I do: Teacher will begin with singing or saying the ABC and encourage students to join in. Next the teacher should open to a poem or song and read aloud to students from the ABC Flip Chart. Or Next the teacher will point and read aloud the title "Alphabet Rescue" and the author Audrey Wood. After that begin reading the story aloud. While reading stop periodically and have students identify which letter they see on the pages, DO NOT stop at every single page, just periodically.
3. *We do*: Then discuss what was happening in the book using the key words first or beginning, middle, and last or at the end. Encourage students to use the key words or terms
4. (5-7 mins max) Review the letters of the alphabet. Show with the magnetic letter or write on white board or chart paper a letter and have students identify the letter. Extension- have students think of a word that begins with the letter.
5. *You do*: Model first; students will break into two small groups. Group 1 will use white lap boards and magnetic letters. Have the student choose a letter, say it, trace it and write it next to it. Group 2 will choose a letter, say it and then take play doh and try to create the letter.
6. *Exit Ticket*: The teacher will choose a letter of the alphabet and write it on the board. Next the teacher will say the incorrect letter. Have students show a silent thumb up if the teacher said the correct letter or a thumb down if the teacher said the wrong letter. Teacher will do a quick scan of the responses, noting any student that showed the incorrect response and then have hands down.

Sight & Sound Words: (9:45-10:15)
1. Have students gather together. The teacher will display the chart paper with the sight words & sound word pre-written on it. Next the teacher will explain that "these words are called sight words and knowing these words will help make you a better reader."
2. *I do*: Teacher will lead a call and response where the teacher will repeat the first word, a student name, while pointing to it and students will repeat it. Continue down the list one time.
3. Next repeat down the list but challenge students to move faster with the teacher still speaking the word first and students repeating clearly. Repeat once more but this time the students will say the words and the teacher will not lead.
4. After that the teacher will slowly say the Sound word: Africa (Ah-fr-i-Ka). Students will repeat the word. If there is a map in the room, the teacher will point to where Africa is located.
5. *We do*: 4 Corners Game- Teacher will place the index cards with the 4 sight words other than the student's names in 4 different corners of the room. Rules of the game: the teacher or leader of the game will say one of the words on the index cards. The players will have 10 seconds to go over to that 'corner' that has the word. Anyone who is at the wrong 'corner' is out.
6. Students and teacher will play the game for 4-5 rounds.
7. *You do*: Handwriting practice. Students will practice writing the sight words on pre-printed handwriting sheets.
8. Exit Ticket: The teacher will write "can" on the board. Have students stand up if they can say the word. Teacher should do a quick scan and note down who is and is not standing. Then on the count of 3 have the students standing say the word written on the board aloud.

Bathroom Break: (10:15-10:20)
Small Groups/Guided Reading: (10:20-10:45)
Small groups should not be larger than 5 students and smaller than 2.

1. Teacher MUST model and go over small group activities and protocols before you send students in groups! Students must work on the assigned task at their group! Students must ask their group questions first if unclear before asking teacher. Students must remain in their small group space unless they are getting another activity for their group or cleaning up. Bathroom, water, etc is not allowed during groups. Students must use whisper voice when talking in groups. Actual student group time will be shorter the first month or so until students become acclimated to the expectations and routines of small group work.
2. *Small Group 1: Guided reading.* In this group the teacher will begin by first reviewing depending on the level of the students either the alphabets or the sight words introduced earlier that day. For alphabets: on individual white lap boards have students write the letter that you name. You can use magnetic letters so students have a reference to what it looks like if needed. For sight words: using the index cards from the 4 Corners game, show the card and have students state the word on the card. Extensions~ have students write the word on white lap boards or use in sentences. Then move into the text that day. Again depending on the level of the students: choose a text close to their level. Teacher will go over the title of the books and the author. Preview the text by looking through the book and making a prediction what the text may be about based on the pictures, title and cover. Teacher must model to students how to use the sentence frame "I predict __ because __." when making a prediction statement to the group about the text or anything. Next have students make predictions about the book using the sentence frame. Then the teacher will either choose to Echo read (you point and read a page at a time and have them repeat you) or Round Robin read (each student reads a page and you go around the group) and begin reading the text together. Once finished reading, briefly discuss the text, what was it about, who was in it: focus on using the key words beginning, middle and end of the story. After that based on what the focus was before reading the text have the students 'hunt' for the sight words or letters in story. Write down each one found on the white lap boards and then share once the students in the group are finished 'hunting'.
3. *Small Group 2 & 3*: Students will use instant learning center kits. Teacher will choose the 2 focused on Letter Recognition & Beginning Sounds. Teacher will MODEL/demonstrate how to use the center kits.

Writing Workshop: (10:45- 11:00)
1. *I/We do*: (6 mins max) The teacher will use the shared reading book or chart used earlier that morning and point and say the author's name. The teacher will then ask if anyone can describe or tell what the author's job is. The teacher will select 2-3 students to share thoughts (do not select more than 3 because answers will begin to repeat).
2. Based on student responses the teacher will explain to students that the author's think of and write the stories. Some author's write many books while some write 1 or 2 books.
3. (If accessible: show other books written by Audrey Wood such as "Silly Sally," "Quick as a Cricket" and others here on the link http://www.audreywood.com/books-written-by-don,-bruce,-and-audrey-wood/all-books-written-and-illustrated-by-the-woods Also the website can be shown using a projector if possible.
4. *You do*: The teacher will then explain to students that each one of them is an author as well. Each time they write and draw something, a sentence, a short story, an idea they are doing some part of what an author that writes and

publishes books do. Today they will think about something they did over the summer and draw it. Then using the sentence frame "This summer I ___." The students will tell/write about their picture. The teacher must walk around and promote inventive spelling (where students try to write it on their own first) and then underneath the teacher writes/spells words correctly.
5. If time remains the teacher will select 2-3 students to share their picture and sentence.

Math: (11:00-11:30)
1. Students will gather together and the teacher will begin counting from 1-10 and show the number with fingers. Encourage students to join in.
2. *I/We do*: Teacher will focus on the numbers 1-5. Teacher will first write the number 1 on the board and then say it. Next write the number 2 on the board and say that. Continue to the number 5. Next the teacher will point to and sequentially repeat all 5 numbers and have students repeat.
3. After that the teacher will take the Bear Counters and display 1 bear. Ask students how many bears to do they see? What number is that? Have a student answer. Teacher will repeat with 3 bears and have a student identify how many bears they see and can students point to which number that is. The teacher will repeat until they have gone through all five numbers.
4. Then the teacher will model how to write each number, step by step. On the board the teacher will begin with the number '1' and model and explain to students that the number one is a straight stick. The teacher will distribute white lap boards, markers and erasers to students. Students will then follow the directions from the model and write the number one on their boards. Underneath or next to the numbers have students draw the number of dots to represent the number. Raise the boards up to show their work.
5. The teacher will then model and explain how to write the number 2. The teacher will explain to begin on the dotted lines on line paper or begin and then hump back down, straight slanted line, stop at the bottom under where you started then trace the bottom like an "L". Students will follow the directions from the model and how to write the number two on their boards. Underneath or next to the numbers have students draw the number of dots to represent the number. Raise board up to show their work.
6. The teacher will then model and explain how to write the number 3. The teacher will explain & show to write the number three as a capital B without the line. Students will follow the directions from the model and how to write the number three on their boards. Underneath or next to the numbers have students draw the number of dots to represent the number. Raise board up to show their work.
7. The teacher will then model and explain how to write the number 4. The teacher will explain & show to write the number 4 with straight lines, beginning with a straight line half way down, then straight line to the right, and the longest line on the right. Students will follow the directions from the model and how to write the number four on their boards. Underneath or next to the numbers have students draw the number of dots to represent the number. Raise board up to show their work.
8. The teacher will then model and explain how to write the number 5. The teacher will explain & show to write the number 5 with straight line to the side, straight line down and then a bubble like a lower case B without closing it. Students will follow the directions from the model and how to write the number five on their boards. Underneath or next to the numbers have students draw the number of dots to represent the number. Raise board up to show their work.

9. *You do*: The teacher will give students the directions that they will work in small groups. Each group will receive a sheet with 5 boxes and each box numbered. As a group students will use the counters to represent each number in the box. The teacher will circulate the room to check each group's work. Once completed, each student will practice writing the numbers on the tracing sheet.
10. *Exit Ticket*: Teacher will say the number 4 and students will represent the number using their fingers. Teacher should take a scan around the room to observe which scholar is correct and incorrect. Record down.

Closing Activity: (11:30-11:45)
1. Gather students together for a closing activity game on the projector & computer. Choices include Reading Eggs (if accessible) or an ABC game on Starfall.com

DEAR (Drop Everything And Read) (11:47-11:57)

Week 3 (9:00-12:00)

ELA Focus/Skill: directionality & letter vs word
Phonics (letter/word family): /a/
Sound Words: apple
Sight Words: I, am, an, me, you
Big Book: Chicka Chicka Boom Boom by Bill Martin Jr.
Writing Focus: What is writing?
Math Focus: Numbers 6-10 & 1-10

Objectives: Students will be able to:
- repeat and identify the day, weather and season
- repeat the letters of the alphabet sequentially
- identify the letter /a/, it's sound and words that begin with /a/
- identify and describe the difference between a letter and word
- categorize words and letters
- identify sight words & use in context
- orally retell a story sequentially using the shared reading
- describe what is writing
- repeat, identify, represent and write the numbers 1-10 using manipulative

Materials:
"All About Today" pocket chart, "Chicka Chicka Boom Boom" big book, white lap boards, dry erase markers, board erasers, post-its, picture of an apple & an ant seperately or be prepared to draw one, coloring & tracing sheet (http://twistynoodle.com/a-words-2-coloring-page/block_outline/), chart paper with sight words pre-written, handwriting sheets with the numbers 1-5 written twice numerically (www.handwritingworksheets.com), index cards with sight-words pre-written on them, Instant Learning Centers: Letter Recognition, Beginning Sounds and Building words, hand writing story paper with picture space and the pre-written sentence frame: I am __., crayons, pencils, erasers, bear & circle counters, projector & computer

ELA
Whole Group: Morning Meeting/Shared Read: (9:00- 9:15)
1. Students will gather together for Morning Meeting where the teacher will model how to use the "All About Today" pocket chart. The teacher will read the information on the pocket chart, using a pointer, starting with the month, date and year using the sentence frame "Today is __." Next have the students repeat the sentence. After that the teacher will continue on with the pocket chart moving to "Yesterday was __." Students will repeat each section after the teacher has pointed and read it aloud. Then teacher will read aloud the objectives for the day, briefly explaining that this is what the goal is by the end of their time together (Use academic language). If extra time, have 1-2 students share something exciting or important news about themselves.

2. (9:15-9:45) *I do*: Teacher will begin with singing or saying the ABC and encourage students to join in. Next the teacher will point and read aloud the title "Chicka Chicka Boom Boom" and the author Bill Martin Jr as well as the illustrator Lois Ehlert. After that begin reading the story aloud. While reading stop periodically and have students identify which letter they see on the pages, DO NOT stop at every single page, just periodically.
3. *We do*: Then discuss what was happening in the book using the key words first or beginning, middle, and last or at the end. Encourage students to use the key words or terms
4. (5-7 mins max) Review the letters of the alphabet orally. The teacher will then focus in on the letter /a/. First write the letter on the board, bother upper case and lower (write clearly so students can see how to write both type of letters. Next the teacher will say the short /a/ sound and students will repeat. After that the teacher with draw or place a picture of an apple next to the letter. The teacher will then point and say A, ah (the /a/ sound), apple. Have students repeat as the teacher points to each. Repeat twice.
5. *You do*: Teacher will distribute a coloring sheet with pictures of words that begin with /a/. http://twistynoodle.com/a-words-2-coloring-page/block_outline/ Have students color in the pictures and letter as well as trace the words (ant, apple).
6. *Exit Ticket*: The teacher will show a picture of an ant on the board. Next the teacher will ask if this picture of an ant begins with /a/. Have students show a silent thumb up if it does or a thumb down if it does not. Teacher will do a quick scan of the responses, noting any student that showed the incorrect response and then have hands down.

Sight & Sound Words: (9:45-10:15)
1. Have students gather together. The teacher will display the chart paper with the sight words & sound word pre-written on it. Next the teacher will explain that "these words are called sight words and knowing these words will help make you a better reader."
2. *I do:* Teacher will lead a call and response where the teacher will repeat the first word, a student name, while pointing to it and students will repeat it. Continue down the list one time.
3. Next repeat down the list but challenge students to move faster with the teacher still speaking the word first and students repeating clearly. Repeat once more but this time the students will say the words and the teacher will not lead.
4. After that the teacher will slowly say the Sound word: apple (Ah-p-le). Students will repeat the word. Point to the picture of the apple previously used.
5. *We do:* Sight word Tic Tac Toe- Teacher will draw the tic tac toe board on the board. Then inside each box the teacher will write the new sight words just introduced and in the extra boxes the sight words from the previous week (no, the, is, can). The teacher will explain the game's rules briefly. There are 2 teams, the X and the O team. 1 player will get picked and they will pick where they want their letter (X or O) to go on the board. To get their spot the player must say the word in the box first. If the word is said correctly then the teacher or player will draw the letter in the box. If the word is incorrect then the next team goes. The first team to 3 in a row wins. The teacher will need to split the class into two teams.
6. Students and teacher will play the game for 2-3 rounds.
7. *You do:* Handwriting practice. Students will practice writing the sight words on pre-printed handwriting sheets.

8. *Exit Ticket:* The teacher will write "am" on the board. Have students stand up if they can say the word. Teacher should do a quick scan and note down who is and is not standing. Then on the count of 3 have the students standing say the word written on the board aloud.

Bathroom Break: (10:15-10:20)

Small Groups/Guided Reading: (10:20-10:45)

Small groups should not be larger than 5 students and smaller than 2.

1. Teacher MUST model and go over small group activities and protocols before you send students in groups! Students must work on the assigned task at their group! Students must ask their group questions first if unclear before asking teacher. Students must remain in their small group space unless they are getting another activity for their group or cleaning up. Bathroom, water, etc is not allowed during groups. Students must use whisper voice when talking in groups. Actual student group time will be shorter the first month or so until students become acclimated to the expectations and routines of small group work.

2. *Small Group 1:* Guided reading. In this group the teacher will begin by first reviewing depending on the level of the students either the alphabets or the sight words introduced earlier that day. For alphabets: on individual white lap boards have students write the letter that you name. You can use magnetic letters so students have a reference to what it looks like if needed. For sight words: using the index cards with the sight words pre-written on them, show the card and have students state the word on the card. Extensions~ have students write the word on white lap boards or use in sentences. Then move into the text that day. Again depending on the level of the students: choose a text close to their level. Teacher will go over the title of the books and the author. Preview the text by looking through the book and making a prediction what the text may be about based on the pictures, title and cover. Teacher must model to students how to use the sentence frame "I predict __ because __." when making a prediction statement to the group about the text or anything. Next have students make predictions about the book using the sentence frame. Then the teacher will either choose to Echo read (you point and read a page at a time and have them repeat you) or Round Robin read (each student reads a page and you go around the group) and begin reading the text together. Once finished reading, briefly discuss the text, what was it about, who was in it: focus on using the key words beginning, middle and end of the story. After that based on what the focus was before reading the text have the students 'hunt' for the sight words or letters in story. Write down each one found on the white lap boards and then share once the students in the group are finished 'hunting'.

3. *Small Group 2 & 3:* Students will use instant learning center kits. Teacher will choose the 2 focused on Letter Recognition, Beginning Sounds & Building Words. Teacher will MODEL/demonstrate how to use the center kits.

Writing Workshop: (10:45- 11:00)

1. *I do:* (6 mins max) The teacher will write the question "What is writing?" on the board. The teacher will then ask if anyone can describe or tell what is writing? The teacher will select 2-3 students to share thoughts (do not select more than 3 because answers will begin to repeat).

2. Based on student responses the teacher will explain to students that writing is the act of putting words on to paper or board. The words usually come together to tell something in what we call a sentence. A sentence is more than word put together to say something like I am a girl. The teacher should write the sentence on the board so students can see.

3. The teacher will then say another example can be He is sitting and write it on the board. Then ask students to help think of another sentence to write. Take 2-3 more suggestions. Write what the students say on the board but be sure it is telling something before you write it.
4. *You do:* The teacher will then explain to students that each one of them is an writer and author as well. Today they will think about something that tells/describe about them. The teacher will write the sentence frame "I am __" on the board and then ask students to help think or brainstorm ideas to fill in the sentence that describe themselves. The teacher should write the first idea of girl/boy. Have students suggest some other things such as tall, short, tall, sitting, standing, coloring, walking, etc). Then using the sentence frame "I am ___." The students will tell about themselves and then draw/color a picture to match. The teacher must walk around and promote inventive spelling (where students try to write it on their own first) and then underneath the teacher writes/spells words correctly.
5. If time remains the teacher will select 2-3 students to share their picture and sentence.

Math: (11:00-11:30)
1. Students will gather together and the teacher will begin counting from 1-10 and show the number with fingers. Encourage students to join in.
2. *I/We do*: Teacher will focus on the numbers 6-10. Teacher will first write the number 6 on the board and then say it. Next write the number 7 on the board and say that. Continue to the number 10. Next the teacher will point to and sequentially repeat all 5 numbers and have students repeat.
3. After that the teacher will take the Bear Counters and display 6 bears. Ask students how many bears to do they see? What number is that? Have a student answer. Teacher will repeat with 8 bears and have a student identify how many bears they see and can students point to which number that is. The teacher will repeat until they have gone through all five numbers.
4. Then the teacher will model how to write each number, step by step. On the board the teacher will begin with the number '6' and model and explain to students that the number six is two circles. The teacher will model and explain that you start off like you are making a circle except before you close the circle where you started you turn and go in towards the middle. The teacher will distribute white lap boards, markers and erasers to students. Students will then follow the directions from the model and write the number six on their boards. Underneath or next to the numbers have students draw the number of dots to represent the number. Raise the boards up to show their work.
5. The teacher will then model and explain how to write the number 7. The teacher will explain and show that to begin you will draw a straight line to the side and then a straight line slanted down. Students will follow the directions from the model and how to write the number seven on their boards. Underneath or next to the numbers have students draw the number of dots to represent the number. Raise board up to show their work.
6. The teacher will then model and explain how to write the number 8. The teacher will explain & show to write the number eight that you draw two circles on top of each other. Students will follow the directions from the model and how to write the number eight on their boards. Underneath or next to the numbers have students draw the number of dots to represent the number. Raise board up to show their work.

7. The teacher will then model and explain how to write the number 9. The teacher will explain & show to write the number nine you start of with a small circle and then draw a line on the right side straight down. Students will follow the directions from the model and how to write the number nine on their boards. Underneath or next to the numbers have students draw the number of dots to represent the number. Raise board up to show their work.

8. The teacher will then model and explain how to write the number 10. The teacher will explain & show to write the number 10 with two numbers, a 1 and a 0 next to each other. Students will follow the directions from the model and how to write the number five on their boards. Underneath or next to the numbers have students draw the number of dots to represent the number. Raise board up to show their work.

9. *You do*: The teacher will give students the directions that they will work in small groups. Each group will receive a sheet with 5 boxes and each box numbered. As a group, students will use the counters to represent each number in the box. The teacher will circulate the room to check each group's work. Once completed, each student will practice writing the numbers on the tracing sheet.

10. *Exit Ticket*: Teacher will say the number 8 and students will represent the number using their fingers. Teacher should take a scan around the room to observe which scholar is correct and incorrect. Record down.

Closing Activity: (11:30-11:45)

11. Gather students together for a closing activity game of Number Bingo.

DEAR (Drop Everything And Read) (11:45-11:57)

Week 4 (9:00-12:00)

ELA Focus/Skill: alliteration & letter vs number
Phonics (letter/word family): /b/ & -at
Sound Words: be, ball, blue
Sight Words: is, at, he, a, so, on
Big Book: Pat the Cat by Colin Hawkins
Writing Focus: Where is writing?
Math Focus: Numbers 1-10

Objectives: Students will be able to:
- repeat and identify the day, weather and season
- repeat the letters of the alphabet sequentially
- identify the letter /b/, it's sound and words that begin with /b/
- identify and sort words that begin with the same letters (alliteration)
- identify and name words in the –at word family
- identify and sort rhyming and non-rhyming words
- identify and describe the difference between a letter and a number
- identify sight words & use in context
- orally identify the sound words and speak phonetically
- orally retell a story sequentially using the shared reading
- locate where writing is found in a variety of locations
- repeat, identify, represent and write the numbers 1-10 using manipulative

Materials:
"All About Today" pocket chart, "Pat the Cat" big book, ABC flash cards, white lap boards, dry erase markers, board erasers, post-its, picture of a bat, play doh, activity sheet to use with the play doh, sheet protectors for the activity sheet, chart paper with sight words pre-written, handwriting sheets with the sight words written twice (www.handwritingworksheets.com), index cards with sight words pre-written on it, Instant Learning Centers: Letter Recognition, Beginning Sounds and Building words, hand writing story paper with picture space and the pre-written sentence frame: I see __., crayons, pencils, erasers, bear & circle counters, ten frames, math worksheet http://printables.scholastic.com/shop/prcontent/Count-and-Color-Counting-Groups-of-1-10-Objects-Math-Practice-Page/9780439553698-012, Number Bingo

ELA
Whole Group: Morning Meeting/Shared Read: (9:00- 9:15)
1. Students will gather together for Morning Meeting where the teacher will model how to use the "All About Today" pocket chart. The teacher will read the information on the pocket chart, using a pointer, starting with the month, date and year using the sentence frame "Today is __." Next have the students repeat the

sentence. After that the teacher will continue on with the pocket chart moving to "Yesterday was ___." Students will repeat each section after the teacher has pointed and read it aloud. Then teacher will read aloud the objectives for the day, briefly explaining that this is what the goal is by the end of their time together (Use academic language). If extra time, have 1-2 students share something exciting or important news about themselves.

2. (9:15-9:45) *I do:* Teacher will begin with ABC flash cards and go through them pointing to or showing each letter (depending on the flash card) while saying them and encourage students to join in. Next the teacher will point and read aloud the title "Pat the Cat" and the author Colin Hawkins. The teacher will ask students if they can describe the author's job. After that begin reading the story aloud. While reading stop periodically and have students identify which letter they see on the pages, DO NOT stop at every single page, just periodically.

3. *We do:* Then discuss what was happening in the book using the key words first or beginning, middle, and last or at the end. Encourage students to use the key words or terms

4. (5-7 mins max) The teacher will then focus in on the letter /b/. First write the letter on the board, bother upper case and lower (write clearly so students can see how to write both type of letters. Next the teacher will say the /b/ sound and students will repeat. After that the teacher with draw or place a picture of a bat next to the letter. The teacher will then point and say b, buh (the b sound), bat. Have students repeat as the teacher points to each. Repeat twice. The teacher will then write the word 'bat' on the board and point to each sound as the word is 'sound out.' Have student's think of and each share a different word that starts with the /b/ sound.

5. Then using the shared read book "Pat the Cat" the teacher will point to the word cat and then say bat and cat. The teacher will ask students what do they hear when both words are said, bat & cat? The teacher should guide students to identify that they sound similar. Add the next word Pat to the list and repeat all three words consecutively. After that the teacher should write all three words on the board & ask students what they notice these three words have in common. The teacher will then explain that these three words are what we call rhyming words. Rhyming words are words that have the same ending sounds so they sound similar except for the first letter(s).

6. *You do*: Teacher will then have students look through each page of the shared reading book as the teacher reads aloud. As students find rhyming words they should raise their hand or tell the teacher to "stop." The teacher will write down each word they stop at that rhymes. Together the students and teacher will review the list that was made by reading down the list & underlining the –at in each word.

7. *Exit Ticket*: The teacher will write & draw a picture for the words cat and sat on the board. Next the teacher will ask if these two words rhyme. Have students show a silent thumb up if it does or a thumb down if it does not. Teacher will do a quick scan of the responses, noting any student that showed the incorrect response and then have hands down.

Sight & Sound Words: (9:45-10:15)

1. Have students gather together. The teacher will display the chart paper with the sight words & sound word pre-written on it.
2. *I do:* Teacher will lead a call and response where the teacher will repeat the first word, a student name, while pointing to it and students will repeat it. Continue down the list one time.

3. Next repeat down the list but challenge students to move faster with the teacher still speaking the word first and students repeating clearly. Repeat once more but this time the students will say the words and the teacher will not lead.
4. After that the teacher will slowly say the Sound words: be (buh ee), ball (buh all) & blue (bl oo). Students will repeat the word. Point to the picture of a ball and the color blue.
5. *We do*: Sight word play doh: Students will use the pre-made activity sheet with the sheet protectors and use the play doh to spell out each word. Students will trade sheets to practice making different words as many times as the time allows.
6. *You do:* Handwriting practice. Students will practice writing the sight words on pre-printed handwriting sheets.
7. *Exit Ticket:* The teacher will write "on" on the board in the sentence: *The bag is on the bat.* Have students write the sight word on a post it. Teacher should collect the post-its and do a quick scan and note down who wrote the correct word and who did not.

Bathroom Break: (10:15-10:20)
Small Groups/Guided Reading: (10:20-10:45)
Small groups should not be larger than 5 students and smaller than 2.
1. Teacher MUST model and go over small group activities and protocols before you send students in groups! Students must work on the assigned task at their group! Students must ask their group questions first if unclear before asking teacher. Students must remain in their small group space unless they are getting another activity for their group or cleaning up. Bathroom, water, etc is not allowed during groups. Students must use whisper voice when talking in groups. Actual student group time will be shorter the first month or so until students become acclimated to the expectations and routines of small group work.
2. *Small Group 1:* Guided reading. In this group the teacher will begin by first reviewing depending on the level of the students either the alphabets or the sight words introduced earlier that day. For alphabets: on individual white lap boards have students write the letter that you name. You can use magnetic letters so students have a reference to what it looks like if needed. For sight words: use the pre-written sight word index cards, show the card and have students state the word on the card. Extensions~ have students write the word on white lap boards or use in sentences. Then move into the text that day. Again depending on the level of the students: choose a text close to their level. Teacher will go over the title of the books and the author. Preview the text by looking through the book and making a prediction what the text may be about based on the pictures, title and cover. Teacher must model to students how to use the sentence frame "I predict __ because __." when making a prediction statement to the group about the text or anything. Next have students make predictions about the book using the sentence frame. Then the teacher will either choose to Echo read (you point and read a page at a time and have them repeat you) or Round Robin read (each student reads a page and you go around the group) and begin reading the text together. Once finished reading, briefly discuss the text, what was it about, who was in it: focus on using the key words beginning, middle and end of the story. After that based on what the focus was before reading the text have the students 'hunt' for the sight words or letters in story. Write down each one found on the white lap boards and then share once the students in the group are finished 'hunting'.

3. *Small Group 2 & 3:* Students will use instant learning center kits. Teacher will choose the 2 focused on Letter Recognition, Beginning Sounds & Building Words. Teacher will MODEL/demonstrate how to use the center kits.

Writing Workshop: (10:45- 11:00)
1. *I do:* (6 mins max) The teacher will write the question "Where is writing?" on the board. The teacher will then ask if anyone can describe or tell where is writing found? The teacher will select 2-3 students to share thoughts (do not select more than 3 because answers will begin to repeat).
2. Based on student responses the teacher will explain to students that writing is found everywhere. Have students get up and take a walk around the room to find writing. The teacher should point out all of the locations that students have found writing, board, charts, their own work, books, door, etc.
3. The teacher should then place some books, magazines, newspapers, anything with writing in it. Students will be given the opportunity to look through them for a few mins (3 mins top).
4. *You do:* The teacher will then explain to students that each one of them will create writing each day. Today they will think about something that they see. The teacher will write the sentence frame "I see __" on the board and then ask students to help think or brainstorm ideas to fill in the sentence that tell what they see around them. The teacher should write the first idea friends. Have students suggest some other things such as chairs, kids, books, door, etc). Then using the sentence frame "I see ___." The students will tell what they see and then draw/color a picture to match. The teacher must walk around and promote inventive spelling (where students try to write it on their own first) and then underneath the teacher writes/spells words correctly.
5. If time remains the teacher will select 2-3 students to share their picture and sentence.

Math: (11:00-11:30)
1. Students will gather together and the teacher will begin counting from 1-10 and show the number with fingers. Encourage students to join in. The teacher will ask students what is the difference between a letter and a number and record responses on the board or chart paper labeled Letter vs Number. Teacher will guide discussion to what each tell or where they are found. The teacher will explain to students that letters are what make words and sounds. Numbers are used to represent the amount of objects. Today we'll focus on the numbers 1-10.
2. *I do:* First the teacher will begin by telling students that they are going to become experts in the 1-10. The teacher will display a ten-place mat. The teacher will have a student volunteer pick an index card from the pile with 1-10 written on it. Once the student chooses the card, he/she should say the number and show peers. The teacher will then model how to use the ten-place mat to represent the number with counters.
3. After that the teacher will take the Bear Counters and display 5 bears. Ask students how many bears to do they see? What number is that? Have a student answer. Teacher will repeat with 7 bears and have a student identify how many bears they see and can students point to which number that is. The teacher will repeat until they have gone through some of the ten numbers.
4. *We do:* Then the teacher will break the students into partners. Each partner group will receive one ten-place mat, index cards or flash cards with the numbers 1-10, and manipulative. Just as the teacher modeled the teacher will re-explain the directions: One partner will pick an index/flash card from the pile, together they will identify the number. The other partner will show that number using the

manipulative on the ten-place mat. The teacher will circulate around the room to check each groups work. Then the students will clear the mat, put the card that was chosen to the side and switch roles. The opposite partner will pick the card this time, together both will say the number, and the other partner will use the manipulative to represent the number. This should continue during the allotted time frame of 8-10 mins.

5. *You do:* The teacher will distribute activity sheet where students will color in the number of pictures that represent the given number.
http://printables.scholastic.com/shop/prcontent/Count-and-Color-Counting-Groups-of-1-10-Objects-Math-Practice-Page/9780439553698-012

6. *Exit Ticket:* Teacher will say the number 7 and students will represent the number using their fingers. Teacher should take a scan around the room to observe which scholar is correct and incorrect. Record down.

Closing Activity: (11:30-11:45)

1. Gather students together for a closing activity game of Number Bingo.

DEAR (Drop Everything And Read) (11:45-11:57)

Week 5 (9:00-12:00)

ELA Focus/Skill: rhyming & title vs author
Phonics (letter/word family): /m/ & -an
Sound Words: me, my, mom, man
Sight Words: in, up, and, am, we
Big Book: This Old Man by McGraw Hill
Writing Focus: Why do we write?
Math Focus: Numbers 1-10

Objectives: Students will be able to:
- repeat and identify the day, weather and season
- repeat the letters of the alphabet sequentially
- identify the letter /m/, it's sound and words that begin with /m/
- identify and name words in the –an word family
- identify and sort rhyming and non-rhyming words
- identify and describe the difference between a title and an author
- identify sight words & use in context
- orally identify the sound words and speak phonetically
- orally retell a story sequentially using the shared reading
- identify why do we write and how writing is used to persuade, inform and entertain
- repeat, identify, represent and write the numbers 1-10 using manipulative
- rote count numbers from 1-10

Materials:
"All About Today" pocket chart, "This Old Man" big book, ABC flash cards, white lap boards, dry erase markers, board erasers, post-its, picture of a man, can, & fan, -ag word family book (see appendix), chart paper with sight words pre-written, inflatable beach ball (or any ball), sticky notes with this week's sight words written on them & then crumbled up, a popcorn container or any container to put the crumbled words in, handwriting sheets with the sight words written twice (www.handwritingworksheets.com), Instant Learning Centers: Rhyming Sounds, Beginning Sounds and Building words, hand writing story paper with picture space and the pre-written sentence frame: I like ___., crayons, pencils, erasers, Play doh Mats (see appendix), Number Bingo

ELA
Whole Group: Morning Meeting/Shared Read: (9:00- 9:15)
1. Students will gather together for Morning Meeting where the teacher will model how to use the "All About Today" pocket chart. The teacher will read the information on the pocket chart, using a pointer, starting with the month, date and year using the sentence frame "Today is ___." Next have the students repeat the

sentence. After that the teacher will continue on with the pocket chart moving to "Yesterday was ___." Students will repeat each section after the teacher has pointed and read it aloud. Then teacher will read aloud the objectives for the day, briefly explaining that this is what the goal is by the end of their time together (Use academic language). If extra time, have 1-2 students share something exciting or important news about themselves.

2. (9:15-9:45) *I do:* Teacher will begin with ABC flash cards and go through them pointing to or showing each letter (depending on the flash card) while saying them and encourage students to join in. Next the teacher will point and read aloud the title "This Old Man" and the author McGraw Hill. The teacher will ask students if they can describe the author's job. After that begin reading the story aloud. While reading stop periodically and have students identify which letter they see on the pages, DO NOT stop at every single page, just periodically.

3. *We do:* Then discuss what was happening in the book using the key words first or beginning, middle, and last or at the end. Encourage students to use the key words or terms. The teacher will then ask student to identify where the author's name is located on the book. Have students point out or have a student come up to the book to point it out. After that the teacher will ask where is the title of the book found and have students point out or have a student come up to the book to show it. The teacher should briefly explain that all titles are found on the front or cover of a book. The author's name is usually on the front, at the bottom or on the title page sometimes. It's important to know the name of the book we read and the person or people who write it.

4. (5-7 mins max) The teacher will then focus in on the letter /m/. First write the letter on the board, bother upper case and lower (write clearly so students can see how to write both type of letters. Next the teacher will say the /m/ sound and students will repeat. After that the teacher with draw or place a picture of a man next to the letter. The teacher will then point and say m, muh (the m sound), man. Have students repeat as the teacher points to each. Repeat twice. The teacher will then write the word 'man' on the board and point to each sound as the word is 'sound out.' Then the teacher will say the following words aloud: man, me, mom, my. Have the students identify what each of the words has in common, guide students to listen to each word. The teacher should repeat the words slowly a second time if needed. Guide students to identify that each of the words begin with the same sound, /m/. After that challenge students to think of other words that begin with /m/. The teacher should have scholars repeat the words that begin with /m/ named by students.

5. Then the teacher will write –an on the board and display a picture of a man, can, and fan. Underneath or next of the pictures write the name of each word. The teacher will then read aloud each word and ask what do they hear when all the words are said? The teacher should guide students to identify that they sound similar or that they rhyme (last week's lesson). The teacher will then remind students that these three words are what we call rhyming words. Rhyming words are words that have the same ending sounds so they sound similar except for the first letter(s).

6. *You do:* Teacher will then have students create an –an book (see appendix). Students will create half books where they will cut & glue the pictures to spell out the –an word next to its matching words and will trace over the –an word.

7. *Exit Ticket:* The teacher will have students look through their books to find the word 'van.' At the count of 3 the students will raise the page to show the teacher.

The teacher should scan the room and note down who is showing the correct page and who isn't.

Sight & Sound Words: (9:45-10:15)
1. Have students gather together. The teacher will display the chart paper with the sight words & sound word pre-written on it.
2. *I do:* Teacher will lead a call and response where the teacher will repeat the first word, a student name, while pointing to it and students will repeat it. Continue down the list one time.
3. Next repeat down the list but challenge students to move faster with the teacher still speaking the word first and students repeating clearly. Repeat once more but this time the students will say the words and the teacher will not lead.
4. After that the teacher will slowly say the Sound words: me (m ee), my (m i), mom (m o m) & man (m -an). Students will repeat the word. Point to the picture of a man.
5. *We do*: Sight Word Popcorn: Sight words written on sticky notes that are balled up and placed in a popcorn container (or any container). The rules of the game: the teacher will toss the beach ball (or any soft ball will do) to a student; that student will pick a crumpled up paper from the container and read the word aloud. If the student reads the word correctly they can toss the ball to another student, if not the teacher will toss the ball to someone else and they will have an attempt to read the word. Continue until all of the crumpled papers have been picked & read.
6. *You do:* Handwriting practice. Students will practice writing the sight words on pre-printed handwriting sheets.
7. *Exit Ticket*: The teacher will write "we" on the board in the sentence: *We are at Sankofa*. Have students write the sight word on their white lap board; then at the count of 3 all students should raise their boards up. Teacher should do a quick scan and note down who wrote the correct word and who did not.

Bathroom Break: (10:15-10:20)

Small Groups/Guided Reading: (10:20-10:45)
Small groups should not be larger than 5 students and smaller than 2.
1. Teacher MUST model and go over small group activities and protocols before you send students in groups! Students must work on the assigned task at their group! Students must ask their group questions first if unclear before asking teacher. Students must remain in their small group space unless they are getting another activity for their group or cleaning up. Bathroom, water, etc is not allowed during groups. Students must use whisper voice when talking in groups. Actual student group time will be shorter the first month or so until students become acclimated to the expectations and routines of small group work.
2. *Small Group 1:* Guided reading. In this group the teacher will begin by first reviewing depending on the level of the students either the alphabets or the sight words introduced earlier that day. For alphabets: on individual white lap boards have students write the letter that you name. You can use magnetic letters so students have a reference to what it looks like if needed. For sight words: using the papers from the Popcorn game, show the card and have students state the word on the card. Extensions~ have students write the word on white lap boards or use in sentences. Then move into the text that day. Again depending on the level of the students: choose a text close to their level. Teacher will go over the title of the books and the author. Preview the text by looking through the book and making a prediction what the text may be about based on the pictures, title and cover. Teacher must model to students how to use the sentence frame "I

predict __ because __." when making a prediction statement to the group about the text or anything. Next have students make predictions about the book using the sentence frame. Then the teacher will either choose to Echo read (you point and read a page at a time and have them repeat you) or Round Robin read (each student reads a page and you go around the group) and begin reading the text together. Once finished reading, briefly discuss the text, what was it about, who was in it: focus on using the key words beginning, middle and end of the story. After that based on what the focus was before reading the text have the students 'hunt' for the sight words or letters in story. Write down each one found on the white lap boards and then share once the students in the group are finished 'hunting'.

3. *Small Group 2 & 3:* Students will use instant learning center kits. Teacher will choose the 2 focused on Rhyming Sound, Beginning Sounds & Building Words. Teacher will MODEL/demonstrate how to use the center kits.

Writing Workshop: (10:45- 11:00)
1. *I do:* (6 mins max) The teacher will write the question "Why do we write?" on the board. The teacher will then ask if anyone can describe or tell why do we write? The teacher will select 2-3 students to share thoughts (do not select more than 3 because answers will begin to repeat).
2. Based on student responses the teacher will explain to students that writing is found everywhere and used to tell others how we feel, what we think, to make someone laugh or smile, what we know, to tell someone to do something or to share information. Have students turn to a neighbor and tell their partner the last thing that they wrote about. The teacher should have 2 or 3 students share what they told their partner.
3. The teacher should then use chart paper to write *a few sentences telling students about themselves.* For example, the teacher can write: *My name is Sister Brenda. I am a first grade teacher at Sankofa Academy Charter School. My favorite color is purple. I like to eat fruits and vegetables.* The information can be of anything the teacher would like to share. As the teacher is writing the sentences down it should also be read aloud. Then have the students identify if the teacher is telling the students something or trying to tell them to do something (3 mins top).
4. *You do:* The teacher will then explain to students that each one of them create writing each day. Today they will think about them. The teacher will write the sentence frame "I like __" on the board and then ask students to help think or brainstorm ideas to fill in the sentence that tells about themself. The teacher should write the first idea friends. Have students suggest some other things such as pizza, bananas, books, the color orange, etc). Then using the sentence frame "I like ___." The students will tell what they like and then draw/color a picture to match. The teacher must walk around and promote inventive spelling (where students try to write it on their own first) and then underneath the teacher writes/spells words correctly.
5. If time remains the teacher will select 2-3 students to share their picture and sentence.

Math: (11:00-11:30)
1. The teacher will show large flash cards with the numbers 1-10 on them and begin counting aloud. Encourage students to join in. Today we'll continue to focus on the numbers 1-10 so that we can become experts in them.
2. *I do:* First the teacher will begin by telling students that they are going to become experts in the 1-10. The teacher will draw 5 shapes on the board and ask

students how many shapes do they see? Once 5 is identified, the teacher will ask what is another way to show the number 5? Accept answers such as with fingers, by drawing 5 of something else, writing the number 5 or showing 5 of something such as bear manipulative or pencils. The teacher will then explain that a number can be shown or represented in more than one way as we heard from your answers. We can use objects, drawings or writing the number and when you learn it, even using the word five. Then the teacher should write the number 5, draw 5 fingers under it, draw 5 circles, draw five flowers or hearts, draw 5 on a die, and/or five on a dominoes piece.

3. *We do:* Then the teacher will ask for ways to show the number 8. As a whole group have students share ways to make/represent the number 8.
4. *You do:* The teacher will explain that students will each receive a "Play doh Mat" (see appendix) and a container of play doh. What students will do is use the play doh to make the number on the mat, show the number with round balls on the tree and then place that many play doh balls on the mat. Students should continue to switch mats with a partner to show/represent a new number until time is up.
5. *Exit Ticket:* Teacher will say the number 4 and students will represent the number using their fingers. Teacher should take a scan around the room to observe which scholar is correct and incorrect. Record down.

Closing Activity: (11:30-11:45)
   2 Gather students together for a closing activity game of Number Bingo.

DEAR (Drop Everything And Read) (11:45-11:57)

Week 6 (9:00-12:00)

ELA Focus/Skill: illustrator vs author
Phonics (letter/word family): /t/ & -ag
Sound Words: to, two, today
Sight Words: will, three, like, see, go, it
Big Book: What I Like About Me by Allia Zobel Nolan
Writing Focus: Why do I write?
Math Focus: Numbers 11-15

Objectives: Students will be able to:
- repeat and identify the day, weather and season
- repeat the letters of the alphabet sequentially
- identify the letter /t/, it's sound and words that begin with /t/
- identify and name words in the –ag word family
- identify and sort rhyming and non-rhyming words
- identify and describe the difference between an illustrator and an author
- orally identify the sound words and speak phonetically
- identify sight words & use in context
- orally retell a story sequentially using the shared reading
- identify why you write
- repeat, identify, represent and write the numbers 11-15 using manipulative
- sort numbers and place in sequential orders from 1-15

Materials:
"All About Today" pocket chart, "What I Like About Me" big book, ABC flash cards, white lap boards, dry erase markers, board erasers, post-its, picture of a two & turtle, a tag, wag and rag, Trace and Paste activity sheet (see appendix), chart paper with sight words pre-written, index cards with sight words pre-written, scotch tape, handwriting sheets with the sight words written twice (www.handwritingworksheets.com), Instant Learning Centers: Rhyming Sounds, Beginning Sounds and Building words, hand writing story paper with picture space and the pre-written sentence frame: I like __., crayons, pencils, erasers, Play doh Mats (see appendix), Number Bingo

ELA
Whole Group: Morning Meeting/Shared Read: (9:00- 9:15)
1. Students will gather together for Morning Meeting where the teacher will model how to use the "All About Today" pocket chart. The teacher will read the information on the pocket chart, using a pointer, starting with the month, date and year using the sentence frame "Today is __." Next have the students repeat the sentence. After that the teacher will continue on with the pocket chart moving to "Yesterday was __." Students will repeat each section after the teacher has pointed and read it aloud. Then teacher will read aloud the objectives for the

day, briefly explaining that this is what the goal is by the end of their time together (Use academic language). If extra time, have 1-2 students share something exciting or important news about themselves.

2. (9:15-9:45) *I do*: Teacher will begin with ABC flash cards and go through them pointing to or showing each letter (depending on the flash card) while saying them and encourage students to join in. Next the teacher will point and read aloud the title "What I Like About Me," the author Allia Zobel Nolan and the illustrator Miki Sakamoto. The teacher will ask students if they can describe the author's job. After that begin reading the story aloud. While reading stop periodically and have students identify which letter they see on the pages or what is happening so far in the story; having students make predictions for the remainder of the story is another good strategy, DO NOT stop at every single page, just periodically.

3. *We do:* Then discuss what was happening in the book using the key words first or beginning, middle, and last or at the end. Encourage students to use the key words or terms. The teacher will then ask student to identify where the author's name is located on the book. Have students point out or have a student come up to the book to point it out and tell what the author's job is. After that the teacher will ask where is the illustrator's name and have students point out or have a student come up to the book to show it. The teacher should briefly explain that the while author writes the story the illustrator draws and colors or paints the pictures in the book.

4. (5-7 mins max) The teacher will then focus in on the letter /t/. First write the letter on the board, bother upper case and lower (write clearly so students can see how to write both type of letters. Next the teacher will say the /t/ sound and students will repeat. After that the teacher with draw or place a picture of the number two next to the letter. The teacher will then point and say t, t-ah (the t sound), man. Have students repeat as the teacher points to each. Repeat twice. The teacher will then write the word 'two' on the board and point to each sound as the word is 'sound out.' Then the teacher will say the following words aloud: two, today, to, turtle. Have the students identify what each of the words have in common, guide students to listen to each word. The teacher should repeat the words slowly a second time if needed. Guide students to identify that each of the words begin with the same sound, /t/. After that challenge students to think of other words that begin with /t/. The teacher should have scholars repeat the words that begin with /m/ named by students.

5. Then the teacher will write –ag on the board and display a picture of a tag, wag, and rag. Underneath or next of the pictures write the name of each word. The teacher will then read aloud each word and ask what do they hear when all the words are said? The teacher should guide students to identify that they sound similar or that they rhyme (last week's lesson). The teacher will then remind students that these three words are what we call rhyming words. Rhyming words are words that have the same ending sounds so they sound similar except for the first letter(s).

6. *You do:* Teacher will then have students complete the Trace and Paste activity sheet (see appendix).

7. *Exit Ticket*: The teacher will write the word wag on the board, then point and say the word wag. Have the students show a thumb up if the word the teacher said matches the word written or a thumb down if it is not correct. The teacher should scan the room and note down who is showing the correct page and who isn't.

Sight & Sound Words: (9:45-10:15)

1. Have students gather together. The teacher will display the chart paper with the sight words & sound word pre-written on it.
2. *I do:* Teacher will lead a call and response where the teacher will repeat the first word, a student name, while pointing to it and students will repeat it. Continue down the list one time.
3. Next repeat down the list but challenge students to move faster with the teacher still speaking the word first and students repeating clearly. Repeat once more but this time the students will say the words and the teacher will not lead.
4. *We do:* 4 Corners Game: Teacher will place the index cards with the 4 sight words other than the student's names in 6 different corners/sections of the room. Rules of the game: the teacher or leader of the game will say one of the words on the index cards. The players will have 10 seconds to go over to that 'corner' that has the word. Anyone who is at the wrong 'corner' is out.
5. Play 4-5 rounds.
6. *You do:* Handwriting practice. Students will practice writing the sight words on pre-printed handwriting sheets.
7. *Exit Ticket:* The teacher will write "will" on the board in the sentence: *We will have lunch soon.* Have students write the sight word on their white lap board; then at the count of 3 all students should raise their boards up. Teacher should do a quick scan and note down who wrote the correct word and who did not.

Bathroom Break: (10:15-10:20)
Small Groups/Guided Reading: (10:20-10:45)
Small groups should not be larger than 5 students and smaller than 2.
1. Teacher MUST model and go over small group activities and protocols before you send students in groups! Students must work on the assigned task at their group! Students must ask their group questions first if unclear before asking teacher. Students must remain in their small group space unless they are getting another activity for their group or cleaning up. Bathroom, water, etc is not allowed during groups. Students must use whisper voice when talking in groups. Actual student group time will be shorter the first month or so until students become acclimated to the expectations and routines of small group work.
2. *Small Group 1:* Guided reading. In this group the teacher will begin by first reviewing depending on the level of the students either the alphabets or the sight words introduced earlier that day. For alphabets: on individual white lap boards have students write the letter that you name. You can use magnetic letters so students have a reference to what it looks like if needed. For sight words: using the index cards from the 4 Corners game, show the card and have students state the word on the card. Extensions~ have students write the word on white lap boards or use in sentences. Then move into the text that day. Again depending on the level of the students: choose a text close to their level. Teacher will go over the title of the books and the author. Preview the text by looking through the book and making a prediction what the text may be about based on the pictures, title and cover. Teacher must model to students how to use the sentence frame "I predict __ because __." when making a prediction statement to the group about the text or anything. Next have students make predictions about the book using the sentence frame. Then the teacher will either choose to Echo read (you point and read a page at a time and have them repeat you) or Round Robin read (each student reads a page and you go around the group) and begin reading the text together. Once finished reading, briefly discuss the text, what was it about, who was in it: focus on using the key words beginning, middle and end of the story. After that based on what the focus was before reading the text have the

students 'hunt' for the sight words or letters in story. Write down each one found on the white lap boards and then share once the students in the group are finished 'hunting'.
3. *Small Group 2 & 3:* Students will use instant learning center kits. Teacher will choose the 2 focused on Rhyming Sound, Beginning Sounds & Building Words. Teacher will MODEL/demonstrate how to use the center kits.

Writing Workshop: (10:45- 11:00)
1. *I do:* (6 mins max) The teacher will write the question "Where do I write?" on the board. The teacher will then ask if anyone can describe or tell where do we/I write? The teacher will select 2-3 students to share thoughts (do not select more than 3 because answers will begin to repeat).
2. Based on student responses the teacher will explain to students that we write in a variety of places, paper, notebooks, books, post-its, walls, some people write on desks. Writing can be done almost anywhere. Have students turn to the person next to them and share a place that they have written on before. Then come back together and the teacher will take 2-3 students responses in a group sharing.
3. The teacher should review what was written last class session on the chart paper telling students about themselves: *My name is Sister Brenda. I am a first grade teacher at Sankofa Academy Charter School. My favorite color is purple. I like to eat fruits and vegetables.* The information can be of anything the teacher would like to share. As the teacher is writing the sentences down it should also be read aloud. Then have the students identify if the teacher is telling the students something or trying to tell them to do something (3 mins top).
4. *You do:* The teacher will then explain to students that each one of them create writing each day. Today they will think about something that tells about them. The teacher will re-write the sentence frame "I like __" on the board and then ask students to help think or brainstorm ideas to fill in the sentence that tell something different about them. The teacher should write the first idea friends. Have students suggest some other things such as pizza, bananas, books, the color orange, etc). Then using the sentence frame "I like ___." The students will tell what they like and then draw/color a picture to match. The teacher must walk around and promote inventive spelling (where students try to write it on their own first) and then underneath the teacher writes/spells words correctly.
5. If time remains the teacher will select 2-3 students to share their picture and sentence.

Math: (11:00-11:30)
1. The teacher will show large flash cards with the numbers 1-10 on them and begin counting aloud. Encourage students to join in. Today we'll continue to focus on the numbers 11-15 so that we can become experts in them.
2. *I do:* First the teacher will begin by telling students that they are going to learn about the numbers that come after 10. The teacher will explain that numbers are called digit and so far we've learned about the most important numbers 0-9. But let's look at the number 10, ask students what two numbers or digits make up the number 10. Look at the number line in the room for reference. Students should identify the numbers 1 and 0. If not, the teacher should point it out. After that continue with the lesson. The teacher will explain that all of the numbers afterwards will be made up of two of those numbers from 0-9. For example, lets look at the number 11. What two digits or numbers make up the number 11? Guide students to identify the two 1's. Then model the number 12 and identify the two numbers that make up 12.

3. *We do:* Then the teacher will distribute the white lap boards, markers and erasers to students. The teacher will then have students write two 1's next to each other and have students repeat eleven. Next the students will draw 11 dots or circles next to the number on the board to represent the number.
4. Continue with 12-15 on the white boards sequentially however do not draw dots for each.
5. *You do:* The teacher will then distribute counters (bears) to students and have them count out 11 bears, lining them up on the desks and showing how to count and touch them aloud. The teacher will then have students add one bear and count them aloud. Students will identify the number 12.
6. Continue with 13-15.
7. *Exit Ticket:* Teacher will say represent the number 12 using shapes on the board. Then have students count and identify how many shapes are on the board. Teacher should take a scan around the room to observe which scholar is correct and incorrect. Record down.

Closing Activity: (11:30-11:45)
1. Gather students together for a closing activity game of Number Bingo.

DEAR (Drop Everything And Read) (11:45-11:57)

Week 7 (9:00-12:00)

ELA Focus/Skill: word vs sentences
Phonics (letter/word family): /s/ & -ap
Sound Words: see, sun, snake
Sight Words: we, look, go, do, the, my, to
Big Book: S Poem from ABC Flip Chart Book by Teddy Slater
Writing Focus: Getting Ideas
Math Focus: Numbers 11-15

Objectives: Students will be able to:
- repeat and identify the day, weather and season
- repeat the letters of the alphabet sequentially
- identify the letter /s/, it's sound and words that begin with /s/
- identify and name words in the –ap word family
- identify and sort rhyming and non-rhyming words
- identify and describe the difference between a word and a sentence
- orally identify the sound words and speak phonetically
- identify sight words & use in context
- orally retell a story sequentially using the shared reading
- identify where ideas come from for writing
- repeat, identify, represent and write the numbers 11-15 using manipulative
- sort numbers and place in sequential orders from 1-15

Materials:
"All About Today" pocket chart, "ABC Flip Chart Book" big book, ABC flash cards, white lap boards, dry erase markers, board erasers, post-its, pictures of a sun, rap, tap & lap, Trace and Paste activity sheet (see appendix), chart paper with sight words pre-written, index cards with sight words pre-written, scotch tape, handwriting sheets with the sight words written twice (www.handwritingworksheets.com), Instant Learning Centers: Rhyming Sounds, Beginning Sounds and Building words, hand writing story paper with picture space and the pre-written sentence frame: Yesterday I __., crayons, pencils, erasers, paper cups with numbers written on the bottom from 1-15, Number Bingo

ELA
Whole Group: Morning Meeting/Shared Read: (9:00- 9:15)
1. Students will gather together for Morning Meeting where the teacher will model how to use the "All About Today" pocket chart. The teacher will read the information on the pocket chart, using a pointer, starting with the month, date and year using the sentence frame "Today is __." Next have the students repeat the sentence. After that the teacher will continue on with the pocket chart moving to "Yesterday was __." Students will repeat each section after the teacher has pointed and read it aloud. Then teacher will read aloud the objectives for the day, briefly explaining that this is what the goal is by the end of their time together (Use academic language). If extra time, have 1-2 students share something exciting or important news about themselves.
2. ((9:15-9:45) *I do:* Teacher will begin with ABC flash cards and go through them pointing to or showing each letter (depending on the flash card) while saying

them and encourage students to join in. Next the teacher will point and read aloud the title "The S Poem" from the ABC Flip Chart the author Teddy Slater and the illustrator Liisa Guida. The teacher will ask students if they can describe the author's job. After that begin reading the story aloud. While reading stop periodically and have students identify which letter they see on the pages or what is happening so far in the story; having students make predictions for the remainder of the story is another good strategy, DO NOT stop at every single page, just periodically.

3. *We do*: Then discuss what was happening in the book using the key words first or beginning, middle, and last or at the end. Encourage students to use the key words or terms. The teacher will then ask student to identify where the author's name is located on the book. Have students point out or have a student come up to the book to point it out and tell what the author's job is. After that the teacher will ask where is the illustrator's name and have students point out or have a student come up to the book to show it. The teacher should briefly explain that the while author writes the story the illustrator draws and colors or paints the pictures in the book.

4. (5-7 mins max) The teacher will then focus in on the letter /s/. First write the letter on the board, bother upper case and lower (write clearly so students can see how to write both type of letters. Next the teacher will say the /s/ sound and students will repeat. After that the teacher with draw or place a picture of the sun next to the letter. The teacher will then point and say s, ss (the t sound), and add the sound word sun. Have students repeat as the teacher points to each. Repeat twice. The teacher will then write the word 'sun' on the board and point to each sound as the word is 'sound out.' Then the teacher will say the following words aloud: see, sun, snake. Have the students identify what each of the words have in common, guide students to listen to each word. The teacher should repeat the words slowly a second time if needed. Guide students to identify that each of the words begin with the same sound, /s/. After that challenge students to think of other words that begin with /s/. The teacher should have scholars repeat the words that begin with /s/ named by students.

5. Then the teacher will write –ap on the board and display a picture of a tap, rap, and lap. Underneath or next of the pictures write the name of each word. The teacher will then read aloud each word and ask what do they hear when all the words are said? The teacher should guide students to identify that they sound similar or that they rhyme (last week's lesson). The teacher will then remind students that these three words are what we call rhyming words. Rhyming words are words that have the same ending sounds so they sound similar except for the first letter(s).

6. *You do:* Teacher will then have students create an –ap book (see appendix). Students will create half books where they will cut & glue the pictures to spell out the –ap word next to its matching words and will trace over the –ap word.

7. *Exit Ticket:* The teacher will have students write the word 'tap' & rap on their white lap board. Next the students will underline the word family that is found in the two words. After that at the count of 3 the students will raise the lap boards. The teacher should scan the room and note down who is showing the correct page and who isn't.

Sight & Sound Words: (9:45-10:15)

1. Have students gather together. The teacher will display the chart paper with the sight words & sound word pre-written on it.

2. *I do:* Teacher will lead a call and response where the teacher will repeat the first word, a student name, while pointing to it and students will repeat it. Continue down the list one time.
3. Next repeat down the list but challenge students to move faster with the teacher still speaking the word first and students repeating clearly. Repeat once more but this time the students will say the words and the teacher will not lead.
4. We do: Sight word Tic Tac Toe- Teacher will draw the tic tac toe board on the board. Then inside each box the teacher will write the new sight words just introduced and in the extra boxes the sight words from the previous week (go, like, will, three, see, it). The teacher will explain the game's rules briefly. There are 2 teams, the X and the O team. 1 player will get picked and they will pick where they want their letter (X or O) to go on the board. To get their spot the player must say the word in the box first. If the word is said correctly, then the teacher or player will draw the letter in the box. If the word is incorrect then the next team goes. The first team to 3 in a row wins. The teacher will need to split the class into two teams.
5. Play 4-5 rounds.
6. *You do:* Handwriting practice. Students will practice writing the sight words on pre-printed handwriting sheets.
7. Exit Ticket: The teacher will write "look" on the board in the sentence: *She will look for it.* Have students write the sight word on their white lap board; then at the count of 3 all students should raise their boards up. Teacher should do a quick scan and note down who wrote the correct word and who did not.

Bathroom Break: (10:15-10:20)
Small Groups/Guided Reading: (10:20-10:45)
Small groups should not be larger than 5 students and smaller than 2.
1. Teacher MUST model and go over small group activities and protocols before you send students in groups! Students must work on the assigned task at their group! Students must ask their group questions first if unclear before asking teacher. Students must remain in their small group space unless they are getting another activity for their group or cleaning up. Bathroom, water, etc is not allowed during groups. Students must use whisper voice when talking in groups. Actual student group time will be shorter the first month or so until students become acclimated to the expectations and routines of small group work.
2. *Small Group 1:* Guided reading. In this group the teacher will begin by first reviewing depending on the level of the students either the alphabets or the sight words introduced earlier that day. For alphabets: on individual white lap boards have students write the letter that you name. You can use magnetic letters so students have a reference to what it looks like if needed. For sight words: using the pre-written index cards with the sight words, show the card and have students state the word on the card. Extensions~ have students write the word on white lap boards or use in sentences. Then move into the text that day. Again depending on the level of the students: choose a text close to their level. Teacher will go over the title of the books and the author. Preview the text by looking through the book and making a prediction what the text may be about based on the pictures, title and cover. Teacher must model to students how to use the sentence frame "I predict __ because __." when making a prediction statement to the group about the text or anything. Next have students make predictions about the book using the sentence frame. Then the teacher will either choose to Echo read (you point and read a page at a time and have them repeat you) or Round Robin read (each student reads a page and you go around

the group) and begin reading the text together. Once finished reading, briefly discuss the text, what was it about, who was in it: focus on using the key words beginning, middle and end of the story. After that based on what the focus was before reading the text have the students 'hunt' for the sight words or letters in story. Write down each one found on the white lap boards and then share once the students in the group are finished 'hunting'.

3. *Small Group 2 & 3:* Students will use instant learning center kits. Teacher will choose the 2 focused on Rhyming Sound, Beginning Sounds & Building Words. Teacher will MODEL/demonstrate how to use the center kits.

Writing Workshop: (10:45- 11:00)

1. *I do:* (6 mins max) The teacher will write the question "Getting Ideas" on the board. The teacher will then ask where a writer may get an idea from. The teacher will select 2-3 students to share thoughts (do not select more than 3 because answers will begin to repeat).
2. Based on student responses the teacher will explain to students that writers get ideas from things that they know about or things that they experienced.
3. The teacher will distribute some fictional and informational library books and have students work in pairs to look through them having them focus on the pictures within the book to predict what it is about and where the author may have gotten their idea from. Share with partners what they found & have students come back together to share what was found (3 mins top).
4. *You do:* The teacher will then explain to students that they will use something that happened to them yesterday to write about. The teacher will write the sentence frame "Yesterday I __" on the board and then ask students to help think or brainstorm ideas to fill in the sentence that tell something that happened yesterday. The teacher should write the first idea made dinner. Have students suggest some other things such as played with friends, read a book, played games, did homework, etc). Then using the sentence frame "Yesterday I ___." The students will tell what they like and then draw/color a picture to match. The teacher must walk around and promote inventive spelling (where students try to write it on their own first) and then underneath the teacher writes/spells words correctly.
5. If time remains the teacher will select 2-3 students to share their picture and sentence.

Math: (11:00-11:30)

1. The teacher will show large flash cards with the numbers 1-15 on them and begin counting aloud. Encourage students to join in. Today we'll continue to focus on the numbers 11-15 so that we can become experts in them.
2. *I/We do:* First the teacher will explain that we will focus on numbers 1-15. The teacher will write the number 11 on the board and have students identify it. Then the teacher will write the number 12 and have students identify that as well. After that the teacher will draw a group of 11 objects, a separate group of 12 objects and then a group of 13. Explain to students that you need volunteers to count a group of objects and match it to its number.
3. *You do:* Students will play Magic Number Cups. Teacher will model and explain the directions: Students will be in groups of 4 and in each group students will take the cups that have numbers on the bottom and place them in order. Then one person in the group (easier if you assign who starts) will have the group close their eyes (no peaking!) and that person will take one of the cups away. When the group has opened their eyes they have to guess which number is missing. The first person who says the correct number will get to go next. The

cup will go back and the group will close their eyes again and a new cup will magically disappear.

4. *Exit Ticket:* Teacher will say represent the number 15 using shapes on the board. Then have students count and identify how many shapes are on the board. Teacher should take a scan around the room to observe which scholar is correct and incorrect. Record down.

Closing Activity: (11:30-11:45)
1. Gather students together for a closing activity game on the projector & computer. Choices include Reading Eggs (if accessible) or an ABC game on Starfall.com.

DEAR (Drop Everything And Read) (11:45-11:57)

Week 8 (9:00-12:00)

ELA Focus/Skill: parts of a book & content
Phonics (letter/word family): /r/ & -ack
Sound Words: red, run, rain
Sight Words: like, are, all, as, are
Big Book: Click Clack Moo Moo by Doreen Cronin
Writing Focus: Making Idea List
Math Focus: Numbers 15-20

Objectives: Students will be able to:
- repeat and identify the day, weather and season
- repeat the letters of the alphabet sequentially
- identify the letter /r/, it's sound and words that begin with /r/
- identify and name words in the –ack word family
- identify and sort rhyming and non-rhyming words
- identify and describe the parts of a book and its contents
- orally identify the sound words and speak phonetically
- identify sight words & use in context
- orally retell a story sequentially using the shared reading
- brainstorm and create a list of ideas to write about
- repeat, identify, represent and write the numbers 11-20 using manipulative
- sort numbers and place in sequential orders from 1-20

Materials:
"All About Today" pocket chart, "ABC Flip Chart Book" big book, ABC flash cards, white lap boards, dry erase markers, board erasers, post-its, pictures of a rain, rack, sack, & back, Trace and Paste activity sheet (see appendix), chart paper with sight words pre-written, index cards with sight words pre-written, scotch tape, handwriting sheets with the sight words written twice (www.handwritingworksheets.com), Instant Learning Centers: Rhyming Sounds, Beginning Sounds and Building words, blank paper with four boxes drawn & space for name, crayons, pencils, erasers, paper cups with numbers written on the bottom from 1-15, Number Bingo

ELA
Whole Group: Morning Meeting/Shared Read: (9:00- 9:15)
1. Students will gather together for Morning Meeting where the teacher will model how to use the "All About Today" pocket chart. The teacher will read the information on the pocket chart, using a pointer, starting with the month, date and year using the sentence frame "Today is __." Next have the students repeat the sentence. After that the teacher will continue on with the pocket chart moving to "Yesterday was __." Students will repeat each section after the teacher has pointed and read it aloud. Then teacher will read aloud the objectives for the day, briefly explaining that this is what the goal is by the end of their time together (Use academic language). If extra time, have 1-2 students share something exciting or important news about themselves.
2. (9:15-9:45) *I do:* Teacher will begin with ABC flash cards and go through them pointing to or showing each letter (depending on the flash card) while saying

them and encourage students to join in. Next the teacher will point and read aloud the title "Click Clack Moo Moo," the author Dorin Cronin and the illustrator Betty Lewin. The teacher will ask students if they can describe the author's job. After that begin reading the story aloud. While reading stop periodically and have students identify which letter they see on the pages or what is happening so far in the story; having students make predictions for the remainder of the story is another good strategy, DO NOT stop at every single page, just periodically.

3. *We do:* Then discuss what was happening in the book using the key words first or beginning, middle, and last or at the end. Encourage students to use the key words or terms. The teacher will then briefly review the parts of a cover on a book (title, author, illustrator & pictures). Next the teacher should explain that there are other parts of most books as well; while modeling, explain all books have a back cover & title page. Most books also have some kind of picture, drawing or painting done by the illustrator. Also, books have words written by the ____ (have students fill in the blank with the answer author). These are the common parts of a book.

4. (5-7 mins max) The teacher will then focus in on the letter /r/. First write the letter on the board, bother upper case and lower (write clearly so students can see how to write both type of letters. Next the teacher will say the /s/ sound and students will repeat. After that the teacher with draw or place a picture of the rain next to the letter. The teacher will then point and say r, rr (the r sound), and add the sound word rain. Have students repeat as the teacher points to each. Repeat twice. The teacher will then write the word 'rain' on the board and point to each sound as the word is 'sound out.' Then the teacher will say the following words aloud: rain, red, run. Have the students identify what each of the words have in common, guide students to listen to each word. The teacher should repeat the words slowly a second time if needed. Guide students to identify that each of the words begin with the same sound, /r/. After that challenge students to think of other words that begin with /r/. The teacher should have scholars repeat the words that begin with /s/ named by students.

5. Then the teacher will write –ack on the board and display a picture of a tack, back, and sack. Underneath or next of the pictures write the name of each word. The teacher will then read aloud each word and ask what do they hear when all the words are said? The teacher should guide students to identify that they sound similar or that they rhyme (last week's lesson). The teacher will then remind students that these three words are what we call rhyming words. Rhyming words are words that have the same ending sounds so they sound similar except for the first letter(s).

6. *You do:* Teacher will then guide students to create an –ack word family book (see appendix). The teacher will assist in reading the sentences on the pages in the book as well as the word bank to fill in the blanks.

7. *Exit Ticket:* The teacher will write the word back on the board and point to it. The teacher will then say the word sack. Have the students put a thumb up if they believe the teacher said the correct word or a thumb down if the wrong word was said. The teacher will scan the room, observe & record student responses.

Sight & Sound Words: (9:45-10:15)
1. Have students gather together. The teacher will display the chart paper with the sight words & sound word pre-written on it.
2. *I do:* Teacher will lead a call and response where the teacher will repeat the first word, a student name, while pointing to it and students will repeat it. Continue down the list one time.

3. Next repeat down the list but challenge students to move faster with the teacher still speaking the word first and students repeating clearly. Repeat once more but this time the students will say the words and the teacher will not lead.
4. *We do:* Sight word play doh: Students will use the pre-made activity sheet with the sheet protectors and use the play doh to spell out each word. Students will trade sheets to practice making different words as many times as the time allows.
5. *You do*: Handwriting practice. Students will practice writing the sight words on pre-printed handwriting sheets.
6. *Exit Ticket:* The teacher will write the word the sentence: I like to eat bananas. On the board. Then each student will receive a post-it. Have students read over the sentence and then on the post-it write down the sight word that they just practiced on the list & handwriting sheet. Students will then get up and put the post-it next to or under the sentence. The teacher should scan over the words on the post-its & record down any incorrect responses.

Bathroom Break: (10:15-10:20)

Small Groups/Guided Reading: (10:20-10:45)

Small groups should not be larger than 5 students and smaller than 2.

1. Teacher MUST model and go over small group activities and protocols before you send students in groups! Students must work on the assigned task at their group! Students must ask their group questions first if unclear before asking teacher. Students must remain in their small group space unless they are getting another activity for their group or cleaning up. Bathroom, water, etc is not allowed during groups. Students must use whisper voice when talking in groups. Actual student group time will be shorter the first month or so until students become acclimated to the expectations and routines of small group work.
2. *Small Group 1, 2 & 3:* Students will use instant learning center kits. Teacher will choose the 2 focused on Rhyming Sound, Beginning Sounds, Building Words, & Story Sequencing. Teacher will MODEL/demonstrate how to use the new center kits.

Writing Workshop: (10:45- 11:00)

1. *I do:* (6 mins max) The teacher will write the words "Make an idea list" on the board. The teacher will then remind students that last week we talked about where a writer may get an idea from and shared ideas; does anyone remember some places where writers get ideas from? Select 4-6 students to share thoughts. The teacher should write down student responses to create a list on the board or chart paper.
2. Once complete the teacher should re-read the 'list' now created to the students. Then point out that what he/she just made is a list of ideas that they could write about. The teacher should then briefly explain that one ways writers help decide what to write about is that they create a list of ideas that they think of and then can pick from there. Some lists are with words like ours and some can be with pictures.
3. *You do:* The teacher will give the directions that students will create a picture list of ideas that they could possibly write about this year. (A blank sheet of paper with four boxes will be distributed). Have students begin to draw four different pictures in the four boxes. Extension- for students finished early or more advanced: have students write words/sentence to tell about their picture/idea. The teacher must walk around and promote inventive spelling (where students try to write it on their own first) and then underneath the teacher writes/spells words correctly.

   4. If time remains the teacher will select 2-3 students to share their picture and sentence.

Math: (11:00-11:30)
   1. The teacher will show large flash cards with the numbers 1-15 on them and begin counting aloud. Encourage students to join in. Today we'll continue to focus on the numbers 16-20.
   2. *I/We do:* First the teacher will explain that we will focus on numbers 16-20. The teacher will write the number 16 on the board and have students identify it. Then the teacher will write the number 17 and have students identify that as well. After that the teacher will draw a group of 16 objects, a separate group of 17 objects and then a group of 18. Explain to students that you need volunteers to count a group of objects and match it to its number.
   3. *You do:* Students will play Magic Number Cups. Teacher will model and explain the directions: Students will be in groups of 4 and in each group students will take the cups that have numbers on the bottom and place them in order. Then one person in the group (easier if you assign who starts) will have the group close their eyes (no peaking!) and that person will take one of the cups away. When the group has opened their eyes they have to guess which number is missing. The first person who says the correct number will get to go next. The cup will go back and the group will close their eyes again and a new cup will magically disappear.
   4. *Exit Ticket:* Teacher "will say represent the number 18" using shapes on the board. Then have students count and identify how many shapes are on the board. Teacher should take a scan around the room to observe which scholar is correct and incorrect. Record down.

Closing Activity: (11:30-11:45)
   1. Gather students together for a closing activity game on the projector & computer. Choices include Reading Eggs (if accessible) or an ABC game on Starfall.com.

DEAR (Drop Everything And Read) (11:45-11:57)

Week 9 (9:00-12:00)

ELA Focus/Skill: sentence structure & periods
Phonics (letter/word family): /k/=c & k & short vowel /a/ review
Sound Words: cat, can & come
Sight Words: good, was, ball, be, boy
Big Book: Pat the Cat by Colin Hawkins
Writing Focus: Asking Questions
Math Focus: Numbers 1-20

Objectives: Students will be able to:
- repeat and identify the day, weather and season
- repeat the letters of the alphabet sequentially
- identify the letter /c/, it's sound (/c/ & /k/) and words that begin with hard /c/
- identify and name words with short vowel /a/
- identify the structure of a sentence
- identify and use the punctuation mark of a period.
- orally identify the sound words and speak phonetically
- identify sight words & use in context
- orally retell a story sequentially using the shared reading
- brainstorm and create a list of ideas to write about
- repeat, identify, represent and write the numbers 1-20 using manipulative
- sort numbers and place in sequential orders from 1-20

Materials:
"All About Today" pocket chart, "Pat the Cat" big book, ABC flash cards, white lap boards, dry erase markers, board erasers, pictures of a cat & can (should have a picture from week 5), short vowel /a/ activity sheet (see appendix), post-its, index cards, chart paper with sight words pre-written, post-it cards with sight words pre-written, container to play popcorn, handwriting sheets with the sight words written twice (www.handwritingworksheets.com), Instant Learning Centers: Rhyming Sounds, Beginning Sounds and Building words, hand writing story paper with picture space and the pre-written sentence frame: Who __?, crayons, pencils, erasers, paper cups with numbers written on the bottom from 1-15, Number Bingo

ELA
Whole Group: Morning Meeting/Shared Read: (9:00- 9:15)
1. Students will gather together for Morning Meeting where the teacher will model how to use the "All About Today" pocket chart. The teacher will read the information on the pocket chart, using a pointer, starting with the month, date and year using the sentence frame "Today is __." Next have the students repeat the sentence. After that the teacher will continue on with the pocket chart moving to "Yesterday was __." Students will repeat each section after the teacher has pointed and read it aloud. Then teacher will read aloud the objectives for the day, briefly explaining that this is what the goal is by the end of their time together (Use academic language). If extra time, have 1-2 students share something exciting or important news about themselves.
2. (9:15-9:45) *I do:* Teacher will begin with ABC flash cards and go through them pointing to or showing each letter (depending on the flash card) while saying them and encourage students to join in. Next the teacher will point and read

aloud the title "Pat the Cat," the author Colin Hawkins and the illustrator Jacqui Hawkins. The teacher will ask students if they recall hearing this story, if yes what do they recall (encourage using key words/terms of "in the beginning, in the middle and the end." After that begin re-reading the story aloud. While reading stop periodically and have students identify which letter they see on the pages or what is happening so far in the story; having students make predictions for the remainder of the story is another good strategy, DO NOT stop at every single page, just periodically.

3. *We do:* Then discuss what was happening in the book using the key words first or beginning, middle, and last or at the end. Encourage students to use the key words or terms. The teacher will review what parts of the book that were talked about last week are seen in this text. Assist students to recall that there should be a cover with a title, picture, author & illustrator, a title page & end cover. Then the teacher will switch the focus to sentence structure asking students if anyone knows what a sentence is? Take 2-3 responses then guide based on responses the teacher will explain that a sentence is a group of words put together that make sense and tell something. Refer back to the shared read "Pat the Cat" & point out & read aloud a sentence from the book. Have student come up to point out sentences within the book.

4. (5-7 mins max) The teacher will then focus in on the letter /c/. First write the letter on the board, bother upper case and lower (write clearly so students can see how to write both type of letters. Next the teacher will say the letter hard /c/ =k sound and students will repeat. After that the teacher with draw or place a picture of a cat next to the letter. The teacher will then point and say c, k (the k sound), and add the sound word cat. Have students repeat as the teacher points to each. Repeat twice. The teacher will then write the word 'cat' on the board and point to each sound as the word is 'sound out.' Then the teacher will say the following words aloud: cat, can, come. Have the students identify what each of the words have in common, guide students to listen to each word. The teacher should repeat the words slowly a second time if needed. Guide students to identify that each of the words begin with the same sound, /c/. After that challenge students to think of other words that begin with the hard /c/. The teacher should have scholars repeat the words that begin with /c/ named by students.

5. Then the teacher will write short vowel /a/ on the board and display a picture of a cat, rag, can, tap and sack. Underneath or next of the pictures write the name of each word. The teacher will then read aloud each word and ask what do they hear when all the words are said? The teacher should guide students to identify that each word have an /a/ in it, in the middle

6. *You do:* Teacher will then guide students to complete short vowel /a/ worksheet (see appendix). The teacher will assist in reading the sentences on the pages in the book as well as the word bank to fill in the blanks.

7. *Exit Ticket:* The teacher will write the word family -an on the board and point to it. Have the student think of and write a word in that word family on an index card with their names. The teacher will collect, scan the pile, observe & record student responses.

Sight & Sound Words: (9:45-10:15)

1. Have students gather together. The teacher will display the chart paper with the sight words & sound word pre-written on it.

2. *I do:* Teacher will lead a call and response where the teacher will repeat the first word, a student name, while pointing to it and students will repeat it. Continue down the list one time.
3. Next repeat down the list but challenge students to move faster with the teacher still speaking the word first and students repeating clearly. Repeat once more but this time the students will say the words and the teacher will not lead.
4. *We do:* Sight Word Popcorn: Sight words written on sticky notes that are balled up and placed in a popcorn container (or any container). The rules of the game: the teacher will toss the beach ball (or any soft ball will do) to a student; that student will pick a crumpled up paper from the container and read the word aloud. If the student reads the word correctly they can toss the ball to another student, if not the teacher will toss the ball to someone else and they will have an attempt to read the word. Continue until all of the crumpled papers have been picked & read.
5. *You do:* Handwriting practice. Students will practice writing the sight words on pre-printed handwriting sheets.
6. *Exit Ticket:* The teacher will write the sentence: He is a good boy. On the board. Then each student will receive a post-it. Have students read over the sentence and then on the post-it write down the sight word that they just practiced on the list & handwriting sheet. Students will then get up and put the post-it next to or under the sentence. The teacher should scan over the words on the post-its & record down any incorrect responses.

Bathroom Break: (10:15-10:20)

Small Groups/Guided Reading: (10:20-10:45)

Small groups should not be larger than 5 students and smaller than 2.

1. Teacher MUST model and go over small group activities and protocols before you send students in groups! Students must work on the assigned task at their group! Students must ask their group questions first if unclear before asking teacher. Students must remain in their small group space unless they are getting another activity for their group or cleaning up. Bathroom, water, etc is not allowed during groups. Students must use whisper voice when talking in groups. Actual student group time will be shorter the first month or so until students become acclimated to the expectations and routines of small group work.
2. *Small Group 1, 2 & 3:* Students will use instant learning center kits. Teacher will choose the 2 focused on Rhyming Sound, Beginning Sounds, Building Words, & Story Sequencing. Teacher will MODEL/demonstrate how to use the new center kits.

Writing Workshop: (10:45- 11:00)

1. *I do:* (6 mins max) The teacher will write the words "Ask a Question" on the board. After that the teacher should then remind students that earlier we talked about sentences and that they are words put together that tell something. Well when we put words together to ask something that is called a question. For example: Who is hungry? Is a question because I am asking you if you are hungry. Let's practice asking question.
2. Begin with posing a question to the class: Who is 5 years old? And have students raise their hands. Next ask if someone else can think of a question. Take 2 or 3 examples of questions. Then have students pair up and practice asking each other a question. Have students come together & have 1 or 2 pairs share their question.
3. *You do:* The teacher will then explain to students that they will know practice writing a question that begins with Who. The teacher will write the question

frame "Who __?" on the board and then ask students to help think or brainstorm ideas to fill in the question that asks who. The teacher should write the first idea is five years old? Have students suggest some other things such as a boy, wants ice cream, wants to play, etc). Then using the sentence frame "Question ___." The students will tell what they like and then draw/color a picture to match. The teacher must walk around and promote inventive spelling (where students try to write it on their own first) and then underneath the teacher writes/spells words correctly.
4. If time remains the teacher will select 2-3 students to share their picture and sentence.

Math: (11:00-11:30)
1. The teacher will show large flash cards with the numbers 1-20 on them and begin counting aloud. Encourage students to join in. Today we'll continue to focus on the numbers 1-20
2. *I/We do:* First the teacher will explain that we will review the numbers 1-20. We want to be experts with these numbers and easily recognize them so let's play a game. Teacher will draw a large tic tac toe board on the board. In each box write a different number from 1-20. Next the teacher will model and explain the directions: Students will break into teams to play tic tac toe: but in order to get a turn your team must identify what number is being shown in the box. If your team gets it right then you will get to put your letter in the space, if your team gets it wrong then the other teams gets a chance. If no one gets it right, we move on.
3. The teacher will break the class into two teams, decide who is going first and then begin to play the game. Play 1-2 rounds depending on time. Change up the numbers in the boxes for each round.
4. *You do:* Roll & stack em': Directions: The teacher will pair students up. Next they will distribute flash cards with the numbers 1-20 and counters or connectors. The teacher should then explain & model the directions: Each person will have the cards face down & choose a number. Then using the counters or connectors that represent that number. Have your partner check your work when done. After both partners have checked the work, put that card to the side & pick new cards.
5. Continue for 3-4 rounds or as long as time allows. The teacher should also circulate the room to check student work.
6. *Exit Ticket:* Teacher will say represent the number 8 using shapes on the board. Then have students count and identify how many shapes are on the board. Teacher should take a scan around the room to observe which scholar is correct and incorrect. Record down.

Closing Activity: (11:30-11:45)
1. Gather students together for a closing activity game on the projector & computer. Choices include Reading Eggs (if accessible) or an ABC game on Starfall.com.

DEAR (Drop Everything And Read) (11:45-11:57)

Week 10 (9:00-12:00)

ELA Focus/Skill: critical thinking & poetry
Phonics (letter/word family): /n/ & -ip word family
Sound Words: no, not, nine
Sight Words: in, like, came, by, did, day
Big Book: "The N Poem" in the ABC Flip Book by Teddy Slater
Writing Focus: Tools Writers Use
Math Focus: Numbers 1-20

Objectives: Students will be able to:
- repeat and identify the day, weather and season
- repeat the letters of the alphabet sequentially
- identify the letter /n/, it's sound and words that begin with /n/
- identify and name words within the –ip word family
- identify the parts of a poem
- identify the tools and strategies used by writers
- orally identify the sound words and speak phonetically
- identify sight words & use in context
- orally retell a story sequentially using the shared reading
- identify the parts of a fiction story (character & setting)
- create a draft during writing focused on telling about themselves
- repeat, identify, represent and write the numbers 1-20 using manipulative
- sort numbers and place in sequential orders from 1-20

Materials:
"All About Today" pocket chart, "The N Poem" big book, ABC flash cards, white lap boards, dry erase markers, board erasers, pictures of the number nine, a rip, lip and a flip, -ip activity sheet (see appendix), post-its, index cards, chart paper with sight words pre-written, post-it cards with sight words pre-written, container to play popcorn, handwriting sheets with the sight words written twice (www.handwritingworksheets.com), Instant Learning Centers: Rhyming Sounds, Beginning Sounds and Building words, hand writing story paper with picture space and the pre-written sentence frame: I like ___., crayons, pencils, erasers, paper cups with numbers written on the bottom from 1-20, Number Bingo

ELA
Whole Group: Morning Meeting/Shared Read: (9:00- 9:15)
1. Students will gather together for Morning Meeting where the teacher will model how to use the "All About Today" pocket chart. The teacher will read the information on the pocket chart, using a pointer, starting with the month, date and year using the sentence frame "Today is ___." Next have the students repeat the sentence. After that the teacher will continue on with the pocket chart moving to "Yesterday was ___." Students will repeat each section after the teacher has pointed and read it aloud. Then teacher will read aloud the objectives for the day, briefly explaining that this is what the goal is by the end of their time together (Use academic language). If extra time, have 1-2 students share something exciting or important news about themselves.
2. (9:15-9:45) *I do:* Teacher will begin with ABC flash cards and go through them pointing to or showing each letter (depending on the flash card) while saying

them and encourage students to join in. Next the teacher will point and read aloud the title "The N Poem," from the ABC Flip Chart Book, the author Teddy Slater and the illustrator Liisa Guida. After that begin reading the poem aloud. While reading be sure to read the poem rhythmically so that the students can hear how most common poems are read.

3. *We do:* Then explain to students that what they heard was a poem. Poems tend to have a rhythm and rhyme when you read them. Re-read & point to the poem & encourage students to use the key words or terms.

4. (5-7 mins max) The teacher will then review the meaning of the poem- what letter was the focus? What sounds did it make? Write the letter on the board, bother upper case and lower (write clearly so students can see how to write both type of letters. Next the teacher will say the letter /n/ sound and students will repeat. After that the teacher with draw or place a picture of the number nine next to the letter. The teacher will then point and say nn (the n sound), and add the sound word cat. Have students repeat as the teacher points to each. Repeat twice. The teacher will then write the word 'nine' on the board and point to each sound as the word is 'sound out.' Then the teacher will say the following words aloud: no, nine, not. Have the students identify what each of the words have in common, guide students to listen to each word. The teacher should repeat the words slowly a second time if needed. Guide students to identify that each of the words begin with the same sound, /n/. After that challenge students to think of other words that begin with /n/. The teacher should have scholars repeat the words that begin with /n/ named by students.

5. Then the teacher will write word family –ip on the board and display a picture of a rip, lip, and flip. Underneath or next of the pictures write the name of each word. The teacher will then read aloud each word and ask what do they hear when all the words are said? The teacher should guide students to identify that each word has an –ip at the end. Also that each word rhyme.

6. *You do:* Teacher will then guide students to complete flip flap /-ip/ book (see appendix). The teacher will assist in reading the sentences on the pages in the book as well as the word bank to fill in the blanks.

7. *Exit Ticket:* The teacher will write the word family -ip on the board and point to it. Have the student think of and write a word in that word family on an index card with their names. The teacher will collect, scan the pile, observe & record student responses.

Sight & Sound Words: (9:45-10:15)

1. Have students gather together. The teacher will display the chart paper with the sight words & sound word pre-written on it.

2. *I do:* Teacher will lead a call and response where the teacher will repeat the first word, a student name, while pointing to it and students will repeat it. Continue down the list one time.

3. Next repeat down the list but challenge students to move faster with the teacher still speaking the word first and students repeating clearly. Repeat once more but this time the students will say the words and the teacher will not lead.

9. *We do:* 4 Corners Game- Teacher will place the index cards with the 4 sight words other than the student's names in 4 different corners of the room. Rules of the game: the teacher or leader of the game will say one of the words on the index cards. The players will have 10 seconds to go over to that 'corner' that has the word. Anyone who is at the wrong 'corner' is out.

10. Students and teachers will play 4-5 rounds.

4. *You do:* Handwriting practice. Students will practice writing the sight words on pre-printed handwriting sheets.
5. *Exit Ticket:* The teacher will write the sentence: What day is your birthday? On the board. Then each student will receive a post-it. Have students read over the sentence and then on the post-it write down the sight word that they just practiced on the list & handwriting sheet. Students will then get up and put the post-it next to or under the sentence. The teacher should scan over the words on the post-its & record down any incorrect responses.

Bathroom Break: (10:15-10:20)

Small Groups/Guided Reading: (10:20-10:45)

Small groups should not be larger than 5 students and smaller than 2.

1. Teacher MUST model and go over small group activities and protocols before you send students in groups! Students must work on the assigned task at their group! Students must ask their group questions first if unclear before asking teacher. Students must remain in their small group space unless they are getting another activity for their group or cleaning up. Bathroom, water, etc is not allowed during groups. Students must use whisper voice when talking in groups. Actual student group time will be shorter the first month or so until students become acclimated to the expectations and routines of small group work.
2. *Small Group 1:* Guided reading. In this group the teacher will begin by first reviewing depending on the level of the students either the alphabets or the sight words introduced earlier that day. For alphabets: on individual white lap boards have students write the letter that you name. You can use magnetic letters so students have a reference to what it looks like if needed. For sight words: using the pre-written index cards with the sight words, show the card and have students state the word on the card. Extensions~ have students write the word on white lap boards or use in sentences. Then move into the text that day. Again depending on the level of the students: choose a text close to their level. Teacher will go over the title of the books and the author. Preview the text by looking through the book and making a prediction what the text may be about based on the pictures, title and cover. Teacher must model to students how to use the sentence frame "I predict __ because __." when making a prediction statement to the group about the text or anything. Next have students make predictions about the book using the sentence frame. Then the teacher will either choose to Echo read (you point and read a page at a time and have them repeat you) or Round Robin read (each student reads a page and you go around the group) and begin reading the text together. Once finished reading, briefly discuss the text, what was it about, who was in it: focus on using the key words beginning, middle and end of the story. After that based on what the focus was before reading the text have the students 'hunt' for the sight words or letters in story. Write down each one found on the white lap boards and then share once the students in the group are finished 'hunting'.
3. *Small Group 2 & 3:* Students will use instant learning center kits. Teacher will choose the 2 focused on Rhyming Sound, Beginning Sounds & Sound Sort. Teacher will MODEL/demonstrate how to use the center kits.

Writing Workshop: (10:45- 11:00)

1. *I do:* (6 mins max) The teacher will write the words "Tools Writers Use" on the board. Have students participate in sharing what we have talked about so far what writers do to help think of ideas to write about, what are some things that they do? The teacher should make a list of student responses (make a list, writing, drawing, ask questions).

2. *We do:* Whole group write: Teacher will explain and model to students that they will get to pick one of the strategies to begin the writing process and take it through the writing stages. The teacher will model how to take a question: What is my favorite food? & write it on the board while reading aloud. Then model to students how to think about it for a second and then make a list of possible answers to the question. The teacher should write a list of 2-3 responses to the questions: "I like to eat pizza, bananas, and spaghetti." Next the teacher should model and explain: now that I have a list, I have to pick one to really write about. I really like spaghetti the best so I will pick that. The teacher should model how to circle, star or mark the one picked. Using the chart paper the teacher will then model how to write a sentence using the frame "I like _____." While reading aloud as it is written. Then model how the drawing/picture matches the sentence. Details are very important.
3. *You do:* The teacher will then explain to students that now they will try this on their own. Give clear, step by step directions. Students will pick their own strategy & then using the sentence frame write a sentence. The students will then draw a picture to match the sentence they created. The teacher must walk around and promote inventive spelling (where students try to write it on their own first) and then underneath the teacher writes/spells words correctly.
4. If time remains the teacher will select 2-3 students to share their picture and sentence.

Math: (11:00-11:30)
1. The teacher will show large flash cards with the numbers 1-20 on them and begin counting aloud. Encourage students to join in. Today we'll continue to focus on the numbers 1-20
2. *I/We do:* First the teacher will explain that we will review the numbers 1-20. Students will break into partners. Each partner will receive a stack of flash cards from 1-20 & counters. Each partner will pick a card, say the number and use the counters to represent the number that was chosen. Students should try to focus on doing as many numbers as time allows. One group can also work on the Math Instant Learning Center of Counting.
3. *You do:* Color by Number Worksheet (See appendix): Students will work on worksheet independently.
4. *Exit Ticket:* Teacher will say represent the number 18 using shapes on the board. Then have students count and identify how many shapes are on the board. Teacher should take a scan around the room to observe which scholar is correct and incorrect. Record down.

Closing Activity: (11:30-11:45)
1. Gather students together for a closing activity game on the projector & computer. Choices include Reading Eggs (if accessible) or an ABC game on Starfall.com.

DEAR (Drop Everything And Read) (11:45-11:57)

Week 11 (9:00-12:00)

ELA Focus/Skill: critical thinking & capitalization
Phonics (letter/word family): /d/ & -ig word family
Sound Words: dad, did, dog, do, day
Sight Words: went, eat, for, girl, get
Big Book: "This Old Man" by Pam Adams
Writing Focus: Making a Flip Book
Math Focus: Numbers 1-20

Objectives: Students will be able to:
- repeat and identify the day, weather and season
- repeat the letters of the alphabet sequentially
- identify the letter /d/, it's sound and words that begin with /d/
- identify and name words within the –ig word family
- identify & apply that the first letter in a sentence is capitalized
- create a flip book about self
- orally identify the sound words and speak phonetically
- identify sight words & use in context
- orally retell a story sequentially using the shared reading
- identify the parts of a fiction story (character & setting)
- repeat, identify, represent and write the numbers 1-20 using manipulative
- sort numbers and place in sequential orders from 1-20

Materials:
"All About Today" pocket chart, "This Old Man" big book, ABC flash cards, white lap boards, dry erase markers, board erasers, post-its, pictures of a dog, a pig, wig and something big, -ig word family flip book (see appendix), post-its, strips of paper with the sight words written for Basketball word game, chart paper with sight words pre-written, index cards with sight words pre-written, handwriting sheets with the sight words written twice (www.handwritingworksheets.com), Instant Learning Centers: Rhyming Sounds, Beginning Sounds and Building words, pre-made flip books with 3-4 pages & sentence frames on each (your choice but focus on telling about themselves The cover should say All About ___, the pages can say I like ___, My favorite color is ___ My family is ___, one completed to show students as an example, crayons, pencils, erasers, large number cards with the numbers 1-20, Dino Dominoes (see appendix), Number Bingo

ELA
Whole Group: Morning Meeting/Shared Read: (9:00- 9:15)
1. Students will gather together for Morning Meeting where the teacher will model how to use the "All About Today" pocket chart. The teacher will read the information on the pocket chart, using a pointer, starting with the month, date and year using the sentence frame "Today is __." Next have the students repeat the sentence. After that the teacher will continue on with the pocket chart moving to "Yesterday was __." Students will repeat each section after the teacher has pointed and read it aloud. Then teacher will read aloud the objectives for the day, briefly explaining that this is what the goal is by the end of their time together (Use academic language). If extra time, have 1-2 students share something exciting or important news about themselves.

2. (9:15-9:45) *I do:* Teacher will begin with ABC flash cards and go through them pointing to or showing each letter (depending on the flash card) while saying the letters & its sound & encourage students to join in. Next the teacher will point and read aloud the title "This Old Man," the author Pam Adams and the illustrator Pam Adams. After that begin reading the poem/story aloud. While reading be sure to read the poem rhythmically so that the students can hear how most common poems are read. Stop half way and ask students if they recall what type of story this is called? The teacher is looking for the answer poem because we have the rhythm and rhyme within it.
3. *We do:* Once the teacher has finished the story go back through and have students identify what was happening in the story? Focus on retelling with the key terms of first, next, last or in the beginning, middle and at the end. Next the teacher will ask students who were the main people/person in the story? Students should identify the old man or the man. The teacher should explain that the people in a story are called characters. When in a story, just like a movie mostly is about one or two people/characters those are called the main character. The teacher should re-ask who is the main character in the story "This Old Man?" Students should answer with the man.
4. (5-7 mins max) Write the letter /d/ on the board, bother upper case and lower (write clearly so students can see how to write both type of letters. Next the teacher will ask what letter do they see on the board? Once answered then the teacher will ask what sound does the letter make? If needed the teacher should begin saying some /d/ words such as dog, dad, did to assist with the sound recognition. Have students practice saying the sound of the letter. After that the teacher with draw or place a picture of a dog next to the letter & have students identify the picture. The teacher will then point and say duh (the d sound), and add the sound word dog. Have students repeat as the teacher points to each. Repeat twice. The teacher will then write the word 'dog' on the board and point to each sound as the word is 'sound out.' Then the teacher will say the following words aloud: dad, day, do & did. Have the students identify what each of the words have in common, guide students to listen to each word. The teacher should repeat the words slowly a second time if needed. Guide students to identify that each of the words begin with the same sound, /d/. After that challenge students to think of other words that begin with /d/ & the teacher should write some of the words on the board or chart paper to provide a visual for students. The teacher should have scholars repeat the words that begin with /d/ named by students.
5. Then the teacher will write word family –ig on the board and display a picture of a pig, wig, and big. Underneath or next of the pictures write the name of each word. The teacher will then read aloud each word and ask what do they hear when all the words are said? The teacher should guide students to identify that each word has –ig at the end. Also that each word rhyme. Have students turn to the person near them and brainstorm another word that has –ig at the end. The teacher should keep in mind that some of the words brainstormed may not be real words but the focus is on keep the words within the –ig word family. If a student says a made-up word such as mig then saying something along the lines of "while that does have –ig in it, mig is not a real word." An option for teachers is to create a t-chart on the board/chart paper where one column is for real words that students' think of and the other side for made up words so that students can see the difference.

    6. *You do:* Teacher will then guide students to complete flip /-ig/ book (see appendix). The teacher will assist in reading the words on the pages in the book so that students can find the picture that matches & glue it.

    7. *Exit Ticket:* The teacher will write the word family -ip on the board and point to it. Have the student think of and write a word in that word family on the white lap board. At the count of 3 all the students should raise their boards up so that the teacher will scan the room, observe & record student responses.

Sight & Sound Words: (9:45-10:15)

1. Have students gather together. The teacher will display the chart paper with the sight words & sound word pre-written on it.
2. *I do:* Teacher will lead a call and response where the teacher will repeat the first word, a student name, while pointing to it and students will repeat it. Continue down the list one time.
3. Next repeat down the list but challenge students to move faster with the teacher still speaking the word first and students repeating clearly. Repeat once more but this time the students will say the words and the teacher will not lead.
4. *We do:* Basketball Word Game- Teacher will have the sight words written on strips of paper, next ball up the papers with the words. After that scatter the balled up papers around the room on the floor. Students will each have a turn to pick up a balled up paper. Once they unfold the paper, the student will have to say the word written; if the word is said correctly then students will have the opportunity to 'shoot' the balled up paper into the trash basket. If the word is said incorrectly then the student must ball up the paper and put it down on the same spot on the ground. It is the next persons turn.
5. The teacher should mix up the remaining words once everyone has gone once before beginning a second round.
6. Students and teachers will play until no other papers remain on the floor. If time, play again.
7. *You do:* Handwriting practice. Students will practice writing the sight words on pre-printed handwriting sheets.
8. *Exit Ticket:* The teacher write the word get on the board & then say the word get. Have students give a thumb up if the word the teacher said matches the word written on the board or give a thumb down if the word said doesn't match what is written.

Bathroom Break: (10:15-10:20)

Small Groups/Guided Reading: (10:20-10:45)

Small groups should not be larger than 5 students and smaller than 2.

1. Teacher MUST model and go over small group activities and protocols before you send students in groups! Students must work on the assigned task at their group! Students must ask their group questions first if unclear before asking teacher. Students must remain in their small group space unless they are getting another activity for their group or cleaning up. Bathroom, water, etc is not allowed during groups. Students must use whisper voice when talking in groups. Actual student group time will be shorter the first month or so until students become acclimated to the expectations and routines of small group work.
2. *Small Group 1:* Guided reading. In this group the teacher will begin by first reviewing depending on the level of the students either the alphabets or the sight words introduced earlier that day. For alphabets: on individual white lap boards have students write the letter that you name. You can use magnetic letters so students have a reference to what it looks like if needed. For sight words: using the pre-written index cards with the sight words, show the card and have

students state the word on the card. Extensions~ have students write the word on white lap boards or use in sentences. Then move into the text that day. Again depending on the level of the students: choose a text close to their level. Teacher will go over the title of the books and the author. Preview the text by looking through the book and making a prediction what the text may be about based on the pictures, title and cover. Teacher must model to students how to use the sentence frame "I predict __ because __." when making a prediction statement to the group about the text or anything. Next have students make predictions about the book using the sentence frame. Then the teacher will either choose to Echo read (you point and read a page at a time and have them repeat you) or Round Robin read (each student reads a page and you go around the group) and begin reading the text together. Once finished reading, briefly discuss the text, what was it about, who was in it: focus on using the key words beginning, middle and end of the story. After that based on what the focus was before reading the text have the students 'hunt' for the sight words or letters in story. Write down each one found on the white lap boards and then share once the students in the group are finished 'hunting'.
3. *Small Group 2 & 3:* Students will use instant learning center kits. Teacher will choose the 2 focused on Rhyming Sound, Beginning Sounds & Sound Sort. Teacher will MODEL/demonstrate how to use the center kits.

Writing Workshop: (10:45- 11:00)
1. *I do:* (6 mins max) The teacher will write the words "Let's Make a Book About Me" on the board. Have students participate in sharing things about themselves such as favorite color, food, like to do, & family. The teacher should have a pre-made book to show students what the finished copy will look like.
2. *We do:* Whole group write: Teacher will explain and model to students how to work on their flip book. Begin with the cover. On the line after "All About" students should write their name. Be sure that each student writes their name with a capital letter. Next, the teacher will read aloud the sentence frames one at a time and allow students to fill it in. (For advanced students allow them to write their own sentence without the frame given.) Be sure to also reiterate to students that sentences begin with capital letters just as they see with the frames in the books. Save the coloring for after all the blanks have been filled in. Remember to allow for inventive writing at first & then circulate to revise any spelling.
3. *You do:* The teacher will give students to work on the illustrations for their flip books. Don't forget the cover and end page.
4. Students should practice reading if finished early or go back to an old writing piece to finish working on.
5. If time remains the teacher will select 2-3 students to share their picture and sentence.

Math: (11:00-11:30)
1. The teacher will show large flash cards with the numbers 1-20 on them and begin counting aloud. Encourage students to join in. Today we'll continue to focus on placing the number in order.
2. *I/We do:* First the teacher will point to a number line in the classroom and explain to students that this row of numbers is called a number line. We use it when we need help remembering how to put numbers in order like in the way we count them. 1,2,3,4,5 is how we count in order. Now let's write these numbers on the board out of order (write the numbers on the board). If I was told to put these numbers in order that are all mixed up I can use this number line to help me if I'm

not sure. So according to the number line which number is first? 1. What comes next? 2. Continue until the five numbers are in order.
3. Then the teacher will explain to students that now we will make our own large number line in class but we all have to help. Based on the number of students each student may be given one or two or the large number cards at a time to hold. Using the number line to assist the teacher should guide students to help put the number cards in order. Once complete, as a whole group review the number line.
4. *You do:* Dino Numbers Match Game (See appendix): Students will work on activity independently to match the numbers together with the dinosaurs.
5. *Exit Ticket:* Teacher will say represent the number 18 using shapes on the board. Then have students count and identify how many shapes are on the board. Teacher should take a scan around the room to observe which scholar is correct and incorrect. Record down.

Closing Activity: (11:30-11:45)
1. Gather students together for a closing activity game of Number Bingo

DEAR (Drop Everything And Read) (11:45-11:57)

Week 12 (9:00-12:00)

ELA Focus/Skill: sequencing, reality vs fantasy
Phonics (letter/word family): /f/ & -it word family
Sound Words: for, four, five, fox
Sight Words: if, got, has, how
Big Book: "The Three Billy Goats Gruff" by Paul Galdone
Writing Focus: Making an Accordion Book
Math Focus: Numbers 1-20

Objectives: Students will be able to:
- repeat and identify the day, weather and season
- repeat the letters of the alphabet sequentially
- identify the letter /f/, it's sound and words that begin with /f/
- identify and name words within the –it word family
- create an accordion book about what students do each morning or focused on the shared read
- orally identify the sound words and speak phonetically
- identify sight words & use in context
- orally retell a story sequentially using the shared reading/ put story picture cards in sequential order
- distinguish between a reality and fantasy in a story
- identify the parts of a fiction story (character & setting)
- repeat, identify, represent and write the numbers 1-20 using manipulative
- sort numbers and place in sequential orders from 1-20

Materials:
"All About Today" pocket chart, "The Three Billy Goats Gruff" big book, ABC flash cards, white lap boards, dry erase markers, board erasers, post-its, copies of pictures from within the shared read story, pictures of the number five, a pit, sit, hit and bit, -it word poster & activity sheet (see appendix), post-its, chart paper with sight words pre-written, index cards with sight words pre-written for small groups, handwriting sheets with the sight words written twice (www.handwritingworksheets.com), Instant Learning Centers: Rhyming Sounds, Beginning Sounds and Building words, pre-made accordion books with 3 pages & sentence frames on each (The cover should say The Three Billy Goats Gruff, the pages can say First ___, Next ___ & Last ___), one completed to show students as an example crayons, pencils, erasers, play-doh, Four-in-a-row Number recognition bingo (see appendix), computer & projector

ELA
Whole Group: Morning Meeting/Shared Read: (9:00- 9:15)
1.
   2. Students will gather together for Morning Meeting where the teacher will model how to use the "All About Today" pocket chart. The teacher will read the information on the pocket chart, using a pointer, starting with the month, date and year using the sentence frame "Today is ___." Next have the students repeat the sentence. After that the teacher will continue on with the pocket chart moving to "Yesterday was ___." Students will repeat each section after the teacher has pointed and read it aloud. Then teacher will read aloud the objectives for the day, briefly explaining that this is what the goal is by the end of their time

together (Use academic language). If extra time, have 1-2 students share something exciting or important news about themselves.

3. (9:15-9:45) *I do:* Teacher will begin with ABC flash cards and go through them pointing to or showing each letter (depending on the flash card) while saying the letters & its sound & encourage students to join in. Or if the students have mastered this then distribute the flash cards to students and have them put them in order on the floor or desks. Next the teacher will point and read aloud the title "The Three Billy Goats Gruff," the author & illustrator Paul Galdone. After that begin reading the story aloud. Stop half way and ask students to identify the characters in the story: remembering that the characters are the people in the book. Also have students identify who are the main characters (who the story is mostly about or who is/are doing most of the talking)?

4. *We do:* Once the teacher has finished the story go back through and have students identify what was happening in the story? Focus on retelling with the key terms of first, next, last or in the beginning, middle and at the end. Next the teacher will ask if this is a story that could really happen or not? Why? Based on student response the teacher should explain that if a story is mostly about things that could never really happen, like a goat talking, then it's called a fantasy story. But if it's a story that could really happen like a story about the first day of school for a kid then it is called a reality story. The teacher should write the words "fantasy vs reality" on the board for students to see visually.

5. Then the teacher said let's look at this fantasy story and see if we can put them it in order sequentially. The teacher should display copies of pictures from the story on the board mixed up (NOT in sequential order). Explain and have students come up and assist in putting the pictures in order to retell the story. Once complete as a whole group go over the order & have students briefly explain what is happening in the pictures, encourage students to use the word first, next, then last or in the beginning, middle and at the end of the story…..

6. (5-7 mins max) Write the letter /f/ on the board, bother upper case and lower (write clearly so students can see how to write both type of letters. Next the teacher will ask what letter do they see on the board? Once answered then the teacher will ask what sound does the letter make? If needed the teacher should begin saying some /f/ words such as for, four, five to assist with the sound recognition. Have students practice saying the sound of the letter. After that the teacher with draw or place a picture of the number five next to the letter & have students identify the picture. The teacher will then point and say ff (the f sound), and add the sound word five. Have students repeat as the teacher points to each. Repeat twice. The teacher will then write the word 'five' on the board and point to each sound as the word is 'sound out.' Then the teacher will say the following words aloud: five, four, for & fox. Have the students identify what each of the words have in common, guide students to listen to each word. The teacher should repeat the words slowly a second time if needed. Guide students to identify that each of the words begin with the same sound, /f/. After that challenge students to think of other words that begin with /f/ & the teacher should write some of the words on the board or chart paper to provide a visual for students. The teacher should have scholars repeat the words that begin with /f/ named by students. If possible show pictures of words that begin with /f/ to allow students a visual.

7. Then the teacher will write word family –it on the board and display a picture of a pit, sit, hit and bit. Underneath or next of the pictures write the name of each word. The teacher will then read aloud each word and ask what do they hear

58

when all the words are said? The teacher should guide students to identify that each word has –it at the end. Also that each word rhyme & are a part of the –it word family. Distribute to students the white lap board & markers and one the board have students listen to the teacher say the word bit aloud & phonetically. The teacher should also cover, erase or take down the –it words displayed. Students will then try to sound out and write the word down on the white lap board. After 20 seconds have students raise their boards up & one student spell the word aloud. The teacher should write the word down on the board. Have students check their words on the boards. Is it spelled correctly?

8. Try again with the word hit, sit & pit. Briefly explain to students that one strategy when sounding out new words is to say the word slowly and listen for any letter or word family they already know. Like in the word bit- we hear it and know that word family & how to spell it. So I just need to listen to what the beginning/first letter/sound is & write it down. That is how we sound out new words or words we're unsure of.
9. *You do:* Teacher will display the –it word family poster (see appendix; pg 10 in doc). Have students use the poster to complete the spelling for each word on the activity sheet (see appendix' pg 38 in docs).
10. *Exit Ticket:* The teacher will write the word family -it on the board and point to it. Have the student think of and write a word in that word family on the white lap board. At the count of 3 all the students should raise their boards up so that the teacher will scan the room, observe & record student responses.

Sight & Sound Words: (9:45-10:15)

1. Have students gather together. The teacher will display the chart paper with the sight words & sound word pre-written on it.
2. *I do:* Teacher will lead a call and response where the teacher will repeat the first word, a student name, while pointing to it and students will repeat it. Continue down the list one time.
3. Next repeat down the list but challenge students to move faster with the teacher still speaking the word first and students repeating clearly. Repeat once more but this time the students will say the words and the teacher will not lead.
4. *We do:* Sight word Tic Tac Toe- Teacher will draw the tic tac toe board on the board. Then inside each box the teacher will write the new sight words just introduced and in the extra boxes the sight words from the previous week (went, eat, for, get, girl). The teacher will explain the game's rules briefly. There are 2 teams, the X and the O team. 1 player will get picked and they will pick where they want their letter (X or O) to go on the board. To get their spot the player must say the word in the box first. If the word is said correctly, then the teacher or player will draw the letter in the box. If the word is incorrect then the next team goes. The first team to 3 in a row wins. The teacher will need to split the class into two teams.
5. Students and teachers will play for 2-3 rounds depending on time.
6. *You do:* Handwriting practice. Students will practice writing the sight words on pre-printed handwriting sheets.
7. *Exit Ticket:* The teacher will write the word how on the board & then say the word has. Have students give a thumb up if the word the teacher said matches the word written on the board or give a thumb down if the word said doesn't match what is written.

Bathroom Break: (10:15-10:20)
Small Groups/Guided Reading: (10:20-10:45)
Small groups should not be larger than 5 students and smaller than 2.

1. Teacher MUST model and go over small group activities and protocols before you send students in groups! Students must work on the assigned task at their group! Students must ask their group questions first if unclear before asking teacher. Students must remain in their small group space unless they are getting another activity for their group or cleaning up. Bathroom, water, etc is not allowed during groups. Students must use whisper voice when talking in groups. Actual student group time will be shorter the first month or so until students become acclimated to the expectations and routines of small group work.
2. *Small Group 1:* Guided reading. In this group the teacher will begin by first reviewing depending on the level of the students either the alphabets or the sight words introduced earlier that day. For alphabets: on individual white lap boards have students write the letter that you name. You can use magnetic letters so students have a reference to what it looks like if needed. For sight words: using the pre-written index cards with the sight words, show the card and have students state the word on the card. Extensions~ have students write the word on white lap boards or use in sentences. Then move into the text that day. Again depending on the level of the students: choose a text close to their level. Teacher will go over the title of the books and the author. Preview the text by looking through the book and making a prediction what the text may be about based on the pictures, title and cover. Teacher must model to students how to use the sentence frame "I predict __ because __." when making a prediction statement to the group about the text or anything. Next have students make predictions about the book using the sentence frame. Then the teacher will either choose to Echo read (you point and read a page at a time and have them repeat you) or Round Robin read (each student reads a page and you go around the group) and begin reading the text together. Once finished reading, briefly discuss the text, what was it about, who was in it: focus on using the key words beginning, middle and end of the story. After that based on what the focus was before reading the text have the students 'hunt' for the sight words or letters in story. Write down each one found on the white lap boards and then share once the students in the group are finished 'hunting'.
3. Then have students take the sequence organizer (see appendix) and draw what happened first, next & last in the story. The teacher should check for details, clarity by speaking with students and accuracy.
4. *Small Group 2 & 3:* Students will use instant learning center kits. Teacher will choose the 2 focused on Rhyming Sound, Beginning Sounds & Sound Sort. Teacher will MODEL/demonstrate how to use the center kits.

Writing Workshop: (10:45- 11:00)
1. *I do:* (6 mins max) The teacher will write the words "Let's Make a Book re-telling The Three Billy Goats Gruff" on the board. Have students participate in sharing things about the story we read this morning. Display the big book for reference. The teacher should have a pre-made accordion book to show students what the finished copy will look like. Also explain that since we're all using one book our own books we make may be similar to our partners and that's ok.
2. *We/You do:* Whole group write: Teacher will explain and model to students how to work on their flip book. Begin with the cover; students will need to draw a cover reflecting the story. Next, the teacher will read aloud the word 'first' & explain to students that in the space they will draw what they think happened first in the story. Allow students time to fill it in. Continue with next and then at the end.

   3. The teacher should also model how to fold the books to create the accordion style if necessary.
   4. Students should practice reading/retelling if finished early or go back to an old writing piece to finish working on.
   5. If time remains the teacher will select 2-3 students to share their picture and sentence.

Math: (11:00-11:30)
   1. The teacher will show large flash cards with the numbers 1-20 on them and begin counting aloud. Encourage students to join in. Today we'll continue to focus on placing the number in order.
   2. *I/We do*: First the teacher will distribute play doh to students. Next explain that the teacher will say a number between 1-20 and with the play doh students will make that number. Remember to use the number line & the teacher should point to it so students can reference it.
   3. Then the teacher will randomly say aloud any number between 1-20 & allow students 30 seconds to make the number. Use a time if needed. Once time is up, students should put their hands on their laps so they will stop working and the teacher should walk around and check work. The teacher should note down any students that still need assistance and those who 'got it.' Once finished checking have students roll up the play doh and wait for the next number.
   4. The teacher should continue for a minimum of 5 numbers. Be sure to say single and double digit numbers between 1-20.
   5. *You do:* Four-in-a-row Number Recognition Bingo (See appendix): Students will work on activity in a whole group setting.
   6. *Exit Ticket*: Teacher will say represent the number 12 using shapes on the board. Then have students count and identify how many shapes are on the board. Teacher should take a scan around the room to observe which scholar is correct and incorrect. Record down.

Closing Activity: (11:30-11:45)
   1. Gather students together for a closing activity game on the projector & computer. Choices include Reading Eggs (if accessible) or an ABC game on Starfall.com.

DEAR (Drop Everything And Read) (11:45-11:57)

Week 13 (9:00-12:00)

ELA Focus/Skill: sequencing, rhyming
Phonics (letter/word family): /h/ & -ill word family
Sound Words: her, he, had, here, have
Sight Words: some, had, her, if
Big Book: "Growing Frog: Read & Wonder" by Vivian French
Writing Focus: Making an ABC Book
Math Focus: Numbers 1-20

Objectives: Students will be able to:
- repeat and identify the day, weather and season
- repeat the letters of the alphabet sequentially
- identify the letter /h/, it's sound and words that begin with /h/
- identify and name words within the –ill word family
- create an abc book
- orally identify the sound words and speak phonetically
- identify sight words & use in context
- orally retell a story sequentially using the shared reading/ frog cycle picture cards in sequential order
- identify and sort rhyming and non-rhyming words
- identify the parts of a fiction story (character & setting)
- repeat, identify, represent and write the numbers 1-20 using manipulative
- sort numbers and place in sequential orders from 1-20

Materials:
"All About Today" pocket chart, "Growing Frog" big book, ABC flash cards, white lap boards, dry erase markers, board erasers, post-its, pictures of a boy, for he, a hill, sill, pill and will, magnetic letters, -ill word family cards (see appendix), post-its, chart paper with sight words pre-written, index cards with sight words pre-written for small groups, handwriting sheets with the sight words written twice (www.handwritingworksheets.com), Instant Learning Centers: Rhyming Sounds, Beginning Sounds and Building words, construction paper, one completed page, the letter A to show students as an example, crayons, pencils, erasers, play-doh, Fill in the missing number activity sheet (see appendix), computer & projector

ELA
Whole Group: Morning Meeting/Shared Read: (9:00- 9:15)
1. Students will gather together for Morning Meeting where the teacher will model how to use the "All About Today" pocket chart. The teacher will read the information on the pocket chart, using a pointer, starting with the month, date and year using the sentence frame "Today is __." Next have the students repeat the sentence. After that the teacher will continue on with the pocket chart moving to "Yesterday was __." Students will repeat each section after the teacher has pointed and read it aloud. Then teacher will read aloud the objectives for the day, briefly explaining that this is what the goal is by the end of their time together (Use academic language). If extra time, have 1-2 students share something exciting or important news about themselves.
2. (9:15-9:45) *I do:* Teacher will begin with ABC flash cards and go through them pointing to or showing each letter (depending on the flash card) while saying the

letters & its sound & encourage students to join in. Or if the students have mastered this then distribute the flash cards to students and have them put them in order on the floor or desks. Next the teacher will point and read aloud the title "Growing Frog," the author Vivian French & illustrator Alison Bartlett. After that begin reading the story aloud. Stop half way and ask students to identify if this is a reality or fantasy book: Remind students to recall that if something can really happen that it is a reality story and if it could never happen then it is a fantasy. Once students identify have them include a reason why that is there answer (evidence from the text).

3. *We do:* Once the teacher has finished the story go back through and have students identify what the story was about? What steps are in the frog's life? How does it start off or come from is a good guiding question. Allow students to refer back to the pages. The teacher should then take a sheet of chart paper and draw & label the cycle of a frog. Then lead a call and response with students naming the steps. Include body motions if able to.

4. (5-7 mins max) Write the letter /h/ on the board, bother upper case and lower (write clearly so students can see how to write both type of letters. Next the teacher will ask what letter do they see on the board? Once answered then the teacher will ask what sound does the letter make? If needed the teacher should begin saying some /h/ words such as have, hi, her & had to assist with the sound recognition. Have students practice saying the sound of the letter. After that the teacher with draw or place a picture of he (boy/male) next to the letter & have students identify the picture. The teacher will then point and say hu (the h sound), and add the sound word he. Have students repeat as the teacher points to each. Repeat twice. The teacher will then write the word 'five' on the board and point to each sound as the word is 'sound out.' Then the teacher will say the following words aloud: he, her, had, here & have. Have the students identify what each of the words have in common, guide students to listen to each word. The teacher should repeat the words slowly a second time if needed. Guide students to identify that each of the words begin with the same sound, /h/. After that challenge students to think of other words that begin with /h/ & the teacher should write some of the words on the board or chart paper to provide a visual for students. The teacher should have scholars repeat the words that begin with /h/ named by students. If possible show pictures of words that begin with /h/ to allow students a visual.

5. Then the teacher will write word family –ill on the board and display a picture of a pill, sill, fill and hill. Underneath or next of the pictures write the name of each word. The teacher will then read aloud each word and ask what do they hear when all the words are said? The teacher should guide students to identify that each word has –ill at the end. Also that each word rhyme & are a part of the –ill word family. Distribute to students the white lap board, markers and magnetic alphabet letters. On the board have students listen to the teacher say the word hill aloud & phonetically. The teacher should also cover, erase or take down the –ill words displayed. Students will then try to sound out and using the magnetic letter sound & spell out the word. After 20 seconds have students raise their hands up to be checked & one student spells the word aloud. The teacher should write the word down on the board. Have students check their words on the boards. Is it spelled correctly? If yes, then with the marker students should re-write the word on the white lap board.

6. Try again with the word pill, sill & fill. Briefly re-explain to students that one strategy when sounding out new words is to say the word slowly and listen for

any letter or word family they already know. Like in the word bit- we hear it and know that word family & how to spell it. So I just need to listen to what the beginning/first letter/sound is & write it down. That is how we sound out new words or words we're unsure of.

7. *You do:* Teacher will distribute the –ill word cards (see appendix; pg 13 in doc). Have students choose a card & use the magnetic letters to spell the words. Then below, write the word on the board using the marker. Continue until all 6 words have been completed.
8. *Exit Ticket:* The teacher will write the word family -ill on the board and point to it. Have the student think of and write a word in that word family on the white lap board. At the count of 3 all the students should raise their boards up so that the teacher will scan the room, observe & record student responses.

Sight & Sound Words: (9:45-10:15)

1. Have students gather together. The teacher will display the chart paper with the sight words & sound word pre-written on it.
2. *I do:* Teacher will lead a call and response where the teacher will repeat the first word, a student name, while pointing to it and students will repeat it. Continue down the list one time.
3. Next repeat down the list but challenge students to move faster with the teacher still speaking the word first and students repeating clearly. Repeat once more but this time the students will say the words and the teacher will not lead.
4. *We do:* (Play again with new sight words) Sight word Tic Tac Toe- Teacher will draw the tic tac toe board on the board. Then inside each box the teacher will write the new sight words just introduced and in the extra boxes the sight words from the previous week (got, if, has, how). The teacher will explain the game's rules briefly. There are 2 teams, the X and the O team. 1 player will get picked and they will pick where they want their letter (X or O) to go on the board. To get their spot the player must say the word in the box first. If the word is said correctly, then the teacher or player will draw the letter in the box. If the word is incorrect then the next team goes. The first team to 3 in a row wins. The teacher will need to split the class into two teams.
5. Students and teachers will play for 2-3 rounds depending on time.
6. *You do:* Handwriting practice. Students will practice writing the sight words on pre-printed handwriting sheets.
7. *Exit Ticket:* The teacher will write the word her on the board & then say the word her. Have students give a thumb up if the word the teacher said matches the word written on the board or give a thumb down if the word said doesn't match what is written.

Bathroom Break: (10:15-10:20)

Small Groups/Guided Reading: (10:20-10:45)

Small groups should not be larger than 5 students and smaller than 2.

1. Teacher MUST model and go over small group activities and protocols before you send students in groups! Students must work on the assigned task at their group! Students must ask their group questions first if unclear before asking teacher. Students must remain in their small group space unless they are getting another activity for their group or cleaning up. Bathroom, water, etc is not allowed during groups. Students must use whisper voice when talking in groups. Actual student group time will be shorter the first month or so until students become acclimated to the expectations and routines of small group work.

2. *Small Group 1, 2 & 3:* Students will use instant learning center kits. Teacher will choose the 2 focused on Rhyming Sound, Beginning Sounds & Sound Sort. Teacher will MODEL/demonstrate how to use any of the center kits if needed.

Writing Workshop: (10:45- 11:00)
1. *I do:* (6 mins max) The teacher will write the words "Let's Make an ABC Book" on the board. The teacher should explain that this is a whole class project & each person will be authors and illustrators in this book. First step is to think of things that begin with each letter. So turn to the person next to you, taking turns, think of and say a word that begins with an A, then do B, C, and all the way to Z. Help your partner if they get stuck. You will have 3 minutes and its ok if you don't get done before time is up. Go!
2. *We/You do:* Whole group write: Based on the number of students, each child should be assigned either 1 or two letters of the alphabet. The teacher should do the letter A so that students know what it should look like. On construction paper the teacher should write an uppercase and lowercase Aa. Underneath should be a colored picture of something that begins with A like an apple. Then the word apple should be under the picture.
3. Once the 3 minutes is up. Gather students and have 2-3 students share some of their ideas. Then depending if each child is assigned 1 or 2 letters, distribute construction paper to students. The teacher should students the letter A page that was made & then explain that each person will have 1 or 2 letters (again depending on the amount of students) and they will make a page for the book with their letter. The letter goes at the top like this one. Both upper case and lower case must be written. Next think of a word that begins with the letter, like the model apple begins with a. The teacher should have students tell what picture/word they are thinking of before beginning to draw.
4. Students must color in the picture. The teacher can either spell out the word for the students on a post-it so that they are able to write it under their pictures or for more advanced students allow them to sound it out.
5. Once everyone is done, gather all of the pages and the teacher should put them in order to staple it. The teacher can work on a cover for the book.
6. If time remains the gather students to share the book with them. If not be sure to do it on the next meeting.

Math: (11:00-11:30)
1. The teacher will show large flash cards with the numbers 1-20 on them and begin counting aloud. Encourage students to join in. Today we'll continue to focus on placing the number in order.
2. *I/We do:* First the teacher will distribute play doh to students. Next explain that the teacher will write a number between 1-20 on the board and with the play doh students will make that many play doh balls. The teacher should model to students how to make play doh balls.
3. Have students take 1-2 minutes to make the play doh balls before coming around to check. Also as the teacher checks have a student identify what number was written on the board. The teacher should note down any students that still need assistance and those who 'got it.' Once finished checking have students roll up the play doh and wait for the next number.
4. The teacher should continue for a minimum of 5-6 numbers. Be sure to say single and double digit numbers between 1-20.
5. *You do:* Number Recognition & Fill-in the missing number activity sheet (See appendix): Students will work on activity independently.

6. *Exit Ticket:* Teacher will distribute post-it or index cards say a number aloud. Have student write the number on the post-it or card along with their name. Collect and go through noting down any students who did not get it correct.

Closing Activity: (11:30-11:45)
1. Gather students together for a closing activity game on the projector & computer. Choices include Reading Eggs (if accessible) or an ABC game on Starfall.com.

DEAR (Drop Everything And Read) (11:45-11:57)

Week 14 (9:00-12:00)

ELA Focus/Skill: Rhyming Verse
Phonics (letter/word family): /w/ & -in word family
Sound Words: with, what, where, when, whale
Sight Words: we, will, jump
Big Book: "Up, Down & Around" by Katherine Ayres
Writing Focus: Making a Number Book
Math Focus: Numbers 1-20

Objectives: Students will be able to:
- repeat and identify the day, weather and season
- repeat the letters of the alphabet sequentially
- identify the letter /w/, it's sound and words that begin with /w/
- identify and name words within the –in word family
- create a number book as a whole class
- orally identify the sound words and speak phonetically
- identify sight words & use in context
- orally retell a story sequentially using the shared reading with key words
- identify and sort rhyming and non-rhyming words
- identify & read a rhyming verse within text; describe what is a rhyme
- repeat, identify, represent and write the numbers 1-20 using manipulative
- sort numbers and place in sequential orders from 1-20

Materials:
"All About Today" pocket chart, "Up, Down & Around" big book, ABC flash cards, white lap boards, dry erase markers, board erasers, post-its, pictures of the whale, a pin, fin, win and bin, magnetic letters, -in word family cards (see Word Family Flip book in appendix), post-its, chart paper with sight words pre-written, index cards with sight words pre-written for small groups, post-its with sight words written on it & crumbled up for Popcorn game, container for Popcorn game, handwriting sheets with the sight words written twice (www.handwritingworksheets.com), Instant Learning Centers: Rhyming Sounds, Beginning Sounds and Building words, construction paper, one completed page of the number 1 to show students as an example, crayons, pencils, erasers, number flash cards (1-20 & 1 set for each student), computer & projector

ELA
Whole Group: Morning Meeting/Shared Read: (9:00- 9:15)
1. Students will gather together for Morning Meeting where the teacher will model how to use the "All About Today" pocket chart. The teacher will read the information on the pocket chart, using a pointer, starting with the month, date and year using the sentence frame "Today is ___." Next have the students repeat the sentence. After that the teacher will continue on with the pocket chart moving to "Yesterday was ___." Students will repeat each section after the teacher has pointed and read it aloud. Then teacher will read aloud the objectives for the day, briefly explaining that this is what the goal is by the end of their time together (Use academic language). If extra time, have 1-2 students share something exciting or important news about themselves.
2. (9:15-9:45) *I do:* Teacher will begin with ABC flash cards and go through them pointing to or showing each letter (depending on the flash card) while saying the

letters & its sound & encourage students to join in. Or if the students have mastered this then distribute the flash cards to students and have them put them in order on the floor or desks. Next the teacher will point and read aloud the title "Up, Down & Around," the author Katherine Ayres & illustrator Nadine Bernard Westcott. After that begin reading the story aloud. Stop half way and ask students to identify if this is a reality or fantasy book: Remind students to recall that if something can really happen that it is a reality story and if it could never happen then it is a fantasy. Once students identify have them include a reason why that is there answer (evidence from the text).

3. *We do:* Once the teacher has finished the story go back through and have students identify what the story was about? What vegetables and fruits were mentioned in the story?

4. (5-7 mins max) Write the letter /w/ on the board, bother upper case and lower (write clearly so students can see how to write both type of letters. Next the teacher will ask what letter do they see on the board? Once answered then the teacher will ask what sound does the letter make? If needed the teacher should begin saying some /w/ words such as why, will, with & what to assist with the sound recognition. Have students practice saying the sound of the letter. After that the teacher with draw or place a picture of a whale next to the letter & have students identify the picture. The teacher will then point and say wu (the w sound), and add the sound word whale. Have students repeat as the teacher points to each. Repeat twice. The teacher will then write the word 'whale' on the board and point to each sound as the word is 'sound out.' Then the teacher will say the following words aloud: with, what, where when & whale. Have the students identify what each of the words has in common, guide students to listen to each word. The teacher should repeat the words slowly a second time if needed. Guide students to identify that each of the words begin with the same sound, /w/. After that challenge students to think of other words that begin with /w/ & the teacher should write some of the words on the board or chart paper to provide a visual for students. The teacher should have scholars repeat the words that begin with /w/ named by students. If possible show pictures of words that begin with /w/ to allow students a visual.

5. Then the teacher will write word family –in on the board and display a picture of a pin, fin, win and bin. Underneath or next of the pictures write the name of each word. The teacher will then read aloud each word and ask what do they hear when all the words are said? The teacher should guide students to identify that each word has –in at the end. Also that each word rhyme & are a part of the –in word family. Distribute to students the white lap board, markers and magnetic alphabet letters. On the board have students listen to the teacher say the word bin aloud & phonetically. The teacher should also cover, erase or take down the –in words displayed. Students will then try to sound out and using the magnetic letter sound & spell out the word. After 20 seconds have students raise their hands up to be checked & one student spells the word aloud. The teacher should write the word down on the board. Have students check their words on the boards. Is it spelled correctly? If yes, then with the marker students should re-write the word on the white lap board.

6. Try again with the word pin, win & fin. Briefly re-explain to students that one strategy when sounding out new words is to say the word slowly and listen for any letter or word family they already know. Like in the word bin we hear it and know that word family & how to spell it. So I just need to listen to what the

beginning/first letter/sound is & write it down. That is how we sound out new words or words we're unsure of.
7. *You do:* Teacher will distribute the –in word family flip book (see appendix; pg 12 in Word Family Flip Book doc). Have students cut and put together the flip book. Either staple the book or use book rings.
8. *Exit Ticket:* The teacher will write the word family -in on the board and point to it. Have the student think of and write a word in that word family on the white lap board. At the count of 3 all the students should raise their boards up so that the teacher will scan the room, observe & record student responses.

Sight & Sound Words: (9:45-10:15)
1. Have students gather together. The teacher will display the chart paper with the sight words & sound word pre-written on it.
2. *I do:* Teacher will lead a call and response where the teacher will repeat the first word, a student name, while pointing to it and students will repeat it. Continue down the list one time.
3. Next repeat down the list but challenge students to move faster with the teacher still speaking the word first and students repeating clearly. Repeat once more but this time the students will say the words and the teacher will not lead.
4. *We do:* Sight Word Popcorn: Sight words written on sticky notes that are balled up and placed in a popcorn container (or any container). The rules of the game: the teacher will toss the beach ball (or any soft ball will do) to a student; that student will pick a crumpled up paper from the container and read the word aloud. If the student reads the word correctly they can toss the ball to another student, if not the teacher will toss the ball to someone else and they will have an attempt to read the word. Continue until all of the crumpled papers have been picked & read.
5. *You do:* Handwriting practice. Students will practice writing the sight words on pre-printed handwriting sheets.
6. *Exit Ticket:* The teacher will write the word her on the board & then say the word her. Have students give a thumb up if the word the teacher said matches the word written on the board or give a thumb down if the word said doesn't match what is written.

Bathroom Break: (10:15-10:20)

Small Groups/Guided Reading: (10:20-10:45)
Small groups should not be larger than 5 students and smaller than 2.
1. Teacher MUST model and go over small group activities and protocols before you send students in groups! Students must work on the assigned task at their group! Students must ask their group questions first if unclear before asking teacher. Students must remain in their small group space unless they are getting another activity for their group or cleaning up. Bathroom, water, etc is not allowed during groups. Students must use whisper voice when talking in groups. Actual student group time will be shorter the first month or so until students become acclimated to the expectations and routines of small group work.
2. *Small Group 1, 2 & 3:* Students will use instant learning center kits. Teacher will choose the 2 focused on Rhyming Sound, Beginning Sounds & Sound Sort. Teacher will MODEL/demonstrate how to use any of the center kits if needed.

Writing Workshop: (10:45- 11:00)
1. *I do:* (6 mins max) Share ABC Book from last week if it wasn't shared. The teacher will write the words "Let's Make a Number Book" on the board. The teacher should explain that this is a whole class project again & each person will be authors and illustrators in this book. First step is to think of what things you

want to draw for each number. So turn to the person next to you, taking turns, think of and say a word that you can draw to show a 1, then 2, 3, and all the way to 20. Help your partner if they get stuck. You will have 3 minutes and its ok if you don't get done before time is up. Go!
2. *We/You do:* Whole group write: Based on the number of students, each child should be assigned either 1 or two numbers. The teacher should do the number 1 page so that students know what it should look like. On construction paper the teacher should write a number 1. Underneath should be a picture of 1 thing to represent the number.
3. Once the 3 minutes is up. Gather students and have 2-3 students share some of their ideas. Then depending if each child is assigned 1 or 2 numbers, distribute construction paper to students. The teacher should show students the number 1 page that was made & then explain that each person will have 1 or 2 numbers (again depending on the amount of students) and they will make a page for the book with their number. The number goes at the top like this one. Next think of an object that you will draw to represent that number like the 1 apple on this page.
4. Students must color in the picture.
5. Once everyone is done, gather all of the pages and the teacher should put them in order to staple it. The teacher can work on a cover for the book.
6. If time remains the gather students to share the book with them. If not be sure to do it on the next meeting.

Math: (11:00-11:30)
1. The teacher will show large flash cards with the numbers 1-20 on them and begin counting aloud. Encourage students to join in. Today we'll continue to focus on placing the number in order.
2. *I/We do:* First the teacher will divide students into groups of 3 or 4. Each group will receive a deck of flash cards from 1-20. Each groups will have 3-4 minutes to put the cards in order. Once each group is done then they will raise their hands for the teacher to check. Be sure to spread each group so that there is enough space in between.
3. *You do:* The teacher should partner each student up and give each group two sets of number cards (1-20). The teacher should explain that each group will play the memory game. Mix both sets together, lay them out face down and the object is for a player to pick two cards. If the cards match they get to keep them, if they do not match place them back face down. The player with the most cards at the end wins.
4. *Exit Ticket:* Teacher will distribute post-it or index cards say a number aloud. Have student write the number on the post-it or card along with their name. Collect and go through noting down any students who did not get it correct.

Closing Activity: (11:30-11:45)
1. Gather students together for a closing activity game on the projector & computer. Choices include Reading Eggs (if accessible) or an ABC game on Starfall.com.

DEAR (Drop Everything And Read) (11:45-11:57)

Week 15 (9:00-12:00)

ELA Focus/Skill: Fiction vs nonfiction & quotation mark
Phonics (letter/word family): /p/ & -ick word family
Sound Words: pat, play, please, pick
Sight Words: his, him, mom, some
Big Book: "The Little Red Hen" by Byron Barton
Writing Focus: Making a Color Book
Math Focus: Numbers 1-20

Objectives: Students will be able to:
- repeat and identify the day, weather and season
- repeat the letters of the alphabet sequentially
- identify the letter /p/, it's sound and words that begin with /p/
- identify and name words within the –ick word family
- create a color book as a whole class
- orally identify the sound words and speak phonetically
- identify sight words & use in context
- identify and locate quotation marks in text; describe its usage in texts
- identify and describe the difference between fiction and non-fiction texts
- repeat, identify, represent and write the numbers 1-20 using manipulative
- sort numbers and place in sequential orders from 1-20
- count on from any given number from 1-20

Materials:
"All About Today" pocket chart, "The Little Red Hen" big book, "Baby Animals" Big book, ABC flash cards, white lap boards, dry erase markers, board erasers, post-its, pictures of kids playing, a baby chick, someone sick, someone kicking and some picking something, magnetic letters, -ick activity (see appendix), post-its, chart paper with sight words pre-written, index cards with sight words pre-written for small groups, post-its with sight words written on it & crumbled up for Basketball game, handwriting sheets with the sight words written twice (www.handwritingworksheets.com), Instant Learning Centers: Rhyming Sounds, Beginning Sounds and Building words, white construction paper, one completed page, the color white to show students as an example, crayons, pencils, erasers, ten frame mats (enough for 2 per student), counters (the two sided chips are good), Monkey in the Middle activity sheets (see appendix), computer & projector

ELA
Whole Group: Morning Meeting/Shared Read: (9:00- 9:15)
1. Students will gather together for Morning Meeting where the teacher will model how to use the "All About Today" pocket chart. The teacher will read the information on the pocket chart, using a pointer, starting with the month, date and year using the sentence frame "Today is __." Next have the students repeat the sentence. After that the teacher will continue on with the pocket chart moving to "Yesterday was __." Students will repeat each section after the teacher has pointed and read it aloud. Then teacher will read aloud the objectives for the day, briefly explaining that this is what the goal is by the end of their time together (Use academic language). If extra time, have 1-2 students share something exciting or important news about themselves.

2. (9:15-9:45) *I do:* Teacher will begin with ABC flash cards and go through them pointing to or showing each letter (depending on the flash card) while saying the letters & its sound & encourage students to join in. Or if the students have mastered this then distribute the flash cards to students and have them put them in order on the floor or desks. Next the teacher will point and read aloud the title "The Little Red Hen," the author and illustrator Byron Barton. After that begin reading the story aloud. Stop half way and ask students to identify if this is a reality or fantasy book: Remind students to recall that if something can really happen that it is a reality story and if it could never happen then it is a fantasy. Once students identify have them include a reason why that is there answer (evidence from the text).
3. *We do:* Once the teacher has finished the story go back through and have students identify what the story was about? Focus on using the key words first, next and last. Then begin a mini-lesson on fiction vs non-fiction. The teacher will explain to students that another way to describe something as real or fantasy is to use the words fiction and non-fiction. Something that is fiction is a fantasy or could never really happen. However, if we have a reality book like this book Baby Animals (show the book) it is called a non-fiction book. Lets practice saying these new words; repeat after me: fiction is fantasy (have students repeat this) & non-fiction is real (have students repeat).
4. *You do:* If time allows have students go through some books in the library or big books and sort to make 2 piles; fiction & non-fiction. Go over after to check.
5. (5-7 mins max) Write the letter /p/ on the board, bother upper case and lower (write clearly so students can see how to write both type of letters. Next the teacher will ask what letter do they see on the board? Once answered then the teacher will ask what sound does the letter make? If needed the teacher should begin saying some /p/ words such as pat, play, please & pick to assist with the sound recognition. Have students practice saying the sound of the letter. After that the teacher with draw or place a picture of someone playing next to the letter & have students identify the picture. The teacher will then point and say pu (the p sound), and add the sound word play. Have students repeat as the teacher points to each. Repeat twice. The teacher will then write the word 'play' on the board and point to each sound as the word is 'sound out.' Then the teacher will say the following words aloud: pay, please, pick & play. Have the students identify what each of the words has in common, guide students to listen to each word. The teacher should repeat the words slowly a second time if needed. Guide students to identify that each of the words begin with the same sound, /p/. After that challenge students to think of other words that begin with /p/ & the teacher should write some of the words on the board or chart paper to provide a visual for students. The teacher should have scholars repeat the words that begin with /p/ named by students. If possible show pictures of words that begin with /p/ to allow students a visual.
6. Then the teacher will write word family –ick on the board and display a picture of a chick, someone sick, pick and someone kicking. Underneath or next of the pictures write the name of each word. The teacher will then read aloud each word and ask what do they hear when all the words are said? Also if anyone recognizes one of the words that we just focused on for /p/. Next the teacher should guide students to identify that each word has –ick at the end. Also that each word rhyme & are a part of the –ick word family. Distribute to students the white lap boards, dry erase markers, eraser & magnetic letters. On the board have students listen to the teacher say the word 'pick' aloud & phonetically. The

72

teacher should also cover, erase or take down the –ick words displayed. Students will then try to sound out and using the magnetic letter sound & spell out the word. After 20 seconds have students raise their hands up to be checked & one student spells the word aloud. The teacher should write the word down on the board. Have students check their words on the boards. Is it spelled correctly? If yes, then with the marker students should re-write the word on the white lap board.

7. Try again with the word sick, kick & chick (which will be a challenge). Briefly re-explain to students that one strategy when sounding out new words is to say the word slowly and listen for any letter or word family they already know. Like in the word bin we hear it and know that word family & how to spell it. So I just need to listen to what the beginning/first letter/sound is & write it down. That is how we sound out new words or words we're unsure of.
8. *You do:* Teacher will model & explain how to make the Chick word Slider (see appendix). Have students independently work on making their own word slider.
9. *Exit Ticket:* The teacher will write the word family -ick on the board and point to it. Have the student think of and write a word in that word family on the white lap board. At the count of 3 all the students should raise their boards up so that the teacher will scan the room, observe & record student responses.

Sight & Sound Words: (9:45-10:15)
1. Have students gather together. The teacher will display the chart paper with the sight words & sound word pre-written on it.
2. *I do:* Teacher will lead a call and response where the teacher will repeat the first word, a student name, while pointing to it and students will repeat it. Continue down the list one time.
3. Next repeat down the list but challenge students to move faster with the teacher still speaking the word first and students repeating clearly. Repeat once more but this time the students will say the words and the teacher will not lead.
4. *We do:* Basketball Word Game- Teacher will have the sight words written on strips of paper, next ball up the papers with the words. After that scatter the balled up papers around the room on the floor. Students will each have a turn to pick up a balled up paper. Once they unfold the paper, the student will have to say the word written; if the word is said correctly then students will have the opportunity to 'shoot' the balled up paper into the trash basket. If the word is said incorrectly then the student must ball up the paper and put it down on the same spot on the ground. It is the next persons turn.
5. The teacher should mix up the remaining words once everyone has gone once before beginning a second round.
6. Students and teachers will play until no other papers remain on the floor. If time, play again.
7. *You do:* Handwriting practice. Students will practice writing the sight words on pre-printed handwriting sheets.
8. *Exit Ticket:* The teacher will write the word him on the board & then say the word her. Have students give a thumb up if the word the teacher said matches the word written on the board or give a thumb down if the word said doesn't match what is written.

Bathroom Break: (10:15-10:20)

Small Groups/Guided Reading: (10:20-10:45)
Small groups should not be larger than 5 students and smaller than 2.
1. Teacher MUST model and go over small group activities and protocols before you send students in groups! Students must work on the assigned task at their

group! Students must ask their group questions first if unclear before asking teacher. Students must remain in their small group space unless they are getting another activity for their group or cleaning up. Bathroom, water, etc is not allowed during groups. Students must use whisper voice when talking in groups. Actual student group time will be shorter the first month or so until students become acclimated to the expectations and routines of small group work.
  2. *Small Group 1, 2 & 3:* Students will use instant learning center kits. Teacher will choose the 2 focused on Rhyming Sound, Beginning Sounds & Sound Sort. Teacher will MODEL/demonstrate how to use any of the center kits if needed.

Writing Workshop: (10:45- 11:00)
  1. Mini-lesson: (5-7 minutes max!) *Quotation Marks-* The teacher will ask students how do we as readers know when someone is talking in a story? Give 15-30 seconds for students to think of a response. Take 1-2 possible answers. Next the teacher should draw and point to the quotation marks. Explain to students that these are called quotation marks and they are used to tell the reader (us) that someone is talking in a book. The teacher should refer back to the shared read "The Little Red Hen" and locate any quotation marks to show to students as an example. Read aloud the quote to students. Explain that when you see this and hear the name then we know that this character is talking to another character in a story. Now we have another hint to help make the stories even better!!!
  2. *I do:* (6 mins max) Share Number Book from last week if it wasn't shared. The teacher will write the words "Let's Make a Color Book" on the board. The teacher should explain that this is a whole class project again & each person will be authors and illustrators in this book. First step is to think of what things you want to draw for each color. So turn to the person next to you, taking turns, think of and say a word that you can draw to show red, then orange, blue, and all the major colors. Help your partner if they get stuck. You will have 3 minutes and its ok if you don't get done before time is up. Go!
  3. *We/You do:* Whole group write: Each child should be assigned a color. The teacher should do a sample page using the color white so that students know what it should look like. On white construction paper the teacher should write the color White. Underneath should be a picture of something white like a cloud or cotton ball to represent the color.
  4. Once the 3 minutes is up. Gather students and have 2-3 students share some of their ideas. Then assign each student a color except white, distribute the white construction paper to students. The teacher should show students the page that was made & then explain that each person will have a color and they will make a page for the book with their color. The color word goes at the top like this one. Next think of an object that you will draw and color to represent that color.
  5. The teacher should write all the of color words on the board being used. Try to write them in their representative color like the word red with a red marker to help students identify the word without asking which says red or orange, etc.
  6. The teacher will work on the cover for the book.
  7. Once everyone is done, gather all of the pages and the teacher should put them in order to staple it.
  8. If time remains the gather students to share the book with them. If not be sure to do it on the next meeting.

Math: (11:00-11:30)

1. The teacher will show large flash cards with the numbers 1-20 on them and begin counting aloud. Encourage students to join in. Today we'll continue to focus on placing the number in order.
2. *I/We do:* First the teacher will model to students using a ten frame mats (each student will need 2 mats to work with the teen numbers) how to count on from a random given number like 12. Ask students what number comes after 12 & observe how many students know automatically versus having to think about it. The teacher should write the number 12 on the board and then a line after for the next number. Explain that it is important that we know the next number quickly because it will help us be better counters and then help us to add and subtract numbers. The teacher will count & place 12 counters on the ten frame mats. Pause after 12 & ask what number comes next when this next counter is put down? Students will/should say 13. The teacher should write the 13 following the 12 on the board.
3. The teacher should draw a line after 13 and ask students what comes next? Use the ten frame mats to help? Have students identify the next number and write it on the board. Next have students clear their ten frames and the teacher should write the number 9 on the board. Again ask what comes next and have students use the counters on their ten frames to find the answer. Write the answer on the board once found by students.
4. Repeat again for 5-6 random numbers from 1-19.
5. *You do:* Have students work independently on the 'Monkey in the Middle Sequencing' (see appendix). The teacher should provide directions on how to complete. There is an advanced for students to practice with all the numbers 1-20 and another version for those who need more focus on numbers 1-10.
6. *Exit Ticket:* Teacher will distribute post-it or index cards say a number aloud. Have student write the number on the post-it or card along with their name. Collect and go through noting down any students who did not get it correct.

Closing Activity: (11:30-11:45)
1. Gather students together for a closing activity game on the projector & computer. Choices include Reading Eggs (if accessible) or an ABC game on Starfall.com.

DEAR (Drop Everything And Read) (11:45-11:57)

Week 16 (9:00-12:00)

ELA Focus/Skill: ABC Sequence Action Words & cause and effect
Phonics (letter/word family): /l/ & short vowel /i/ review with word family
Sound Words: little, love, like, look
Sight Words: or, man, not, now
Big Book: "Rainbow Fish" by Marcus Pfister
Writing Focus: Full Names on Paper
Math Focus: Counting on using any numbers from 1-20

Objectives: Students will be able to:
- repeat and identify the day, weather and season
- repeat the letters of the alphabet sequentially
- identify the letter /l/, it's sound and words that begin with /l/
- sort and identify short vowel /i/ word families
- write their full names
- orally identify the sound words and speak phonetically
- identify sight words & use in context
- sort and write action words in ABC order
- identify the cause and effect in a story
- repeat, identify, represent and write the numbers 1-20 using manipulative
- sort numbers and place in sequential orders from 1-20
- count on from any given number from 1-20

Materials:
"All About Today" pocket chart, "Rainbow Fish" big book (be sure to pre-read & identify pages with action words- write on a sticky note to help you remember), ABC flash cards, white lap boards, dry erase markers, board erasers, post-its, large story map drawn on chart paper, pictures of hearts for love, short vowel review (see appendix), post-its, chart paper with sight words pre-written, index cards with sight words pre-written for small groups & 4 Corners game, handwriting sheets with the sight words written twice (www.handwritingworksheets.com), Instant Learning Centers: Rhyming Sounds, Beginning Sounds and Building words, handwriting paper with each students name written twice, construction paper, crayons, pencils, erasers, glue, paper plates, an assortment of shapes cut as pizza toppings for students to use, number flash cards (atleast 1 for each group/table of students), computer & projector

ELA
Whole Group: Morning Meeting/Shared Read: (9:00- 9:15)
1. Students will gather together for Morning Meeting where the teacher will model how to use the "All About Today" pocket chart. The teacher will read the information on the pocket chart, using a pointer, starting with the month, date and year using the sentence frame "Today is __." Next have the students repeat the sentence. After that the teacher will continue on with the pocket chart moving to "Yesterday was __." Students will repeat each section after the teacher has pointed and read it aloud. Then teacher will read aloud the objectives for the day, briefly explaining that this is what the goal is by the end of their time together (Use academic language). If extra time, have 1-2 students share something exciting or important news about themselves.

2. (9:15-9:45) *I do:* Teacher will begin with ABC flash cards and go through them pointing to or showing each letter (depending on the flash card) while saying the letters & its sound & encourage students to join in. Or if the students have mastered this then distribute the flash cards to students and have them put them in order on the floor or desks. Next the teacher will point and read aloud the title "Rainbow Fish," the author Marcus Pfister and illustrator J Alison James. After that begin reading the story aloud. Stop half way and ask students to identify if this is a reality or fantasy book: Remind students to recall that if something can really happen that it is a reality story and if it could never happen then it is a fantasy. Once students identify have them include a reason why that is there answer (evidence from the text).
3. *We do:* Once the teacher has finished the story go back through and have students identify what the story was about? Focus on using the key words first, next and last. Have students identify who the characters are in the story & begin filling in a story map. Model & explain how organizers help us keep our information in one place & organized.
4. Mini-lesson: Action words- Teacher will then explain to students that there are some words in a story and when we write that help readers know that something is happening like walking, running, talking, etc. Let's see if we can find some. The teacher should refer back to the sticky note that was created before class to turn to specific pages with action words on them. The teacher should read aloud sentences with the action words and have students identify the word within the sentence. Write the words on the board. When you have a list of 4-5 words, stop and read aloud to the class.
5. Challenge students to see if we can put this list in what we call ABC order. Ask students how many people know their ABC's? The teacher should explain that it's important to know your ABC's to put words in ABC order. First you underline the first letter of each word & then use the ABC chart on the wall to help us just like how we can use the number line to help us put numbers in order. Together with the students look at the list and put the words in ABC order. If needed show students to use the second letter in a word to help with words that begin with the same letter.
6. (5-7 mins max) Write the letter /l/ on the board, bother upper case and lower (write clearly so students can see how to write both type of letters. Next the teacher will ask what letter do they see on the board? Once answered then the teacher will ask what sound does the letter make? If needed the teacher should begin saying some /l/ words such as love, little, like & look to assist with the sound recognition. Have students practice saying the sound of the letter. After that the teacher with draw or place a picture of hearts to show love next to the letter & have students identify the picture. The teacher will then point and say ll (the l sound), and add the sound word love. Have students repeat as the teacher points to each. Repeat twice. The teacher will then write the word 'love' on the board and point to each sound as the word is 'sound out.' Then the teacher will say the following words aloud: little, like, look & love. Have the students identify what each of the words has in common, guide students to listen to each word. The teacher should repeat the words slowly a second time if needed. Guide students to identify that each of the words begin with the same sound, /l/. After that challenge students to think of other words that begin with /p/ & the teacher should write some of the words on the board or chart paper to provide a visual for students. The teacher should have scholars repeat the words that begin with /l/

named by students. If possible show pictures of words that begin with /l/ to allow students a visual.

7. Then the teacher will write short vowel /i/ on the board and display a picture of a lip, pig, sit, hill, pin and chick. Underneath or next of the pictures write the name of each word. The teacher will then read aloud each word and ask what do they hear when all the words are said? The teacher should guide students to identify that each word has an /i/ in it, in the middle. Write the word wig on the board & have students identify in which group would that word belong in. The teacher should also try with the words brick, rip, hit, will and win.
8. *You do:* Teacher will then guide students to complete short vowel /i/ worksheet (see appendix). The teacher will assist in reading the sentences on the pages in the book as well as the word bank to fill in the blanks.
9. *Exit Ticket:* The teacher will write the word family -ick on the board and point to it. Have the student think of and write a word in that word family on the white lap board. At the count of 3 all the students should raise their boards up so that the teacher will scan the room, observe & record student responses.

Sight & Sound Words: (9:45-10:15)
1. Have students gather together. The teacher will display the chart paper with the sight words & sound word pre-written on it.
2. *I do:* Teacher will lead a call and response where the teacher will repeat the first word, a student name, while pointing to it and students will repeat it. Continue down the list one time.
3. Next repeat down the list but challenge students to move faster with the teacher still speaking the word first and students repeating clearly. Repeat once more but this time the students will say the words and the teacher will not lead.
4. *We do:* 4 Corners Game- Teacher will place the index cards with the 4 sight words other than the student's names in 4 different corners of the room. Rules of the game: the teacher or leader of the game will say one of the words on the index cards. The players will have 10 seconds to go over to that 'corner' that has the word. Anyone who is at the wrong 'corner' is out.
5. Students and teachers will play 4-5 rounds.
6. *You do:* Handwriting practice. Students will practice writing the sight words on pre-printed handwriting sheets.
7. *Exit Ticket:* The teacher will write the word not on the board & then say the word not. Have students give a thumb up if the word the teacher said matches the word written on the board or give a thumb down if the word said doesn't match what is written.

Bathroom Break: (10:15-10:20)

Small Groups/Guided Reading: (10:20-10:45)

Small groups should not be larger than 5 students and smaller than 2.
1. Teacher MUST model and go over small group activities and protocols before you send students in groups! Students must work on the assigned task at their group! Students must ask their group questions first if unclear before asking teacher. Students must remain in their small group space unless they are getting another activity for their group or cleaning up. Bathroom, water, etc is not allowed during groups. Students must use whisper voice when talking in groups. Actual student group time will be shorter the first month or so until students become acclimated to the expectations and routines of small group work.
2. *Small Group 1, 2 & 3:* Students will use instant learning center kits. Teacher will choose the 2 focused on Rhyming Sound, Beginning Sounds & Sound Sort. Teacher will MODEL/demonstrate how to use any of the center kits if needed.

Writing Workshop: (10:45- 11:00)
1. *I do:* (6 mins max) Share Color Book from last week if it wasn't shared. The teacher will write "Know our Full Names" on the board. The teacher should explain that it is so important that we know how to spell and write our full names. We need when we write our names on papers for school, for jobs, to get a car, house, for almost everything! The teacher should write their full name on the board for students to see & also explain that some of us have shorter full names than others but that's ok!
2. *We/You do:* Have each student will turn to their partner and practice saying their full name. Next the teacher will pass out handwriting sheets with each student's name pre-written twice. Once as a reference and the second time to trace for practice. Students should write their names at least 2-3 times depending on the space on the paper.
3. Once everyone is done, the teacher should take out the shared read "Rainbow Fish" again & write the words cause and effect on the board. Read the words aloud to students and briefly explain that this means that something happened because of something else. The teacher should turn to the part of the story where the fish refused to share his shiny scales. Next ask students to describe what is happening on this page. Once students finish sharing then the teacher should ask what happened when the fish refused to share his scales. Students should describe that no one wanted to be friends with him any more and he was alone. Then explain that the cause is him refusing to share his beautiful scales and the effect is the fish having no friends.
4. If time, distribute a white sheet of construction paper, model to students how to fold in half. On the top of one side write the word cause and the on the top of the other side write the word effect. Have students draw the scene in Rainbow Fish where the fish refused to share his scales on the cause side. Allow 3-4 minutes (can color afterwards). Then on the effect side have students draw how the fish felt after he refused and no one wanted to be his friend. Students can take the time to color both pictures if time allows.
5. If time remains the gather students to share their work.

Math: (11:00-11:30)
1. The teacher will show large flash cards with the numbers 1-20 on them and begin counting aloud. Encourage students to join in. Today we'll continue to focus on placing the number in order.
2. *I/We do:* First the teacher will model and explain the activity: each student will receive a paper plate & an array of shapes. Students will choose a number from the deck of number flash cards as well as that amount of one shape from the table. Students will create a pizza with the shape. Next choose a different number & a different shape & add the topping to the pizza. The teacher should explain that students should have at least 2 different toppings but can add more. Each topping must represent a different number picked from the deck of cards.
3. Once all the materials are distributed students should begin working independently.
4. *You do:* Have students work independently on the What's for Lunch? (see appendix- Math back to school packet). The teacher should provide directions on how to complete.
5. *Exit Ticket:* Teacher will distribute post-it or index cards say a number aloud. Have student write the number on the post-it or card along with their name. Collect and go through noting down any students who did not get it correct.

Closing Activity: (11:30-11:45)

1. Gather students together for a closing activity game on the projector & computer. Choices include Reading Eggs (if accessible) or an ABC game on Starfall.com.

DEAR (Drop Everything And Read) (11:45-11:57)

Week 17 (9:00-12:00) – Mid-Year Review should take place this class or by the end of Week 19 class.

ELA Focus/Skill: Sequence (Beg, Middle, End) & Dialogue
Phonics (letter/word family): /g/ & -op word family
Sound Words: get, got, girl, good
Sight Words: but, went, play
Big Book: "Click Clack Moo Cows that Type" by Doreen Cronin
Writing Focus: Talking Pictures
Math Focus: Numbers 21-25

Objectives: Students will be able to:
- repeat and identify the day, weather and season
- place the letters of the alphabet sequentially
- identify the letter /g/, it's sound and words that begin with /g/
- sort and identify -op word family words
- create pictures with dialogue
- orally identify the sound words and speak phonetically
- identify sight words & use in context
- draw and tell story in sequential order
- identify dialogue in a story
- repeat, identify, represent and write the numbers 21-25 using manipulative
- sort numbers and place in sequential orders from 21-25
- count on from any given number from 21-25

Materials:
"All About Today" pocket chart, "Click Clack Moo Cows that Type" Big book, ABC flash cards, white lap boards, dry erase markers, board erasers, post-its, large sequence map drawn on chart paper with labels for beginning, middle & end written in, pictures of a girl, top, popcorn, mop & cop, red, blue & white construction paper, post-its, chart paper with sight words pre-written, index cards with sight words pre-written for small groups & 4 Corners game, handwriting sheets with the sight words written twice (www.handwritingworksheets.com), Instant Learning Centers: Rhyming Sounds, Beginning Sounds and Building words, sequence organizer for small group, handwriting paper with each students name written twice, construction paper, crayons, pencils, erasers, glue, paper plates, an assortment of shapes cut as pizza toppings for students to use, number flash cards (at least 1 for each group/table of students), computer & projector

ELA
Whole Group: Morning Meeting/Shared Read: (9:00- 9:15)
1. Students will gather together for Morning Meeting where the teacher will model how to use the "All About Today" pocket chart. The teacher will read the information on the pocket chart, using a pointer, starting with the month, date and year using the sentence frame "Today is __." Next have the students repeat the sentence. After that the teacher will continue on with the pocket chart moving to "Yesterday was __." Students will repeat each section after the teacher has pointed and read it aloud. Then teacher will read aloud the objectives for the day, briefly explaining that this is what the goal is by the end of their time

together (Use academic language). If extra time, have 1-2 students share something exciting or important news about themselves.

2. (9:15-9:45) *I do:* Teacher will begin with ABC flash cards and go through them pointing to or showing each letter (depending on the flash card) while saying the letters & its sound & encourage students to join in. Or if the students have mastered this then distribute the flash cards to students and have them put them in order on the floor or desks. Next the teacher will point and read aloud the title "Click Clack Moo Cows that Type," the author Doreen Cronin and illustrator Betsy Lewin. After that begin reading the story aloud. Stop half way and ask students to retell what has happened so far in the beginning of the story. Listen if students use the key words. Continue reading the story

3. *We do:* Once the teacher has finished the story go back through and have students identify what the story was about? Focus on hearing if the key words first, next and last or beginning, middle and end are used. Model & explain how organizers help us keep our information in one place & organized. Today we are using the Sequence organizer to re-tell the story. Display a large sequence map drawn on chart paper to students. Label each section with beginning, middle, & end. Have students re-tell what happened in the beginning of the story and the teacher should write it in that section. If comfortable include a quick drawing. Continue with middle and end of the story. Re-read the sequence map when completed and have students confirm if the sequence chart matches the story they heard. Feel free to make any adjustments if needed.

4. (5-7 mins max) Write the letter /g/ on the board, bother upper case and lower (write clearly so students can see how to write both type of letters. Next the teacher will ask what letter do they see on the board? Once answered then the teacher will ask what sound does the letter make? If needed the teacher should begin saying some /g/ words such as got, get, good & girl to assist with the sound recognition. Have students practice saying the sound of the letter. After that the teacher with draw or place a picture of a girl next to the letter & have students identify the picture. The teacher will then point and say gu (the g sound), and add the sound word girl. Have students repeat as the teacher points to each. Repeat twice. The teacher will then write the word 'girl' on the board and point to each sound as the word is 'sound out.' Then the teacher will say the following words aloud: get, got, good & girl. Have the students identify what each of the words has in common, guide students to listen to each word. The teacher should repeat the words slowly a second time if needed. Guide students to identify that each of the words begin with the same sound, /g/. After that challenge students to think of other words that begin with /g/ & the teacher should write some of the words on the board or chart paper to provide a visual for students. The teacher should have scholars repeat the words that begin with /g/ named by students. If possible show pictures of words that begin with /g/ to allow students a visual.

5. Then the teacher will write word family –op on the board and display a picture of a top, pop, mop and a cop. Underneath or next of the pictures write the name of each word. The teacher will then read aloud each word and ask what do they hear when all the words are said? Next the teacher should guide students to identify that each word has –op at the end. Also that each word rhyme & are a part of the –op word family. Distribute to students the white lap boards, dry erase markers & erasers. On the board have students listen to the teacher say the word cop aloud & phonetically. The teacher should also cover, erase or take down the –op words displayed. Students will then try to sound out and write it

out on their white lap boards. After 20 seconds have students raise their hands up to be checked & one student spells the word aloud. The teacher should write the word down on the board. Have students check their words on the boards. Is it spelled correctly? If yes, then with the marker students should re-write the word on the white lap board.

6. Try again with the word top, mop & pop. Briefly re-explain to students that one strategy when sounding out new words is to say the word slowly and listen for any letter or word family they already know. Like in the word bin we hear it and know that word family & how to spell it. So I just need to listen to what the beginning/first letter/sound is & write it down. That is how we sound out new words or words we're unsure of.
7. *You do:* Teacher will then guide students to create popcorn kernels with -op (see appendix). The directions are with the activity.
8. *Exit Ticket:* The teacher will write the word family -op on the board and point to it. Have the student think of and write a word in that word family on the white lap board. At the count of 3 all the students should raise their boards up so that the teacher will scan the room, observe & record student responses.

Sight & Sound Words: (9:45-10:15)
1. Have students gather together. The teacher will display the chart paper with the sight words & sound word pre-written on it.
2. *I do:* Teacher will lead a call and response where the teacher will repeat the first word, a student name, while pointing to it and students will repeat it. Continue down the list one time.
3. Next repeat down the list but challenge students to move faster with the teacher still speaking the word first and students repeating clearly. Repeat once more but this time the students will say the words and the teacher will not lead.
4. *We do:* Sight word Tic Tac Toe- Teacher will draw the tic tac toe board on the board. Then inside each box the teacher will write the new sight words just introduced and in the extra boxes the sight words from the previous week (or, not, man, now). The teacher will explain the game's rules briefly. There are 2 teams, the X and the O team. 1 player will get picked and they will pick where they want their letter (X or O) to go on the board. To get their spot the player must say the word in the box first. If the word is said correctly, then the teacher or player will draw the letter in the box. If the word is incorrect then the next team goes. The first team to 3 in a row wins. The teacher will need to split the class into two teams.
5. Students and teachers will play for 2-3 rounds depending on time.
6. *You do:* Handwriting practice. Students will practice writing the sight words on pre-printed handwriting sheets.
7. *Exit Ticket:* The teacher will write the word play on the board & then say the word play. Have students give a thumb up if the word the teacher said matches the word written on the board or give a thumb down if the word said doesn't match what is written.

Bathroom Break: (10:15-10:20)

Small Groups/Guided Reading: (10:20-10:45)
Small groups should not be larger than 5 students and smaller than 2.
1. Teacher MUST model and go over small group activities and protocols before you send students in groups! Students must work on the assigned task at their group! Students must ask their group questions first if unclear before asking teacher. Students must remain in their small group space unless they are getting another activity for their group or cleaning up. Bathroom, water, etc is not allowed

during groups. Students must use whisper voice when talking in groups. Actual student group time will be shorter the first month or so until students become acclimated to the expectations and routines of small group work.

2. *Small Group 1:* Guided reading. In this group the teacher will begin by first reviewing depending on the level of the students either the alphabets or the sight words introduced earlier that day. For alphabets: on individual white lap boards have students write the letter that you name. You can use magnetic letters so students have a reference to what it looks like if needed. For sight words: using the pre-written index cards with the sight words, show the card and have students state the word on the card. Extensions~ have students write the word on white lap boards or use in sentences. Then move into the text that day. Again depending on the level of the students: choose a text close to their level. Teacher will go over the title of the books and the author. Preview the text by looking through the book and making a prediction what the text may be about based on the pictures, title and cover. Teacher must model to students how to use the sentence frame "I predict __ because __." when making a prediction statement to the group about the text or anything. Next have students make predictions about the book using the sentence frame. Then the teacher will either choose to Echo read (you point and read a page at a time and have them repeat you) or Round Robin read (each student reads a page and you go around the group) and begin reading the text together. Once finished reading, briefly discuss the text, what was it about, who was in it: focus on using the key words beginning, middle and end of the story. After that based on what the focus was before reading the text have the students 'hunt' for the sight words or letters in story. Write down each one found on the white lap boards and then share once the students in the group are finished 'hunting'.

3. Then have students take the sequence organizer (see appendix) and draw what happened first, next & last in the story. The teacher should check for details, clarity by speaking with students and accuracy.

4. *Small Groups 2 & 3:* Students will use instant learning center kits. Teacher will choose the 2 focused on Rhyming Sound, Beginning Sounds & Sound Sort. Teacher will MODEL/demonstrate how to use any of the center kits if needed.

Writing Workshop: (10:45- 11:00)

1. *I do:* (6 mins max) Mini-lesson dialogue in writing and text. The teacher will refer to "Click Clack Moo Cows that Type" and have students recall what the mark was that indicates talking in a story. Accept drawings if students do not recall the name of quotation marks. Have students locate a set of quotation marks in the text. Explain that another word for talking is a dialogue. Many stories have dialogue in them. But there are pictures that show talking too! The teacher should display a picture of a comic or a book such as "Don't Let the Pigeon Drive the Bus" by Moe Williems that has lots of talking pictures. Explain that the words are inside of a speech bubble and usually whoever the speech bubble is pointing is the character that is talking or saying those words. Read an example of a dialogue.

2. *We/You do:* The teacher should model and explain to students that they will draw a picture and include speech bubbles in it. The teacher will use a sheet of construction paper and draw a picture with two people engaging in some activity like catch. Next model how to draw a picture a speech bubble and then writing something in them to show them talking. Maybe something like 'catch this!' and 'yes!'

3. The teacher should distribute construction paper to students along with pencils & crayons. Have students begin with an idea first and then the drawing. The teacher should circulate around to monitor drawings and assist in drawing the speech bubbles. Remember to allow for inventive spelling first before assisting in editing & revising.
4. If time remains the gather students to share their work.

Math: (11:00-11:30)
1. The teacher will show large flash cards with the numbers 1-20 on them and begin counting aloud. Encourage students to join in. Today we'll focus on the numbers 21-25.
2. *I/We do:* First the teacher will model and explain how the numbers up to 25 are double digit as well. Just like the numbers from 10-19 begin with 1's, from 20-25 will all start with 2. So twenty-one is written with a 2 and 1 together like this. Model on the board how to write 21. Continue with showing 22. Have students assist in what 23 may look like. Continue up to 25.
3. Next have students locate the number 21 on a number line. Ask students what number comes before 21? Using the number line, students should locate 20. Then beginning from 20 have the students count along the number line for 20-25 aloud.
4. The teacher should then distribute white lap boards, markers and erasers. Explain that now students will practice writing the numbers from 21-25. The teacher will say the number 22 and students will write the number on their boards. At the count of 3 have students raise the board up. The teacher will scan the room to see who has it the number correct and who does not. Have a volunteer either tell how to write the number or come up to the board to write them. Have students check their work.
5. *You do:* Have students work independently on completing a chart listing numbers sequentially from 1-25 (see appendix- missing numbers).
6. *Exit Ticket:* Teacher will distribute post-it or index cards say a number aloud. Have student write the number on the post-it or card along with their name. Collect and go through noting down any students who did not get it correct.

Closing Activity: (11:30-11:45)
1. Gather students together for a closing activity game on the projector & computer. Choices include Reading Eggs (if accessible) or an ABC game on Starfall.com.

DEAR (Drop Everything And Read) (11:45-11:57)

Week 18 (9:00-12:00)

ELA Focus/Skill: Prediction, nouns, characters & setting
Phonics (letter/word family): /j/ & -og word family
Sound Words: jump
Sight Words: into, out, down, read
Big Book: "Tog the Dog" by Colin Hawkins
Writing Focus: Writing labels
Math Focus: Numbers 26-30

Objectives: Students will be able to:
- repeat and identify the day, weather and season
- place the letters of the alphabet sequentially
- identify the letter /j/, it's sound and words that begin with /j/
- sort and identify -og word family words
- to write labels & identify nouns
- orally identify the sound words and speak phonetically
- identify sight words & use in context
- predict a text based on illustrations & the title
- identify the characters and setting of a text
- repeat, identify, represent and write the numbers 26-30 using manipulative
- sort numbers and place in sequential orders from 26-30
- count on from any given number from 26-30

Materials:
"All About Today" pocket chart, "Tog the Dog" Big book, ABC flash cards, white lap boards, dry erase markers, board erasers, post-its, large story map drawn on chart paper with labels for character, setting, beginning, middle & end written in, pictures of a child jumping, log, frog, dog & jog, post-its, chart paper with sight words pre-written, index cards with sight words pre-written for small groups, sight words pre-written on post-its & then crumbled up for Sight Word Popcorn, a popcorn container or a container for Sight word popcorn, handwriting sheets with the sight words written twice (www.handwritingworksheets.com), Instant Learning Centers: Rhyming Sounds, Beginning Sounds and Building words & for math: Making Tens & Counting, story map organizer for small groups, blank chart paper, white paper with the title "Nouns" at the top & 4 sections drawn, each labeled with the 4 types of nouns & space to draw/write an example of each, crayons, pencils, erasers, glue, paper plates, an assortment of shapes cut as pizza toppings for students to use, number flash cards (at least 1 for each group/table of students), computer & projector

ELA
Whole Group: Morning Meeting/Shared Read: (9:00- 9:15)
1. Students will gather together for Morning Meeting where the teacher will model how to use the "All About Today" pocket chart. The teacher will read the information on the pocket chart, using a pointer, starting with the month, date and year using the sentence frame "Today is __." Next have the students repeat the sentence. After that the teacher will continue on with the pocket chart moving to "Yesterday was __." Students will repeat each section after the teacher has pointed and read it aloud. Then teacher will read aloud the objectives for the day, briefly explaining that this is what the goal is by the end of their time

together (Use academic language). If extra time, have 1-2 students share something exciting or important news about themselves.

2. (9:15-9:45) *I do:* Teacher will begin with ABC flash cards and go through them pointing to or showing each letter (depending on the flash card) while saying the letters & its sound & encourage students to join in. Or if the students have mastered this then distribute the flash cards to students and have them put them in order on the floor or desks. Next the teacher will point and read aloud the title "Tog the Dog," the author Colin Hawkins and illustrator Jacqui Hawkins. After that begin reading the story aloud. Stop half way and ask students to turn to a partner and make a prediction of what will happen in the rest of the story. Have students use the sentence frame I predict ___. Give 1 minute and then have 1-2 students share their predictions with the group. Continue reading the story

3. *We do:* (7 mins max) Once the teacher has finished the story go back through and have students identify what the story was about? Focus on hearing if the key words first, next and last or beginning, middle and end are used, if not then remind students to use them. Next have students identify the characters in this story, reminding if necessary that the characters are the people in the story. Using chart paper, draw a story map (should have characters, setting, beginning, middle & end sections) and the teacher should remind students that this is called a story map (write the label story map at the top of the organizer that has been drawn. Explain that these are the elements or parts that all fictions, made-up, stores have. *We've talked about all except the setting. Before we do that can you help me fill in this organizer? Who are the characters? What happened in the beginning again? Middle? End?* (The teacher should be filling in the organizer either with writing or pictures with the student responses). *Now what's the setting you may ask? Well the setting is where most of the story takes place. Are they in a house? School? Outside? Inside? So, where does Tog the Dog take place?* Have students respond & when a correct response is given write/draw it on the organizer. Once completed the teacher should review the completed organizer with students.

4. (5-7 mins max) Write the letter /j/ on the board, bother upper case and lower (write clearly so students can see how to write both type of letters. Next the teacher will ask what letter do they see on the board? Once answered then the teacher will ask what sound does the letter make? If needed the teacher should begin saying some /j/ words such as jump, just, joke & jug to assist with the sound recognition. Have students practice saying the sound of the letter. After that the teacher with draw or place a picture of a child jumping next to the letter & have students identify the picture. The teacher will then point and say ju (the h sound), and add the sound word jump. Have students repeat as the teacher points to each. Repeat twice. The teacher will then write the word 'jump' on the board and point to each sound as the word is 'sound out.' Guide students to identify that each of the words begin with the same sound, /j/. After that challenge students to think of other words that begin with /j/ & the teacher should write some of the words on the board or chart paper to provide a visual for students. The teacher should have scholars repeat the words that begin with /j/ named by students. If possible show pictures of words that begin with /j/ to allow students a visual.

5. Then the teacher will write word family –og on the board and display a picture of a log, dog, frog and someone jogging. Underneath or next of the pictures write the name of each word. The teacher will then read aloud each word and ask what do they hear when all the words are said? Next the teacher should guide

students to identify that each word has –og at the end. Also that each word rhyme & are a part of the –og word family. Distribute to students the writing paper & pencils. On the board have students listen to the teacher say the word dog aloud & phonetically. The teacher should also cover, erase or take down the –og words displayed. Students will then try to sound out and using the magnetic letter sound & spell out the word. After 20 seconds have students raise their hands up to be checked & one student spells the word aloud. The teacher should write the word down on the board. Have students check their words on the boards. Is it spelled correctly? If yes, then with the marker students should re-write the word on the white lap board.

6. Try again with the word log, jog & frog (which will be a challenge). Briefly re-explain to students that one strategy when sounding out new words is to say the word slowly and listen for any letter or word family they already know. Like in the word bin we hear it and know that word family & how to spell it. So I just need to listen to what the beginning/first letter/sound is & write it down. That is how we sound out new words or words we're unsure of.
7. *You do:* Teacher will then guide students to create flip book with -og (see appendix- pg 10 of Word Family Flip Books docs). Have students cut and put together the flip book. Either staple the book or use book rings.
8. *Exit Ticket:* The teacher will write the word family -og on the board and point to it. Have the student think of and write a word in that word family on the white lap board. At the count of 3 all the students should raise their boards up so that the teacher will scan the room, observe & record student responses.

Sight & Sound Words: (9:45-10:15)
1. Have students gather together. The teacher will display the chart paper with the sight words & sound word pre-written on it.
2. *I do:* Teacher will lead a call and response where the teacher will repeat the first word, a student name, while pointing to it and students will repeat it. Continue down the list one time.
3. Next repeat down the list but challenge students to move faster with the teacher still speaking the word first and students repeating clearly. Repeat once more but this time the students will say the words and the teacher will not lead.
4. *We do:* Sight Word Popcorn: Sight words written on sticky notes that are balled up and placed in a popcorn container (or any container). The rules of the game: the teacher will toss the beach ball (or any soft ball will do) to a student; that student will pick a crumpled up paper from the container and read the word aloud. If the student reads the word correctly they can toss the ball to another student, if not the teacher will toss the ball to someone else and they will have an attempt to read the word. Continue until all of the crumpled papers have been picked & read.
5. *You do:* Handwriting practice. Students will practice writing the sight words on pre-printed handwriting sheets.
6. *Exit Ticket:* The teacher will write the word play on the board & then say the word play. Have students give a thumb up if the word the teacher said matches the word written on the board or give a thumb down if the word said doesn't match what is written.

Bathroom Break: (10:15-10:20)
Small Groups/Guided Reading: (10:20-10:45)
Small groups should not be larger than 5 students and smaller than 2.
1. Teacher MUST model and go over small group activities and protocols before you send students in groups! Students must work on the assigned task at their

group! Students must ask their group questions first if unclear before asking teacher. Students must remain in their small group space unless they are getting another activity for their group or cleaning up. Bathroom, water, etc is not allowed during groups. Students must use whisper voice when talking in groups. Actual student group time will be shorter the first month or so until students become acclimated to the expectations and routines of small group work.

2. *Small Group 1:* Guided reading. In this group the teacher will begin by first reviewing depending on the level of the students either the alphabets or the sight words introduced earlier that day. For alphabets: on individual white lap boards have students write the letter that you name. You can use magnetic letters so students have a reference to what it looks like if needed. For sight words: using the pre-written index cards with the sight words, show the card and have students state the word on the card. Extensions~ have students write the word on white lap boards or use in sentences. Then move into the text that day. Again depending on the level of the students: choose a text close to their level. Teacher will go over the title of the books and the author. Preview the text by looking through the book and making a prediction what the text may be about based on the pictures, title and cover. Teacher must model to students how to use the sentence frame "I predict __ because __." when making a prediction statement to the group about the text or anything. Next have students make predictions about the book using the sentence frame. Then the teacher will either choose to Echo read (you point and read a page at a time and have them repeat you) or Round Robin read (each student reads a page and you go around the group) and begin reading the text together. Once finished reading, briefly discuss the text, what was it about, who was in it: focus on using the key words beginning, middle and end of the story. After that based on what the focus was before reading the text have the students 'hunt' for the sight words or letters in story. Write down each one found on the white lap boards and then share once the students in the group are finished 'hunting'.

3. Then have students take the story map organizer (see appendix) and draw what happened first, next & last in the story. The teacher should check for details, clarity by speaking with students and accuracy.

4. *Small Groups 2 & 3:* Students will use instant learning center kits. Teacher will choose the 2 focused on Rhyming Sound, Beginning Sounds & Sound Sort. Teacher will MODEL/demonstrate how to use any of the center kits if needed.

Writing Workshop: (10:45- 11:00)

1. *I do:* (6 mins max) Mini-lesson on nouns. The teacher will use chart paper and draw a line horizontally & vertically. Next label a box/section "person," another one 'place,' 'animal,' & 'thing.' The label at the top of the chart paper should say "noun" & the teacher should explain that *a noun is a word that tells about a person, place, animal or thing. You and I are nouns because we are persons or people, this chair is a noun because it is a thing, the cat outside is an animal so it's a nouns and Sankofa is a noun because it's a place.*

2. *We do:* The teacher should pull out the shared read "Tog the Dog" and begin to turn the pages. Have students look at the pictures and raise their hand when they see a noun. Students must tell what is the noun they see & if it's a person, place, animal or thing. The teacher will draw/write the noun the student names in the appropriate box on the chart paper. Go through the whole book or as much as space & time allows. The teacher should review the completed chart with students.

3. *You do:* The teacher will distribute the pre-made worksheets that match the chart paper drawing of the 4 boxes/sections. The top should say "Nouns" & each section labeled with the 4 types of nouns. Have students brainstorm and draw (write & draw for those students advanced enough) an example of each type of nouns.
4. The teacher should circulate around to monitor drawings and assist in brainstorming for those who need it. Remember to allow for inventive spelling first before assisting in editing & revising.
5. If time remains the gather students to share their work.

Math: (11:00-11:30)
1. The teacher will show large flash cards with the numbers 1-20 on them and begin counting aloud. Encourage students to join in. Today we'll focus on the numbers 26-30.
2. *I/We do:* First the teacher will briefly review the last lesson on numbers 21-25. And then introduce the 26 and the number 2 and 6 together & write it on the board so that it is visual for students. Draw 26 objects as well & model counting from 1-26 for auditory learners & so that students hear how to count sequentially. Re-count & have students join in. Continue with showing 27 but the drawing of objects isn't necessary. Have students assist in what 28 & 29 may look like. Then have students guess how 30 may be written, hinting at how the number is said.....thir—tee.
3. Next have students locate the number 26 on a number line. Ask students what number comes before 26? Using the number line, students should locate 20. Then beginning from 20 have the students count along the number line from 20-30 aloud.
4. The teacher should then distribute white lap boards, markers and erasers. Explain that now students will practice writing the numbers from 26-30. The teacher will say the number 27 and students will write the number on their boards. At the count of 3 have students raise the board up. The teacher will scan the room to see who has it the number correct and who does not. Have a volunteer either tell how to write the number or come up to the board to write them. Have students check their work.
5. *You do:* Have students work in small groups on stations/centers. of no more than 4. Use the instant learning centers of Making Tens & Counting. One group can also take number flash cards from 1-30, mix them up and then put them back in order.
6. *Exit Ticket:* Teacher will distribute post-it or index cards say a number aloud. Have student write the number on the post-it or card along with their name. Collect and go through noting down any students who did not get it correct.

Closing Activity: (11:30-11:45)
1. Gather students together for a closing activity game on the projector & computer. Choices include Reading Eggs (if accessible) or an ABC game on Starfall.com.

DEAR (Drop Everything And Read) (11:45-11:57)

Week 19 (9:00-12:00)

ELA Focus/Skill: ABC Sequence, Humor/silly stories
Phonics (letter/word family): /z/ & -ot word family
Sound Words: zoo, zip
Sight Words: came, after, put, run
Big Book: "The Three Billy Goats Gruff" by Paul Galdone
Writing Focus: Captions for Pictures
Math Focus: Numbers 20-30

Objectives: Students will be able to:
- repeat and identify the day, weather and season
- place the letters of the alphabet sequentially
- identify the letter /z/, it's sound and words that begin with /z/
- sort and identify -ot word family words
- to create & write captions & labels for pictures
- orally identify the sound words and speak phonetically
- identify sight words & use in context
- identify a silly or humorous stories elements
- identify the characters and setting of a text
- place letters of the alphabet in order sequentially
- repeat, identify, represent and write the numbers 20-30 using manipulative
- sort numbers and place in sequential orders from 20-30
- count on from any given number from 20-30

Materials:
"All About Today" pocket chart, "The Three Billy Goats Gruff" Big book, ABC flash cards, white lap boards, dry erase markers, board erasers, post-its, large story map drawn on chart paper with labels for character, setting, beginning, middle & end written in, pictures of a zipper, pot, hot, dot & knot, post-its, chart paper with sight words pre-written, index cards with sight words pre-written for small groups, play-doh, Word family flip book (pg 11- see appendix), handwriting sheets with the sight words written twice (www.handwritingworksheets.com), Instant Learning Centers: Rhyming Sounds, Ending Sounds, Building Words & Story Sequencing & for math: Making Tens & Counting, story map organizer for small groups, an informational text like Baby Animals or Growing Frog, crayons, pencils, erasers, glue, number flash cards (at least 1 for each group/table of students), computer & projector

ELA
Whole Group: Morning Meeting/Shared Read: (9:00- 9:15)
1. Students will gather together for Morning Meeting where the teacher will model how to use the "All About Today" pocket chart. The teacher will read the information on the pocket chart, using a pointer, starting with the month, date and year using the sentence frame "Today is __." Next have the students repeat the sentence. After that the teacher will continue on with the pocket chart moving to "Yesterday was __." Students will repeat each section after the teacher has pointed and read it aloud. Then teacher will read aloud the objectives for the day, briefly explaining that this is what the goal is by the end of their time together (Use academic language). If extra time, have 1-2 students share something exciting or important news about themselves.

2. *(9:15-9:45) I do:* Teacher will begin with ABC flash cards and distribute the flash cards to students and have them put them in order on the floor or desks as a whole group. Next the teacher will point and read aloud the title "Three Billy Goats Gruff," the author & illustrator Paul Galdone. The teacher will remind students that they have *heard this story before but it is great to go back and re-read books, you may hear or see something that was missed the first time, just like in movies.* After that begin reading the story aloud. Stop half way and ask students to turn to a partner and make a prediction of what will happen in the rest of the story. Have students use the sentence frame I predict ___. Give 1 minute and then have 1-2 students share their predictions with the group. Continue reading the story
3. *We do:* (10 mins max) Once the teacher has finished the story go back through and have students identify what the story was about? Have students assist in completing a story map organizer on chart paper. Extension- advanced or higher students should fill an organizer out simultaneously with the class.
4. Next the teacher should ask how did students *feel as they heard this story? Did the story make you feel sad? mad? happy? laugh?* Explain that *stories are written with a purpose, to give us information, to tell us something, to make us laugh, to help us and lots of other reasons. The purpose of this story is to be silly or make us smile or maybe even laugh. What are some parts that you found silly or made you smile or laugh?* Have students turn to a partner and share for 1 minute. Then come back together and have 2-3 students share. If time, have students illustrate what they felt was funny or silly in the story.
5. (5-7 mins max) Write the letter /z/ on the board, bother upper case and lower (write clearly so students can see how to write both type of letters. Next the teacher will ask what letter do they see on the board? Once answered then the teacher will ask what sound does the letter make? If needed the teacher should begin saying some /z/ words such as zip, zoo & zebra to assist with the sound recognition. Have students practice saying the sound of the letter. After that the teacher with draw or place a picture of a zipper next to the letter & have students identify the picture. The teacher will then point and say zu (the z sound), and add the sound word zip. Have students repeat as the teacher points to each. Repeat twice. The teacher will then write the word 'zip' on the board and point to each sound as the word is 'sounded out.' Guide students to identify that each of the words begin with the same sound, /z/. After that challenge students to think of other words that begin with /z/ & the teacher should write some of the words on the board or chart paper to provide a visual for students. The teacher should have scholars repeat the words that begin with /z/ named by students. If possible show pictures of words that begin with /z/ to allow students a visual.
6. Then the teacher will write word family –ot on the board and display a picture of a pot, hot, dot and a knot. Underneath or next of the pictures write the name of each word. The teacher will then read aloud each word and ask what do they hear when all the words are said? Next the teacher should guide students to identify that each word has –ot at the end. Also that each word rhyme & are a part of the –ot word family. Distribute to students the writing paper & pencils. On the paper have students listen to the teacher say the word pot aloud & phonetically. The teacher should also cover, erase or take down the –ot words displayed. Students will then try to sound out and spell out the word. After 20 seconds have students raise their hands up to be checked & one student spells the word aloud. The teacher should write the word down on the board. Have students check their words on the paper. Is it spelled correctly? If yes, then with

the marker students should re-write the word on the paper next to underneath their first spelling.
7. Try again with the word hot, dot & knot (which will be a challenge). Briefly re-explain to students that one strategy when sounding out new words is to say the word slowly and listen for any letter or word family they already know. Like in the word bin we hear it and know that word family & how to spell it. So I just need to listen to what the beginning/first letter/sound is & write it down. That is how we sound out new words or words we're unsure of.
8. *You do:* Teacher will then guide students to create flip book with -ot (see appendix- pg 11 of Word Family Flip Books docs). Have students cut and put together the flip book. Either staple the book or use book rings.
9. *Exit Ticket:* The teacher will write the word family -ot on the board and point to it. Have the student think of and write a word in that word family on index cards. At the count of 3 all the students should raise their cards up so that the teacher will collect them, scan the deck, note & record student responses.

Sight & Sound Words: (9:45-10:15)
1. Have students gather together. The teacher will display the chart paper with the sight words & sound word pre-written on it.
2. *I do:* Teacher will lead a call and response where the teacher will repeat the first word, a student name, while pointing to it and students will repeat it. Continue down the list one time.
3. Next repeat down the list but challenge students to move faster with the teacher still speaking the word first and students repeating clearly. Repeat once more but this time the students will say the words and the teacher will not lead.
4. *We do:* Playdoh sight words: Students will use playdoh to spell out the sight words written on the chart paper.
5. Students will practice writing the sight words on pre-printed handwriting sheets.
6. *Exit Ticket*: Students will each receive a post it where they will write their name and leave room below it. The teacher will write a sight word on the board, came, and then say the sentence *We came to school today.* If students believe the word came is used correctly in the sentence, it makes sentence then they will write the letter y on their post-it. If it doesn't make sense, then they will write the letter N. Then the teacher should collect post-its & scan over them to observe & record student responses.

Bathroom Break: (10:15-10:20)

Small Groups/Guided Reading: (10:20-10:45)
Small groups should not be larger than 5 students and smaller than 2.
1. Teacher MUST model and go over small group activities and protocols before you send students in groups! Students must work on the assigned task at their group! Students must ask their group questions first if unclear before asking teacher. Students must remain in their small group space unless they are getting another activity for their group or cleaning up. Bathroom, water, etc is not allowed during groups. Students must use whisper voice when talking in groups. Actual student group time will be shorter the first month or so until students become acclimated to the expectations and routines of small group work.
2. *Small Group 1:* Guided reading. In this group the teacher will begin by first reviewing depending on the level of the students either the alphabets or the sight words introduced earlier that day. For alphabets: on individual white lap boards have students write the letter that you name. You can use magnetic letters so students have a reference to what it looks like if needed. For sight words: using the pre-written index cards with the sight words, show the card and have

students state the word on the card. Extensions~ have students write the word on white lap boards or use in sentences. Then move into the text that day. Again depending on the level of the students: choose a text close to their level. Teacher will go over the title of the books and the author. Preview the text by looking through the book and making a prediction what the text may be about based on the pictures, title and cover. Teacher must model to students how to use the sentence frame "I predict __ because __." when making a prediction statement to the group about the text or anything. Next have students make predictions about the book using the sentence frame. Then the teacher will either choose to Echo read (you point and read a page at a time and have them repeat you) or Round Robin read (each student reads a page and you go around the group) and begin reading the text together. Once finished reading, briefly discuss the text, what was it about, who was in it: focus on using the key words beginning, middle and end of the story. After that based on what the focus was before reading the text have the students 'hunt' for the sight words or letters in story. Write down each one found on the white lap boards and then share once the students in the group are finished 'hunting'.

3. Then have students take the story map organizer (see appendix) and draw what happened first, next & last in the story. The teacher should check for details, clarity by speaking with students and accuracy.
4. *Small Groups 2 & 3:* Students will use instant learning center kits. Teacher will choose the 2 focused on Ending Sound, Beginning Sounds, Sound Sort & Story Sequencing. Teacher will MODEL/demonstrate how to use any of the new center kits if needed.

Writing Workshop: (10:45- 11:00)
1. *I do:* (6 mins max) Mini-lesson on labels & caption for picture. The teacher will draw or display a picture that can be written on, on the board/chart paper for students to see. Then the teacher will then show students a photo/picture from an informational text that has labels & captions such as a picture from Baby Animals or Growing Frog. The teacher should show & explain to students that *one way photographers and illustrators help others understand their picture or share information.* The teacher should point to the captions and labels as they are being explained. Explain that captions are sentences or phrases that tell about the picture. Labels are one or two words that tell what the picture is like a cat or dog.
2. *We/You do:* The teacher will distribute construction paper and instruct students to draw a picture of the classroom. Once students have completed drawing, gather everyone back together and have students label the picture with "My Room" or "My Classroom." Then proceed to model, spell words that you will use as labels in the picture. Label the desks, door, chairs, etc. Do not exceed more than 3-4 labels in the picture.
3. The teacher should circulate around to monitor drawings and assist those who need it.
4. If time remains the gather students to share their work.

Math: (11:00-11:30)
1. The teacher will show large flash cards with the numbers 1-20 on them and begin counting aloud. Encourage students to join in. Today we'll focus on the numbers 20-30.
2. *I/We do:* The teacher will practice rote counting from 20 to 30 using the whole group. The teacher will start from 10 and instruct students to join in once 20 is

said and together they will stop at 30. The second time the teacher should begin at 15 & have students join in when 20 is said.
3. *You do:* Have students work in small groups on stations/centers of no more than 4. Use the instant learning centers of Making Tens & Counting. One group can also take number flash cards from 1-30, mix them up and then put them back in order.
4. *Exit Ticket:* Teacher will distribute post-it or index cards say a number aloud. Have student write the number on the post-it or card along with their name. Collect and go through noting down any students who did not get it correct.

Closing Activity: (11:30-11:45)
1. Gather students together for a closing activity game on the projector & computer. Choices include Reading Eggs (if accessible) or an ABC game on Starfall.com.

DEAR (Drop Everything And Read) (11:45-11:57)

Week 20 (9:00-12:00)

ELA Focus/Skill: Main Idea, Dialogue & Speech Bubbles
Phonics (letter/word family): /y/ & -ock word family
Sound Words: yellow, you, your, yes
Sight Words: look, about, saw
Big Book: "Click Clack Moo Cows that Type" by Doreen Cronin
Writing Focus: Copying Environmental Print
Math Focus: Numbers 20-30

Objectives: Students will be able to:
- repeat and identify the day, weather and season
- place the letters of the alphabet sequentially
- identify the letter /y/, it's sound and words that begin with /y/
- sort and identify -ock word family words
- to identify & write environmental print labels
- orally identify the sound words and speak phonetically
- identify sight words & use in context
- identify the main idea of a text
- identify & describe the usage of speech bubbles & dialogue in a text
- repeat, identify, represent and write the numbers 20-30 using manipulative
- sort numbers and place in sequential orders from 20-30
- count on from any given number from 20-30

Materials:
"All About Today" pocket chart, "Click Clack Moo Cows that Type" Big book, ABC flash cards, white lap boards, dry erase markers, board erasers, post-its, Cows template (appendix), brown lunch bags, blank speech bubbles drawn or printed, pictures of a yellow blotch, clock, lock, sock & block, post-its, chart paper with sight words pre-written, index cards with sight words pre-written for small groups, post-its with sight words written on them, -ock folding book (see appendix), handwriting sheets with the sight words written twice (www.handwritingworksheets.com), Instant Learning Centers: Rhyming Sounds, Ending Sounds, Building Words & Story Sequencing & for math: Making Tens & Counting, main idea organizer for small groups, crayons, pencils, erasers, make sure that the classroom has items labeled for writing such as the door, clock, wall, board, etc., story writing paper, glue, paper plates, an assortment of shapes cut as pizza toppings for students to use, number flash cards (at least 1 for each group/table of students), computer & projector

ELA
Whole Group: Morning Meeting/Shared Read: (9:00- 9:15)
1. Students will gather together for Morning Meeting where the teacher will model how to use the "All About Today" pocket chart. The teacher will read the information on the pocket chart, using a pointer, starting with the month, date and year using the sentence frame "Today is __." Next have the students repeat the sentence. After that the teacher will continue on with the pocket chart moving to "Yesterday was __." Students will repeat each section after the teacher has pointed and read it aloud. Then teacher will read aloud the objectives for the day, briefly explaining that this is what the goal is by the end of their time

together (Use academic language). If extra time, have 1-2 students share something exciting or important news about themselves.

2. (9:15-9:45) *I do:* Teacher will begin with ABC flash cards and distribute the flash cards to students and have them put them in order on the floor or desks as a whole group. Next the teacher will point and read aloud the title "Click Clack Moo Cows that Type," the author Doreen Cronin & illustrator Betsy Lewin. The teacher will remind students that they have *heard this story before but it is great to go back a re-read books, you may hear or see something that was missed the first time, just like in movies.* After that begin reading the story aloud. Stop half way and ask students to turn to a partner and make a prediction of what will happen in the rest of the story. Observe if students use the sentence frame I predict ___. Give 1 minute and then have 1-2 students share their predictions with the group. Continue reading the story

3. *We do:* (10 mins max) Once the teacher has finished the story go back through and have students identify what the story was about? The teacher will then write the words "Main Idea" on the board & begin to explain that the main idea is found after you ask 'what is the story mostly/mainly about? Or what is the main point/big idea of the story?' It is usually a sentence long and we are not telling the entire story. Next the teacher should ask students what was the main point/big idea of the story? Allow students a few moments to think about it & have 3-4 students share their responses. Main idea: cows are upset about some of their living conditions in the barn so they type a letter to Farmer Brown. Record the main idea on the board & have students echo read it using the sentence frame The main idea is __

4. Next the teacher will ask students how is speech or dialogue found in a story? Students should respond with either quotation marks or speech bubbles (or a response close to this). If not, then the teacher should remind students that authors will use these two elements to show talking or dialogue in a story. Draw them on the board to help remind students. Go through the story book and allow students to locate either speech bubbles or quotation marks.

5. Then have students create a cow puppet from the story on brown lunch bags & add a speech bubble to the top say "Click" or "Clack" or "Moo." Students can either decide or teacher can assign. (Use the cow template in appendix)

6. (5-7 mins max) Write the letter /y/ on the board, bother upper case and lower (write clearly so students can see how to write both type of letters. Next the teacher will ask what letter do they see on the board? Once answered then the teacher will ask what sound does the letter make? If needed the teacher should begin saying some /y/ words such as yellow, you & yes to assist with the sound recognition. Have students practice saying the sound of the letter. After that the teacher with draw or place a picture of a yellow blotch next to the letter & have students identify the picture. The teacher will then point and say yu (the y sound), and add the sound word yellow. Have students repeat as the teacher points to each. Repeat twice. The teacher will then write the word 'yellow' on the board and point to each sound as the word is 'sound out.' Guide students to identify that each of the words begin with the same sound, /y/. After that challenge students to think of other words that begin with /y/ & the teacher should write some of the words on the board or chart paper to provide a visual for students. The teacher should have scholars repeat the words that begin with /y/ named by students. If possible show pictures of words that begin with /y/ to allow students a visual.

7. Then the teacher will write word family –ock on the board and display a picture of a clock, lock, sock and a block. Underneath or next of the pictures write the name of each word. The teacher will then read aloud each word and ask what do they hear when all the words are said? Next the teacher should guide students to identify that each word has –ock at the end. Also that each word rhyme & are a part of the –ock word family. Distribute to students the writing paper & pencils. On the paper have students listen to the teacher say the word sock aloud & phonetically. The teacher should also cover, erase or take down the –ock words displayed. Students will then try to sound out and & spell out the word. After 20 seconds have students raise their hands up to be checked & one student spells the word aloud. The teacher should write the word down on the board. Have students check their words on the paper. Is it spelled correctly? If yes, then with the marker students should re-write the word on the paper underneath or next to their spelling.
8. Try again with the word lock, clock & block (which will both be a challenge). Briefly re-explain to students that one strategy when sounding out new words is to say the word slowly and listen for any letter or word family they already know. Like in the word bin we hear it and know that word family & how to spell it. So I just need to listen to what the beginning/first letter/sound is & write it down. That is how we sound out new words or words we're unsure of.
9. *You do:* Teacher will then guide students to create folding book with -ock (see appendix). Have students complete the –ock word and then color the pictures. Staple to hold together.
10. *Exit Ticket:* The teacher will write the word family -ock on the board and point to it. Have the student think of and write a word in that word family on index cards. At the count of 3 all the students should raise their cards up so that the teacher will collect them, scan the deck, note & record student responses.

Sight & Sound Words: (9:45-10:15)
1. Have students gather together. The teacher will display the chart paper with the sight words & sound word pre-written on it.
2. *I do:* Teacher will lead a call and response where the teacher will repeat the first word, a student name, while pointing to it and students will repeat it. Continue down the list one time.
3. Next repeat down the list but challenge students to move faster with the teacher still speaking the word first and students repeating clearly. Repeat once more but this time the students will say the words and the teacher will not lead.
4. *We do:* Basketball Word Game- Teacher will have the sight words written on strips of paper, next ball up the papers with the words. After that scatter the balled up papers around the room on the floor. Students will each have a turn to pick up a balled up paper. Once they unfold the paper, the student will have to say the word written; if the word is said correctly then students will have the opportunity to 'shoot' the balled up paper into the trash basket. If the word is said incorrectly then the student must ball up the paper and put it down on the same spot on the ground. It is the next persons turn.
5. The teacher should mix up the remaining words once everyone has gone once before beginning a second round.
6. Students and teachers will play until no other papers remain on the floor. If time, play again.
7. Students will practice writing the sight words on pre-printed handwriting sheets.
8. *Exit Ticket*: Students will each receive a post it where they will write their name and leave room below it. The teacher will write a sight word on the board, came,

and then say the sentence *Can you look for it?* If students believe the word look is used correctly in the sentence, it makes sentence then they will write the letter y on their post-it. If it doesn't make sense, then they will write the letter N. Then the teacher should collect post-its & scan over them to observe & record student responses.

Bathroom Break: (10:15-10:20)

Small Groups/Guided Reading: (10:20-10:45)

Small groups should not be larger than 5 students and smaller than 2.

1. Teacher MUST model and go over small group activities and protocols before you send students in groups! Students must work on the assigned task at their group! Students must ask their group questions first if unclear before asking teacher. Students must remain in their small group space unless they are getting another activity for their group or cleaning up. Bathroom, water, etc is not allowed during groups. Students must use whisper voice when talking in groups. Actual student group time will be shorter the first month or so until students become acclimated to the expectations and routines of small group work.

2. *Small Group 1:* Guided reading. In this group the teacher will begin by first reviewing depending on the level of the students either the alphabets or the sight words introduced earlier that day. For alphabets: on individual white lap boards have students write the letter that you name. You can use magnetic letters so students have a reference to what it looks like if needed. For sight words: using the pre-written index cards with the sight words, show the card and have students state the word on the card. Extensions~ have students write the word on white lap boards or use in sentences. Then move into the text that day. Again depending on the level of the students: choose a text close to their level. Teacher will go over the title of the books and the author. Preview the text by looking through the book and making a prediction what the text may be about based on the pictures, title and cover. Teacher must model to students how to use the sentence frame "I predict __ because __." when making a prediction statement to the group about the text or anything. Next have students make predictions about the book using the sentence frame. Then the teacher will either choose to Echo read (you point and read a page at a time and have them repeat you) or Round Robin read (each student reads a page and you go around the group) and begin reading the text together. Once finished reading, briefly discuss the text, what was it about, who was in it: focus on using the key words beginning, middle and end of the story. After that based on what the focus was before reading the text have the students 'hunt' for the sight words or letters in story. Write down each one found on the white lap boards and then share once the students in the group are finished 'hunting'.

3. Then have students take the main idea organizer (see appendix) and draw/write what the main idea of the story is. The teacher should check for details, clarity by speaking with students and accuracy.

4. *Small Groups 2 & 3:* Students will use instant learning center kits. Teacher will choose the 2 focused on Ending Sound, Beginning Sounds, Sound Sort & Story Sequencing. Teacher will MODEL/demonstrate how to use any of the new center kits if needed.

Writing Workshop: (10:45- 11:00)

1. *I do:* (6 mins max) The teacher will remind students that we've talked about labeling pictures and creating captions in pictures. Today we will go hunting for labels around our room. The teacher will distribute a sheet of story writing paper to students.

2. *We do:* Explain and model to students that they will take the writing paper and a pencil with them to walk around the room looking for things labeled. The teacher should point out what the labels look like that is around the room. Once students locate a label have them write down the word on the label on their writing paper. Next to the word quickly draw (not color) what the item is so that students can recognize the word once they sit down. Make sure students take something to lean their papers on as they walk (allows 5-6 mins or possibly longer if time allows).
3. *You do:* Once students have completed the hunt around them room, have them sit with a partner and compare lists. How many labels were found? Can I re-read the labels? Have students re-write the labels once more for handwriting practice.
4. The teacher should circulate around to monitor list work and assist those who need it.
5. If time remains the gather students to share their work.

Math: (11:00-11:30)
5. The teacher will show large flash cards with the numbers 1-20 on them and begin counting aloud. Encourage students to join in. Today we'll focus on the numbers 20-30.
6. *I/We do:* The teacher will practice rote counting from 20 to 30 using the whole group. The teacher will start from 10 and instruct students to join in once 15 is said and together they will stop at 30. The second time the teacher should begin at 15 & have students join in when 17 is said.
7. *You do:* Have students work in small groups on stations/centers of no more than 4. Use the instant learning centers of Making Tens & Counting. One group can also take number flash cards from 1-30, mix them up and then put them back in order.
8. *Exit Ticket:* Teacher will distribute post-it or index cards say a number aloud. Have student write the number on the post-it or card along with their name. Collect and go through noting down any students who did not get it correct.

Closing Activity: (11:30-11:45)
1. Gather students together for a closing activity game on the projector & computer. Choices include Reading Eggs (if accessible) or an ABC game on Starfall.com.

DEAR (Drop Everything And Read) (11:45-11:57)

Week 21 (9:00-12:00)

ELA Focus/Skill: Parts of a Book, Content, Labels & Animals
Phonics (letter/word family): final /y/ & short vowel /o/ review
Sound Words: my, by, why, fly
Sight Words: daddy, mommy, baby, say
Big Book: "Baby Animals" by Sue Davis & Jeni Wilson
Writing Focus: Directionality
Math Focus: Numbers 20-30

Objectives: Students will be able to:
- repeat and identify the day, weather and season
- place the letters of the alphabet sequentially
- identify the letter final/y/, it's sound and words that end with final/y/
- review, sort and identify short vowel /o/ words
- to identify the direction words and writing follows
- orally identify the sound words and speak phonetically
- identify sight words & use in context
- identify and locate the parts of a book, its contents, labels and animals
- repeat, identify, represent and write the numbers 20-30 using manipulative
- sort numbers and place in sequential orders from 20-30
- count on from any given number from 20-30

Materials:
"All About Today" pocket chart, "Baby Animals" Big book, ABC flash cards, white lap boards, dry erase markers, board erasers, post-its, pictures of a house fly, clock, lock, sock & block, post-its, chart paper with sight words pre-written, index cards with sight words pre-written for 4 Corners & small groups, post-its with sight words written on them, short vowel review (see appendix), handwriting sheets with the sight words written twice (www.handwritingworksheets.com), Instant Learning Centers: Rhyming Sounds, Ending Sounds, Building Words & Story Sequencing & for math: Making Tens & Counting, crayons, pencils, erasers, story writing paper, ten frame mats (enough for each student to get 3), counters, number flash cards (atleast 1 for each group/table of students), computer & projector

ELA
Whole Group: Morning Meeting/Shared Read: (9:00- 9:15)
1. Students will gather together for Morning Meeting where the teacher will model how to use the "All About Today" pocket chart. The teacher will read the information on the pocket chart, using a pointer, starting with the month, date and year using the sentence frame "Today is __." Next have the students repeat the sentence. After that the teacher will continue on with the pocket chart moving to "Yesterday was __." Students will repeat each section after the teacher has pointed and read it aloud. Then teacher will read aloud the objectives for the day, briefly explaining that this is what the goal is by the end of their time together (Use academic language). If extra time, have 1-2 students share something exciting or important news about themselves.
2. (9:15-9:45) *I do:* Teacher will begin with ABC flash cards and distribute the flash cards to students to put them in order on the floor or desks as a whole group. Next the teacher will point and read aloud the title "Baby Animals," the authors

Sue Davis & Jeni Wilson. The teacher will remind students that they have *heard this story before but it is great to go back and re-read books, you may hear or see something that was missed the first time, just like in movies.* After that begin reading the story aloud. Stop half way and ask students to turn to a partner and share one fact about animals that has been heard in the text so far that surprises you, is new to you or you find cool/interesting. Allow students 1 min to share & then have 2-3 students share with the class.

3. *We do:* (10 mins max) Once the teacher has finished the story go back through the book and identify what type of book is it? (Real or not real/ fiction or non-fiction) by listening/looking through the content of the book. The parts of a book (cover, title, author, pictures and labels/captions) and what type of animals are mentioned in this text. Explain to students that what we just did was a book hunt, some times this can be done before you read a book to help you decide if this book may be interesting to you or after you have read like we did to help review the information, the type of book or where to find things in the book that you may need to find.

4. *You do:* If time, allow students to go to the class library and look through other books to see if they have the same things/parts as the shared read. Have students raise their hand each time they find something similar & share the title of the book or show its cover for others to see.

5. (5-7 mins max) Write the letter /y/ on the board, bother upper case and lower (write clearly so students can see how to write both type of letters). Have students identify the sound /y/ makes and next the teacher will explain that this week we are looking at words that end in /y/ instead of beginning. After that the teacher with draw or place a picture of a house fly next to the letter & have students identify the picture. The teacher will then point say the sound word fly. Have students repeat as the teacher points to each. Repeat twice. Explain to students that when /y/ is at the end of a word instead of the beginning it can sometime take on the sound of another letter like /i/. Think of a villain in a super hero movie or cartoon that steals a super hero's power & can then use it. The /y/ does that with other letter sounds. The teacher will then write the word 'fly' on the board and point to each sound as the word is 'sound out.' Guide students to identify that each of the words begin with the same ending sound, /y/. After that challenge students to think of other words that end with /y/ & the teacher should write some of the words on the board or chart paper to provide a visual for students if possible. Some options for words are my, by, & why. The teacher should have scholars repeat the words that end with /y/ named by students. If possible show pictures of words that end with /y/ to allow students a visual.

6. Then the teacher will write short vowel /o/ on the board and display a picture of a cop, log, pot and sock. Underneath or next of the pictures write the name of each word. The teacher will then read aloud each word and ask what do they hear when all the words are said? The teacher should guide students to identify that each word has an /o/ in it, in the middle. Write the word pop on the board & have students identify in which group would that word belong in. The teacher should also try with the words block, jog and hot.

7. *You do:* Teacher will then guide students to complete short vowel /o/ worksheet (see appendix). The teacher will assist in reading the sentences on the pages in the book as well as the word bank to fill in the blanks.

8. *Exit Ticket:* The teacher will write the word family -op on the board and point to it. Have the student think of and write a word in that word family on the white lap

board. At the count of 3 all the students should raise their boards up so that the teacher will scan the room, observe & record student responses.

Sight & Sound Words: (9:45-10:15)
1. Have students gather together. The teacher will display the chart paper with the sight words & sound word pre-written on it.
2. *I do:* Teacher will lead a call and response where the teacher will repeat the first word, a student name, while pointing to it and students will repeat it. Continue down the list one time. The teacher should also note & mention to students that this time the /y/ at the end does not sound like /i/ but sounds like /e/ or /y/.
3. Next repeat down the list but challenge students to move faster with the teacher still speaking the word first and students repeating clearly. Repeat once more but this time the students will say the words and the teacher will not lead.
4. *We do:* 4 Corners Game- Teacher will place the index cards with the 4 sight words other than the student's names in 4 different corners of the room. Rules of the game: the teacher or leader of the game will say one of the words on the index cards. The players will have 10 seconds to go over to that 'corner' that has the word. Anyone who is at the wrong 'corner' is out.
5. Students and teachers will play 4-5 rounds.
6. *You do:* Students will practice writing the sight words on pre-printed handwriting sheets.
7. *Exit Ticket*: Students will each receive a post it where they will write their name and leave room below it. The teacher will write a sight word on the board, came, and then say the sentence *You talk baby.* If students believe the word baby is used correctly in the sentence, it makes sentence then they will write the letter y on their post-it. If it doesn't make sense, then they will write the letter N. Then the teacher should collect post-its & scan over them to observe & record student responses.

Bathroom Break: (10:15-10:20)

Small Groups/Guided Reading: (10:20-10:45)
Small groups should not be larger than 5 students and smaller than 2.
1. Teacher MUST model and go over small group activities and protocols before you send students in groups! Students must work on the assigned task at their group! Students must ask their group questions first if unclear before asking teacher. Students must remain in their small group space unless they are getting another activity for their group or cleaning up. Bathroom, water, etc is not allowed during groups. Students must use whisper voice when talking in groups. Actual student group time will be shorter the first month or so until students become acclimated to the expectations and routines of small group work.
2. *All Small Groups:* Students will use instant learning center kits. Teacher will choose the 2 focused on Ending Sound, Beginning Sounds, Sound Sort & Story Sequencing. Teacher will MODEL/demonstrate how to use any of the new center kits if needed.

Writing Workshop: (10:45- 11:00)
1. *I do:* (6 mins max) The teacher will pose a question to students: which side of a paper or book do we begin writing or reading from. Display a blank sheet of writing paper for a student volunteer to come up and point to. Afterwards ask students if anyone can tell you which side of the paper is that? What is it called? The teacher is looking for the key word of 'left.'
2. Explain to students that *when we start to read or write we know that we begin on this side of the paper/book. That is called the "left" side. The word left is a direction word just like the word right, up, down and many, many more. It is so*

important that we learn our direction word because at times here in class and especially as you get older many people will say go to the right, or turn right or use your left hand or one of the many other ways to use the words.

3. *We do:* Have students have raise both hands up in the air. Next with their fingers they will make an uppercase "L." Bring their arms so their hands are in front of them & can see the letter "L." Then raise the hand up that has the "L" facing the right way & isn't backwards (this should be their left hands). Explain to students *that this is a secret way to remember that the hand up in the air is their left hand! The "L" gives you the hint, L for left!* Then ask students to identify if the left hand is now up which hand is left? Students should identify that the right hand is left. Have students put both arms down for a break & then try again but this time have students put their right hands in the air. The teacher should observe and fix any hands that need to be switched.
4. *You do:* The teacher should distribute story writing paper, pencil & crayons. Model to students how to fold their paper in half vertically. Have students fold their paper in half, the teacher should circulate to help fold any papers if needed. Next at the top of the left side, the teacher should model first, have students write an upper case "L" and at the top of the right side, have students write an upper case "R." The teacher should briefly state *the "L" stands for left and the "R" right*.
5. Have students then draw a picture of 18 of anything they would like (flowers, lightning bolts, hearts, cars, etc) on the left side. Underneath the picture write the number 18. Then on the right side draw a picture of their family & label it "My Family."
6. The teacher should circulate around to monitor list work and assist those who need it. Place an example for students to reference.
7. If time remains the gather students to share their work.

Math: (11:00-11:30)

1. The teacher will show large flash cards with the numbers 1-20 on them and begin counting aloud. Encourage students to join in. Today we'll focus on the counting on and making numbers from 20-30.
2. *I/We do:* The teacher will distribute 3 ten frames per student with counters. Have students place 14 counters on the mats. Next instruct students to add 4 more counters to their mats. Have students count how many counters they now have. Explain that they had 14 and by putting or adding 4 more they now made the number 18. Then have students clear the mat and place 20 counters on the mats. Instruct students to add 3 more counters and find out how many they have all together. Again explain that there were 20 and then when you put 3 more you have now made 23. Try again but this time start with 12. Model to students how take 3 counters in their hands but continue to 'count on' from 12 as they place one counter down at a time, saying 13, 14 & 15,
3. Practice with 2 other numbers such as 18 and adding 3 more, 25 and adding 2 more. The teacher should explain that this activity is helping students really become experts in their numbers up to 30! Soon they'll be able to count from any number so fast that it'll blow their minds!
4. *You do:* Have students work in small groups on stations/centers of no more than 4. Use the instant learning centers of Making Tens & Counting. One group can also take number flash cards from 1-30, mix them up and then put them back in order.
5. *Exit Ticket:* Teacher will distribute post-it or index cards say a number aloud. Have student write the number on the post-it or card along with their name. Collect and go through noting down any students who did not get it correct.

Closing Activity: (11:30-11:45)
1. Gather students together for a closing activity game on the projector & computer. Choices include Reading Eggs (if accessible) or an ABC game on Starfall.com.

DEAR (Drop Everything And Read) (11:45-11:57)

Week 22 (9:00-12:00)

ELA Focus/Skill: Dialogue, Character, Plot, Zoo Animals
Phonics (letter/word family): /v/ & /a/, /i/, /o/
Sound Words: very, van, vet
Sight Words: friend, eat, yes
Big Book: "Mig the Pig" by Colin Hawkins
Writing Focus: Top-Bottom
Math Focus: Numbers 20-30

Objectives: Students will be able to:
- repeat and identify the day, weather and season
- place the letters of the alphabet sequentially
- identify the letter /v/, it's sound and words that begin with /v/
- sort and identify short vowel /a/, /i/, & /o/ words
- to identify the direction of top-bottom in writing
- orally identify the sound words and speak phonetically
- identify sight words & use in context
- identify and locate dialogue in a text, the characters and zoo animals
- repeat, identify, represent and write the numbers 20-30 using manipulative
- sort numbers and place in sequential orders from 20-30
- count on from any given number from 20-30

Materials:
"All About Today" pocket chart, "Mig the Pig" Big book, ABC flash cards, white lap boards, dry erase markers, board erasers, post-its, pictures of a van, sock, can, pig & block, post-its, chart paper with sight words pre-written, post-its with sight words written on them, Short Vowel Color by Sound (see appendix), handwriting sheets with the sight words written twice (www.handwritingworksheets.com), Instant Learning Centers: Rhyming Sounds, Ending Sounds, Building Words & Story Sequencing & for math: Making Tens & Counting, crayons, pencils, erasers, story writing paper, ten frame mats (enough for each student to get 3), counters, number flash cards (at least 1 for each group/table of students), computer & projector

ELA
Whole Group: Morning Meeting/Shared Read: (9:00- 9:15)
1. Students will gather together for Morning Meeting where the teacher will model how to use the "All About Today" pocket chart. The teacher will read the information on the pocket chart, using a pointer, starting with the month, date and year using the sentence frame "Today is __." Next have the students repeat the sentence. After that the teacher will continue on with the pocket chart moving to "Yesterday was __." Students will repeat each section after the teacher has pointed and read it aloud. Then teacher will read aloud the objectives for the day, briefly explaining that this is what the goal is by the end of their time together (Use academic language). If extra time, have 1-2 students share something exciting or important news about themselves.
2. (9:15-9:45) *I do:* Teacher will begin with ABC flash cards and distribute the flash cards to students to put them in order on the floor or desks as a whole group. Next the teacher will point and read aloud the title "Mig the Pig," the author Colin Hawkins & the illustrator Jaqui Hawkins. After that begin reading the story aloud.

Stop half way and ask students to turn to a partner and make a prediction of what will happen in the rest of the story. Observe if students use the sentence frame I predict ___. Give 1 minute and then have 1-2 students share their predictions with the group. Continue reading the story.

3. *We do:* (10 mins max) Once the teacher has finished the story go back through the book and have students identify who the characters are in the story? The setting? And the main idea (what was the story mostly about)? Also have students locate one type of the dialogue that occurred in the story.
4. Mini-lesson: Using the shared story, the teacher will write the word "plot" on the board & explain to students that the plot in a story is the big event(s) that happens in a story. When we read Rainbow Fish, one big event was Rainbow Fish feeling alone with no friends. Have teacher and students go back through the shared read and identify the big event(s) in the story. Keep in mind this is not a summary. It is similar to the main idea at times.
5. Once students & teacher agree on the plot, write them on the board under the word so that students can see the connection and their thoughts in writing.
6. *You do:* Have students begin the "Short Vowel Color by Sound" activity sheet. Begin with the short vowel a, I & o. Keep in mind that students can complete this sheet after the review of short vowels.
7. (5-7 mins max) Write the letter /v/ on the board, bother upper case and lower (write clearly so students can see how to write both type of letters. Next the teacher will ask what letter do they see on the board? Once answered then the teacher will ask what sound does the letter make? If needed the teacher should begin saying some /v/ words such as very, vet & van to assist with the sound recognition. Have students practice saying the sound of the letter. After that the teacher with draw or place a picture of a van next to the letter & have students identify the picture. The teacher will then point and say vv (the v sound), and add the sound word van. Have students repeat as the teacher points to each. Repeat twice. The teacher will then write the word 'van' on the board and point to each sound as the word is 'sound out.' Guide students to identify that each of the words begin with the same sound, /v/. After that challenge students to think of other words that begin with /v/ & the teacher should write some of the words on the board or chart paper to provide a visual for students. The teacher should have scholars repeat the words that begin with /v/ named by students. If possible show pictures of words that begin with /v/ to allow students a visual.
8. Then the teacher will write short vowels /o/, /a/ & /i/ on the board and display a picture of a can, pig, sock and fat. Underneath or next of the pictures write the name of each word. The teacher will then read aloud each word and ask what vowels do they hear when all the words are said? The teacher should guide students to identify that each word has a short vowel in it, in the middle. Review each individual sound for the vowels. Write the word win on the board & have students identify in which short vowel group would that word belong in. The teacher should also try with the words flag, jog and pick.
9. *You do:* Teacher will allow students time to work on completing the short vowel coloring sheet. Have students leave the u and e words un-colored.
10. *Exit Ticket:* The teacher will write the word family -ag on the board and point to it. Have the students identify which short vowel this word family contains. On white lap boards students should write the vowel letter on the board & raise it up at the count of 3. Teacher should scan the room & note down any students who show the incorrect answer.

Sight & Sound Words: (9:45-10:15)

1. Have students gather together. The teacher will display the chart paper with the sight words & sound word pre-written on it.
2. *I do:* Teacher will lead a call and response where the teacher will repeat the first word, a student name, while pointing to it and students will repeat it. Continue down the list one time.
3. Next repeat down the list but challenge students to move faster with the teacher still speaking the word first and students repeating clearly. Repeat once more but this time the students will say the words and the teacher will not lead.
8. *We do:* Sight word Tic Tac Toe- Teacher will draw the tic tac toe board on the board. Then inside each box the teacher will write the new sight words just introduced and in the extra boxes the sight words from the previous weeks (under, until, friend, over, daddy, baby, look). The teacher will explain the game's rules briefly. There are 2 teams, the X and the O team. 1 player will get picked and they will pick where they want their letter (X or O) to go on the board. To get their spot the player must say the word in the box first. If the word is said correctly, then the teacher or player will draw the letter in the box. If the word is incorrect then the next team goes. The first team to 3 in a row wins. The teacher will need to split the class into two teams.
4. *You do:* Students and teachers will play for 2-3 rounds depending on time.
5. Students will practice writing the sight words on pre-printed handwriting sheets.
6. *Exit Ticket:* The teacher will distribute post-its to students and they will write their names on them. Then on the board the teacher will write I __ to eat now. Read aloud the sentence. On the post-it students should write which sight word would fill in the blank- allow students to refer back to the chart paper for spelling. The teacher should collect the post-its and scan to see who chose the incorrect word. Record!

Bathroom Break: (10:15-10:20)
Small Groups/Guided Reading: (10:20-10:45)
Small groups should not be larger than 5 students and smaller than 2.
1. Teacher MUST model and go over small group activities and protocols before you send students in groups! Students must work on the assigned task at their group! Students must ask their group questions first if unclear before asking teacher. Students must remain in their small group space unless they are getting another activity for their group or cleaning up. Bathroom, water, etc is not allowed during groups. Students must use whisper voice when talking in groups. Actual student group time will be shorter the first month or so until students become acclimated to the expectations and routines of small group work.
2. *All Small Groups:* Students will use instant learning center kits. Teacher will choose the 2 focused on Ending Sound, Beginning Sounds, Sound Sort & Story Sequencing. Teacher will MODEL/demonstrate how to use any of the new center kits if needed.

Writing Workshop: (10:45- 11:00)
1. *I do:* (6 mins max) The teacher will pose a question to students: do we begin writing at the bottom or top of a paper? Where is the top located? Why do we begin at the top?
2. Have students share their responses to the last question of why do we begin at the top (HOT question) with a partner or class. Repeat/restate any responses that showcase deep thought!
3. *We do:* The teacher should display a sheet of paper (preferably chart paper) and have students each come up and write their first names at the top of the paper. Afterwards have students come back up and write a short a word at the bottom of

the paper. Observe students to see if they identify the top and bottom of the paper accurately.
4. *You do:* The teacher should distribute story writing paper, pencil & crayons. Model to students how to fold their paper in half horizontally. Have students fold their paper in half, the teacher should circulate to help fold any papers if needed. Next at the top, the teacher should model first, have students write an upper case "T" and at the bottom have students write an upper case "B." The teacher should briefly state *the "T" stands for top and the "B" bottom*.
5. Have students then draw a picture of 20 of anything they would like (flowers, lightning bolts, hearts, cars, etc) on the top. Underneath the picture write the number 20. Then on the bottom draw a picture of their favorite food & label it "Food."
6. The teacher should circulate around to monitor list work and assist those who need it. Place an example for students to reference.
7. If time remains the gather students to share their work.

Math: (11:00-11:30)
1. The teacher will show large flash cards with the numbers 1-20 on them and begin counting aloud. Encourage students to join in. Today we'll focus on the counting on and making numbers from 20-30.
2. *I/We do:* The teacher will distribute 3 ten frames per student with counters. Have students place 26 counters on the mats. Next instruct students to add 3 more counters to their mats. Have students count on from 26 to see how many they now have. Then have students clear the mat and place 10 counters on the mats. Instruct students to add 3 more counters and find out how many they have all together. Re-explain that there were 10 and then when you put 3 more you have now made 13. Try again but this time start with 8 and add 5 more counters.
3. Practice with 2 other numbers such as 19 and adding 3 more, 23 and adding 2 more. The teacher should explain that this activity is helping students really become experts in their numbers up to 30! Soon they'll be able to count from any number so fast that it'll blow their minds!
4. *You do:* Have students work in small groups on stations/centers of no more than 4. Use the instant learning centers of Making Tens & Counting. One group can also take number flash cards from 1-30, mix them up and then put them back in order.
5. *Exit Ticket:* Teacher will distribute post-it or index cards say a number aloud. Have student write the number on the post-it or card along with their name. Collect and go through noting down any students who did not get it correct.

Closing Activity: (11:30-11:45)
1. Gather students together for a closing activity game on the projector & computer. Choices include Reading Eggs (if accessible) or an ABC game on Starfall.com.

DEAR (Drop Everything And Read) (11:45-11:57)

Week 23 (9:00-12:00)

ELA Focus/Skill: Questions
Phonics (letter/word family): qu/kw/ & -un word family
Sound Words: queen, quack
Sight Words: under, until, over
Big Book: "Up, Down & Around" by Katherine Ayres
Writing Focus: Return Sweep
Math Focus: Shapes

Objectives: Students will be able to:
- repeat and identify the day, weather and season
- place the letters of the alphabet sequentially
- identify the digraph qu/kw/, it's sound and words that begin with qu/kw/
- sort and identify words within the –un word family
- to identify the rule of 'return sweep' in writing
- orally identify the sound words and speak phonetically
- identify sight words & use in context
- identify and locate questions in texts
- identify and represent shapes using manipulative

Materials:

"All About Today" pocket chart, "Up, Down & Around" Big book, ABC flash cards, white lap boards, dry erase markers, board erasers, post-its, pictures of a queen, sun, run, spun & fun, post-its, chart paper with sight words pre-written, post-its with sight words written on them, -un word family book see appendix, handwriting sheets with the sight words written twice (www.handwritingworksheets.com), Instant Learning Centers: Rhyming Sounds, Ending Sounds, Building Words & Story Sequencing & for math: Making Tens & Counting, crayons, pencils, erasers, story writing paper, ten frame mats (enough for each student to get 3), counters, number flash cards (at least 1 for each group/table of students), computer & projector

ELA
Whole Group: Morning Meeting/Shared Read: (9:00- 9:15)
1. Students will gather together for Morning Meeting where the teacher will model how to use the "All About Today" pocket chart. The teacher will read the information on the pocket chart, using a pointer, starting with the month, date and year using the sentence frame "Today is __." Next have the students repeat the sentence. After that the teacher will continue on with the pocket chart moving to "Yesterday was __." Students will repeat each section after the teacher has pointed and read it aloud. Then teacher will read aloud the objectives for the day, briefly explaining that this is what the goal is by the end of their time together (Use academic language). If extra time, have 1-2 students share something exciting or important news about themselves.
2. (9:15-9:45) *I do:* Teacher will begin with ABC flash cards and distribute the flash cards to students to put them in order on the floor or desks as a whole group. Next the teacher will point and read aloud the title "Up, Down & Around," the author Katherine Ayres & the illustrator Nadine Bernard Westcott. The teacher will remind students that they have *heard this story before but it is great to go*

back and re-read books, you may hear or see something that was missed the first time, just like in movies. After that begin reading the story aloud. Stop half way and ask students to turn to a partner and share one fact about plants that has been heard in the text so far that surprises you, is new to you or you find cool/interesting. Allow students 1 min to share & then have 2-3 students share with the class.

3. *We do:* (10 mins max) Once the teacher has finished the story go back through the book and have students identify the type of text it is (non-fiction or real), the setting of this story (in the garden, outside) and some of the vegetables/plants mentioned. Challenge- have students identify the main idea of this text. What was the story mostly about is a guiding question if needed?

4. *Mini-lesson:* Using the shared story, the teacher will write the word "question" on the board & remind students that a question asks something. We are going to practice asking questions about the story. On chart paper, the teacher should write the question words (who, what, where, when, why & how) & then remind students that most questions usually start with one of these words. Model to students the question- what grows down? The teacher will explain that the answer to this question comes from the story, carrots and beets grow down. Have students think of a question using one of the question words on the chart paper about the story, then turn to a partner next to them and share the question they have thought of. After a minute or two of sharing with partners have 2 or 3 students share with the class their question. The teacher should underline, mark or note which question word students used.

5. (5-7 mins max) Write the letter qu/kw/ on the board (write clearly so students can see how to write both type of letters. Next the teacher will ask if students if they know what sound the two letters make that are next to each other on the board. The teacher should begin saying some qu/kw/ words such as queen, quack & quick to assist with the sound recognition. The teacher will then correct or reiterate the sound that /qu/ makes. Explain to students that the two letters put together are called a digraph and they make one sound together. Have students practice saying the sound of the letter. After that the teacher with draw or place a picture of a queen next to the letter & have students identify the picture. The teacher will then point and say kw (the qu sound), and add the sound word queen. Have students repeat as the teacher points to each. Repeat twice. The teacher will then write the word 'queen' on the board and point to each sound as the word is 'sound out.' Guide students to identify that each of the words begin with the same sound, /v/. After that challenge students to think of other words that begin with /qu/ & the teacher should write some of the words on the board or chart paper to provide a visual for students. The teacher should have scholars repeat the words that begin with /qu/ named by students. If possible show pictures of words that begin with /qu/ to allow students a visual.

6. Then the teacher will write word family –un on the board and display a picture of a sun, run, a web that was spun and someone having fun. Underneath or next of the pictures write the name of each word. The teacher will then read aloud each word and ask what do they hear when all the words are said? Next the teacher should guide students to identify that each word has –un at the end. Also that each word rhyme & are a part of the –un word family. Distribute to students the white lap boards, erasers & dry erase markers. On the board have students listen to the teacher say the word sun aloud & phonetically. The teacher should also cover, erase or take down the –un words displayed. Students will then try to sound out and & spell out the word. After 20 seconds have students raise their

boards up to be checked & one student spells the word aloud. The teacher should write the word down on the board. Have students check their words on their boards. Is it spelled correctly? If yes, then with the marker students should re-write the word on the paper underneath or next to their spelling.

7. Try again with the word fun, run & spun (which will be a challenge). Briefly re-explain to students that one strategy when sounding out new words is to say the word slowly and listen for any letter or word family they already know. Like in the word bin we hear it and know that word family & how to spell it. So I just need to listen to what the beginning/first letter/sound is & write it down. That is how we sound out new words or words we're unsure of.
8. *You do:* Teacher will then guide students to create folding book with -un (see appendix for word family pic book pgs 32 & 33). Have students complete the –un word and then color the pictures. Staple to hold together.
9. *Exit Ticket:* The teacher will write the word family -un on the board and point to it. Have the student think of and write a word in that word family on index cards. At the count of 3 all the students should raise their cards up so that the teacher will collect them, scan the deck, note & record student responses.

Sight & Sound Words: (9:45-10:15)
7. Have students gather together. The teacher will display the chart paper with the sight words & sound word pre-written on it.
8. *I do:* Teacher will lead a call and response where the teacher will repeat the first word, a student name, while pointing to it and students will repeat it. Continue down the list one time.
9. Next repeat down the list but challenge students to move faster with the teacher still speaking the word first and students repeating clearly. Repeat once more but this time the students will say the words and the teacher will not lead.
10. *We do:* Playdoh sight words. Students will use playdoh to spell out the sight words written on the chart paper. Students will practice writing the sight words on pre-printed handwriting sheets.
11. *Exit Ticket:* Students will each receive a post it where they will write their name and leave room below it. The teacher will write a sight word on the board, over, and then say the sentence *We over wall.* If students believe the word over is used correctly in the sentence, it makes sentence then they will write the letter y on their post-it. If it doesn't make sense, then they will write the letter N. Then the teacher should collect post-its & scan over them to observe & record student responses.

Bathroom Break: (10:15-10:20)

Small Groups/Guided Reading: (10:20-10:45)
Small groups should not be larger than 5 students and smaller than 2.
1. Teacher MUST model and go over small group activities and protocols before you send students in groups! Students must work on the assigned task at their group! Students must ask their group questions first if unclear before asking teacher. Students must remain in their small group space unless they are getting another activity for their group or cleaning up. Bathroom, water, etc is not allowed during groups. Students must use whisper voice when talking in groups. Actual student group time will be shorter the first month or so until students become acclimated to the expectations and routines of small group work.
2. *All Small Groups:* Students will use instant learning center kits. Teacher will choose the 2 focused on Ending Sound, Beginning Sounds, Sound Sort & Story Sequencing. Teacher will MODEL/demonstrate how to use any of the new center kits if needed.

Writing Workshop: (10:45- 11:00)
1. *I do:* (6 mins max) The teacher will pose a question to students: as we are writing and we get to an end of a line but we are not finished our sentence, what do we do?
2. Have students share their responses to the question of with a partner or class. Repeat/restate any responses that showcase deep thought!
3. *We do:* The teacher should draw lines on the white board or use chart paper for this demonstration. Begin writing sentences telling about yourself or the day thus far. Stop when you get to the end of the line. Have students direct the teacher where to go next to continue. If the students give the correct direction that the writing will continue on the left side of the next line be sure to praise. If not be sure to clearly demonstrate that since we begin writing on the left side of the paper, where the red line is, where take our pencil to the next line underneath and then all the way to the left. The teacher must be sure to model that step to all students and label this as the "return sweep." We sweep under (the next line) and return to where we begin on the left.
4. The teacher will begin writing some additional sentence and again once the end of the line is reached, have students direct as to where to go next on the paper to continue writing.
5. *You do:* The teacher should distribute story writing paper, pencil & crayons. Model to students how to write the sentence "My name is ____." Students should do their best to copy the sentence and complete it. Move to the next sentence when ready "I am __ years old." Emphasize the return sweep if it was used in the model or needs to be used by students. The last sentence students should write "I love my __."
6. The teacher should circulate around to monitor list work and assist those who need it. Place an example for students to reference.
7. Allow students time to illustrate a picture to match their sentences.
8. If time remains the gather students to share their work.

Math: (11:00-11:30)
1. The teacher will show large flash cards with the numbers 1-30 on them and begin counting aloud. Encourage students to join in. Today we'll focus on our shapes!
2. *I/We do:* The teacher will draw a circle, triangle, square and rectangle on the board. Have students identify any of the shapes if possible. If all the shapes are identified correctly than skip this next part, 3, to 4. If not continue.
3. Call and response- point to each shape, say its name & write it below the shape. Then have students repeat its name. Continue with all the shapes drawn.
4. Then write the name of each shape underneath their picture. The teacher will ask students to think if the shapes remind them of any objects they recognize around them now or can think of that aren't in here. Tissue box, ball, box are acceptable responses.
5. Explain that shapes are all around us, what shape is the board or your desks. The teacher will distribute white lap boards, markers & erasers. Step by step, the teacher will begin with the circle & have students draw each shape on their white boards. Raise the board up once each shape is drawn to check-in with students that what they are drawing is somewhat recognizable. Assist as needed.
6. *You do:* Distribute the pattern shapes to students and have them sort all of the triangles, circles, rectangles, and squares together. Then practice drawing them on their white boards.

7. *Exit Ticket:* Teacher will distribute post-it or index cards say a shape aloud. Have student draw the shape on the post-it or card along with their name. Collect and go through noting down any students who did not get it correct.

Closing Activity: (11:30-11:45)
1. Gather students together for a closing activity game on the projector & computer. Choices include Reading Eggs (if accessible) or an ABC game on Starfall.com.

DEAR (Drop Everything And Read) (11:45-11:57)

Week 24 (9:00-12:00)

ELA Focus/Skill: Characters, Sequencing, Ideas & Events
Phonics (letter/word family): /ks/= final x & -ug word family
Sound Words: fox, box, six
Sight Words: want, because
Big Book: "Little Red Hen" by Byron Barton
Writing Focus: Letter vs Words
Math Focus: Shapes

Objectives: Students will be able to:
- repeat and identify the day, weather and season
- place the letters of the alphabet sequentially
- identify the ending sound of /x/, it's sound and words that end with x/ks/
- sort and identify words within the –ug word family
- to identify & describe the difference between letters and words
- sort & classify letters vs words
- orally identify the sound words and speak phonetically
- identify sight words & use in context
- identify the elements of a story (characters, setting, beginning, middle, end)
- identify and represent shapes using manipulative

Materials:
"All About Today" pocket chart, "Little Red Hen" Big book, ABC flash cards, white lap boards, dry erase markers, board erasers, story map organizer (appendix), post-its, pictures of a box, rug, big, jug & mug, post-its, chart paper with sight words pre-written, post-its with sight words written on them & bawled up, popcorn container to throw the words in, -ug word family worksheet see appendix, handwriting sheets with the sight words written twice (www.handwritingworksheets.com), Instant Learning Centers: Rhyming Sounds, Ending Sounds, Building Words & Story Sequencing & for math: Making Tens & Counting, story map organizer for small groups, "Concepts of Print Activities" pgs 3-10, 14-17 (appendix), crayons, pencils, erasers, story writing paper, Shapes Tracing Activity (see appendix), counters, number flash cards (at least 1 for each group/table of students), computer & projector

ELA
Whole Group: Morning Meeting/Shared Read: (9:00- 9:15)
1. Students will gather together for Morning Meeting where the teacher will model how to use the "All About Today" pocket chart. The teacher will read the information on the pocket chart, using a pointer, starting with the month, date and year using the sentence frame "Today is __." Next have the students repeat the sentence. After that the teacher will continue on with the pocket chart moving to "Yesterday was __." Students will repeat each section after the teacher has pointed and read it aloud. Then teacher will read aloud the objectives for the day, briefly explaining that this is what the goal is by the end of their time together (Use academic language). If extra time, have 1-2 students share something exciting or important news about themselves.
2. (9:15-9:45) *I do:* Teacher will begin with ABC flash cards and distribute the flash cards to students to put them in order on the floor or desks as a whole group from a given letter (for example- sort the letters beginning from F to Z in order).

Next the teacher will point and read aloud the title "The Little Red Hen," the author & illustrator Byron Barton. The teacher will remind students that they have *heard this story before but it is great to go back and re-read books, you may hear or see something that was missed the first time, just like in movies.* After that begin reading the story aloud. Stop half way (about when she is threshing the wheat) and ask the students: Why have the friends not helped Little Red Hen yet? Have students ponder for about 10 seconds & then turn to a neighbor and share their thoughts. Call on 2-3 students to share with group. Then continue reading.

3. *We do:* (10 mins max) Once the teacher has finished the story begin a short class discussion- ask students what were the consequences of Pig, Duck & Cat not helping Red Hen? (They did not get to enjoy any bread.) How did that make them feel? How can you tell? (textual evidence). What lesson do you think the three friends learned?
4. Review with students the elements of a story (character, setting, beginning, middle & end). Orally discuss these elements in the story "The Little Red Hen."
5. *Mini-lesson:* Based on student's levels at this time; drawing or writing of answers is acceptable. Story Map- The teacher will pair students up (can be based on level with high-low together or high-high and low-low) to complete a story map organizer (see appendix). A combination of writing and drawing is encouraged for answers as well as inventive spelling/writing to foster independence.
6. (5-7 mins max) Write the letter x/ks/ on the board (write clearly so students can see how to write both type of letters. Next the teacher will ask if students if they recall what sound this letter makes. The teacher should begin saying some final x/ks/ words such as fox, box & six to assist with the sound recognition. The teacher will then correct or reiterate the sound that final /x/ makes. Have students identify where they hear the /x/. Explain to students that we are going to look at the ending sound that /x/ makes. We know that words can begin with /x/ but they also end with it and it sounds slightly different. Have students practice saying the sound of the letter at the end of words, the /ks/ sound. After that the teacher with draw or place a picture of a box next to the letter & have students identify the picture. The teacher will then point and say ks (the x ending sound), and add the sound word box. Have students repeat as the teacher points to each. Repeat twice. The teacher will then write the word 'box' on the board and point to each sound as the word is 'sound out.' Guide students to identify that each of the words end with the same sound, /x/. After that challenge students to think of other words that end with the final x /ks/ & the teacher should write some of the words on the board or chart paper to provide a visual for students. The teacher should have scholars repeat the words that end with final x /ks/ named by students. If possible show pictures of words that end with x /ks/ to allow students a visual.
7. Then the teacher will write word family –ug on the board and display a picture of a rug, bug, a jug and a mug. Underneath or next of the pictures write the name of each word. The teacher will then read aloud each word and ask what do they hear when all the words are said? Next the teacher should guide students to identify that each word has –ug at the end. Also that each word rhyme & are a part of the –ug word family. Distribute play doh to students and have students listen to the teacher say the word rug aloud & phonetically. The teacher should also cover, erase or take down the –ug words displayed. Students will then try to sound out and & spell out the word with the play doh. After 35 seconds have students raise their hands to be checked & one student spells the word aloud.

    The teacher should write the word down on the board. Have students check their spelling. Is it spelled correctly? If no, then correct spelling.
8. Try again with the word bug, jug & mug. Briefly re-explain to students that one strategy when sounding out new words is to say the word slowly and listen for any letter or word family they already know. Like in the word bin we hear it and know that word family & how to spell it. So I just need to listen to what the beginning/first letter/sound is & write it down. That is how we sound out new words or words we're unsure of.
9. *You do:* Teacher will then guide students to complete –ug worksheet (see appendix 'short u word family' pg 2).
10. *Exit Ticket:* The teacher will write the word family -ug on the board and point to it. Have the student think of and write a word in that word family on index cards. At the count of 3 all the students should raise their cards up so that the teacher will collect them, scan the deck, note & record student responses.

Sight & Sound Words: (9:45-10:15)
1. Have students gather together. The teacher will display the chart paper with the sight words & sound word pre-written on it.
2. *I do:* Teacher will lead a call and response where the teacher will repeat the first word, a student name, while pointing to it and students will repeat it. Continue down the list one time.
3. Next repeat down the list but challenge students to move faster with the teacher still speaking the word first and students repeating clearly. Repeat once more but this time the students will say the words and the teacher will not lead.
4. *We do:* Sight Word Popcorn: Sight words written on sticky notes that are balled up and placed in a popcorn container (or any container). The rules of the game: the teacher will toss the beach ball (or any soft ball will do) to a student; that student will pick a crumpled up paper from the container and read the word aloud. If the student reads the word correctly they can toss the ball to another student, if not the teacher will toss the ball to someone else and they will have an attempt to read the word. Continue until all of the crumpled papers have been picked & read.
5. *You do:* Teacher will distribute handwriting practice sheets with the words written on them once- students will trace and then write the words at least twice.
6. *Exit Ticket:* Students will each receive a post it where they will write their name and leave room below it. The teacher should write the word 'want' on the board & read it aloud. On the post-it students will either write the letter 'y' or 'n' if the word the teacher said matches what is written on the board. The teacher will collect the post-its & check to see who answered correctly & who did not. Record any incorrect post-its.

Bathroom Break: (10:15-10:20)

Small Groups/Guided Reading: (10:20-10:45)
Small groups should not be larger than 5 students and smaller than 2.
1. Teacher MUST model and go over small group activities and protocols before you send students in groups! Students must work on the assigned task at their group! Students must ask their group questions first if unclear before asking teacher. Students must remain in their small group space unless they are getting another activity for their group or cleaning up. Bathroom, water, etc is not allowed during groups. Students must use whisper voice when talking in groups. Actual student group time will be shorter the first month or so until students become acclimated to the expectations and routines of small group work.

2. *Small Group 1*: Guided reading. In this group the teacher will begin by first reviewing depending on the level of the students either the alphabets or the sight words introduced earlier that day. For alphabets: on individual white lap boards have students write the letter that you name. You can use magnetic letters so students have a reference to what it looks like if needed. For sight words: using the pre-written index cards with the sight words, show the card and have students state the word on the card. Extensions~ have students write the word on white lap boards or use in sentences. Then move into the text that day. Again depending on the level of the students: choose a text close to their level. Teacher will go over the title of the books and the author. Preview the text by looking through the book and making a prediction what the text may be about based on the pictures, title and cover. Teacher must model to students how to use the sentence frame "I predict __ because __." when making a prediction statement to the group about the text or anything. Next have students make predictions about the book using the sentence frame. Then the teacher will either choose to Echo read (you point and read a page at a time and have them repeat you) or Round Robin read (each student reads a page and you go around the group) and begin reading the text together. Once finished reading, briefly discuss the text, what was it about, who was in it: focus on using the key words beginning, middle and end of the story. After that based on what the focus was before reading the text have the students 'hunt' for the sight words or letters in story. Write down each one found on the white lap boards and then share once the students in the group are finished 'hunting'.
3. Finally have students independently complete a story map.
4. *All Small Groups:* Students will use instant learning center kits. Teacher will choose the 2 focused on Ending Sound, Beginning Sounds, Sound Sort & Story Sequencing. Teacher will MODEL/demonstrate how to use any of the new center kits if needed.

Writing Workshop: (10:45- 11:00)
1. *I do:* (6 mins max) The teacher will display the letter, words & sentences from the "Concepts of Print" packet (see appendix) on the board. Next the teacher will ask students to look at what's on the board- how can we sort them? (If that question is too difficult then ask what can they tell you about what they see on the board?) Look for responses that focus on they are words, letters & sentences on the board- or we can sort them that way.
2. The teacher will remind students that letters are the individual letters of the alphabet, words are letters put together to make a word, and sentences are words that are put together.
3. *We do:* The teacher will display the labels "word," "letter," & "sentences" from the "Concepts of Print" packet on the board. Have students assist & come up individually to each move one of the words, letters, or sentences under their correct label. Review once complete.
4. *You do:* The teacher should distribute the 'letter, word, sentences' paper (pg 17 of "Concepts of Print Activities"), pencil & crayons. Explain to students the direction at the top of the activity sheet. Then have students independently complete it.
5. The teacher should circulate around to monitor list work and assist those who need it.
6. If time remains the gather students to go over.

Math: (11:00-11:30)

1. The teacher will show large flash cards with the numbers 1-30 on them and begin counting aloud. Encourage students to join in. Today we'll focus on our shapes!
2. *I/We do:* The teacher will draw a hexagon, triangle, square and rectangle on the board. Engage students in reviewing the names of the shapes, how many sides & corners each have.
3. Next, gather students together to complete the "Shapes Tree Map" activity (see appendix- includes directions & picture of activity).
4. *You do:* Distribute shapes tracing activity sheet (see appendix) which will allow students to practice drawing their shapes. There are some shapes that we did not name during the tree activity but please name them for students, pentagon, octagon, diamond & heart.
5. *Exit Ticket:* Teacher will distribute post-it or index cards say a shape aloud. Have student draw the shape on the post-it or card along with their name. Collect and go through noting down any students who did not get it correct.

Closing Activity: (11:30-11:45)
1. Gather students together for a closing activity game on the projector & computer. Choices include Reading Eggs (if accessible) or an ABC game on Starfall.com. Shapes Bingo is an option as well. Review the sight words we've done so far this year is another option (boys vs girls or any variation).

DEAR (Drop Everything And Read) (11:45-11:57)

Week 25 (9:00-12:00)

ELA Focus/Skill: Compare and Contrast
Phonics (letter/word family): digraph /sh/ & -ut word family
Sound Words: she, sheep, shop
Sight Words: said, say, saw
Big Book: "Rainbow Fish" by Marcus Pfister
Writing Focus: Invented Spelling
Math Focus: All About Shapes

Objectives: Students will be able to:
- repeat and identify the day, weather and season
- place the letters of the alphabet sequentially
- identify the digraph /sh/, it's sound and words that begin with /sh/
- sort and identify words within the –ut word family
- to identify & describe the difference between letters and words
- to write with invented spelling- using the word families & letters we've learned thus far
- orally identify the sound words and speak phonetically
- identify sight words & use in context
- compare and contrast elements in a text
- identify the number of sides & corners in common 2D shapes

Materials:
"All About Today" pocket chart, "Rainbow Fish" Big book, ABC flash cards, white lap boards, dry erase markers, board erasers, 2 chart paper with a top-hat organizer drawn on it, post-its, pictures of a sheep, scissors cutting, a door shutting, hut & nut, post-its, chart paper with sight words pre-written, post-its with sight words written on them & bawled up, popcorn container to throw the words in, -ut word family worksheet in short u review (see appendix), handwriting sheets with the sight words written twice (www.handwritingworksheets.com), Instant Learning Centers: Rhyming Sounds, Ending Sounds, Building Words & Story Sequencing & for math: Making Tens & Counting, story map organizer for small groups, "Concepts of Print Activities" pgs 3-10, 14-17 (appendix), crayons, pencils, erasers, story writing paper, number flash cards (1-30), shape manipulative, Shape Tree (see appendix), computer & projector or Shapes Bingo or chart paper with sight words taught thus far

ELA

Whole Group: Morning Meeting/Shared Read: (9:00- 9:15)
1. Students will gather together for Morning Meeting where the teacher will model how to use the "All About Today" pocket chart. The teacher will read the information on the pocket chart, using a pointer, starting with the month, date and year using the sentence frame "Today is __." Next have the students repeat the sentence. After that the teacher will continue on with the pocket chart moving to "Yesterday was __." Students will repeat each section after the teacher has pointed and read it aloud. Then teacher will read aloud the objectives for the day, briefly explaining that this is what the goal is by the end of their time together (Use academic language). If extra time, have 1-2 students share something exciting or important news about themselves.

2. (9:15-9:45) *I do:* Teacher will begin with ABC flash cards and distribute the flash cards to students to put them in order on the floor or desks as a whole group from a given letter (for example- sort the letters beginning from L to Z in order). Next the teacher will point and read aloud the title "Rainbow Fish," the author Marcus Pfister. The teacher will remind students that they have *heard this story before but it is great to go back and re-read books, you may hear or see something that was missed the first time, just like in movies.* After that begin reading the story aloud. Stop half way (about when he sees the Wise Octopus) and ask the students: Why do you think Rainbow Fish won't share his shiny scales? Have students ponder for about 10 seconds & then turn to a neighbor and share their thoughts. Call on 2-3 students to share with group. Then continue reading.
3. *We do:* (10 mins max) Once the teacher has finished the story begin a short class discussion- Why do the other fish want some of Rainbow fish shiny scales? Why does Rainbow Fish go see the Wise Octopus? What causes Rainbow Fish to feel funny inside? Would you tell a friend to read this book? Why?
4. *Mini-lesson:* Compare and Contrast. The teacher should display the Top Hat Organizer drawn on the chart paper. Above the Top Hat write "Compare and Contrast." The teacher should then begin to explain to students that *the words compare and contrast means that we are going to look at how something is the same and how are they different. I need two volunteers (try to pick 1 boy & 1 girl. Have the volunteers stand side by side looking at their peers.) Look at our two classmates. Can someone name me one way they are different? Look at everything about them.* Take 2 or 3 responses from students & the answers can range from their clothes, gender, height, etc. No assumptions, only what can be seen. Once the student share responses the teacher should then ask, *who remembers everything that was said?* Then explain that it *can be hard to remember everything that everyone said so this is where this hat comes in handy. Just like we used a map to share information about books we read, we use this hat to share how something is different and the same. On the top part of the hat is where we're going to write their names & in the top hat section we're going to write how they are different. So remind me what you said again.* As students state the differences again, the teacher should record it on the organizer. Next explain that the bottom part of the hat, the brim, is where the similarities go, how they are the same. Have students share 2-3 responses telling how the two students are the same. The teacher should record the responses on the organizer. Again only take responses where students can visually see.
5. The teacher should display the 2nd Top Hat organizer. Using the story, Rainbow Fish have students compare and contrast Rainbow Fish and the Blue Fish. There should be a minimum of 2 differences & 2 similarities. Record responses on the organizer and read aloud when it is completed.
6. (5-7 mins max) Write the letter /sh/ on the board (write clearly so students can see how to write both type of letters. Next the teacher will ask if students if they know what sound this letter makes. The teacher should begin saying some letters when they are next to each other make one sound together. Does anyone recall the letters/sound we looked at a few weeks ago that do that? Hopefully students recall the /qu/ sound. If not, then remind students. The teacher should use words such as she, sheep, shop & shut to assist with the sound recognition. The teacher will then correct or reiterate the sound that digraph /sh/ makes. Have students identify where they hear the /sh/. Explain to students that we are

going to look at the beginning sound that /sh/ makes. After that the teacher with draw or place a picture of a sheep next to the letter & have students identify the picture. The teacher will then point and say sh and add the sound word sheep. Have students repeat as the teacher points to each. Repeat twice. The teacher will then write the word 'sheep' on the board and point to each sound as the word is 'sound out.' After that challenge students to think of other words that begin with /sh/ & the teacher should write some of the words on the board or chart paper to provide a visual for students. The teacher should have scholars repeat the words that begin with /sh/ named by students. If possible show pictures of words as a visual.

7. Then the teacher will write word family –ut on the board and display a picture of cutting, a hut, a door shutting and a nut. Underneath or next of the pictures write the name of each word. The teacher will then read aloud each word and ask what do they hear when all the words are said? Next the teacher should guide students to identify that each word has –ut at the end. Also that each word rhyme & are a part of the –ut word family. Distribute play doh to students and have students listen to the teacher say the word cut aloud & phonetically. The teacher should also cover, erase or take down the –ut words displayed. Students will then try to sound out and & spell out the word with the play doh. After 35 seconds have students raise their hands to be checked & one student spells the word aloud. The teacher should write the word down on the board. Have students check their spelling. Is it spelled correctly? If no, then correct spelling.

8. Try again with the word hut, nut & shut. Briefly re-explain to students that one strategy when sounding out new words is to say the word slowly and listen for any letter or word family they already know. Like in the word bin we hear it and know that word family & how to spell it. So I just need to listen to what the beginning/first letter/sound is & write it down. That is how we sound out new words or words we're unsure of.

9. *You do:* Teacher will then guide students to complete –ut worksheet (see appendix 'short u word family' pg 4).

10. *Exit Ticket:* The teacher will write the word family -ut on the board and point to it. Have the student think of and write a word in that word family on index cards. At the count of 3 all the students should raise their cards up so that the teacher will collect them, scan the deck, note & record student responses.

Sight & Sound Words: (9:45-10:15)

1. Have students gather together. The teacher will display the chart paper with the sight words & sound word pre-written on it.
2. *I do:* Teacher will lead a call and response where the teacher will repeat the first word, a student name, while pointing to it and students will repeat it. Continue down the list one time.
3. Next repeat down the list but challenge students to move faster with the teacher still speaking the word first and students repeating clearly. Repeat once more but this time the students will say the words and the teacher will not lead.
4. *We do:* Sight Word Popcorn: Sight words written on sticky notes that are balled up and placed in a popcorn container (or any container). The rules of the game: the teacher will toss the beach ball (or any soft ball will do) to a student; that student will pick a crumpled up paper from the container and read the word aloud. If the student reads the word correctly they can toss the ball to another student, if not the teacher will toss the ball to someone else and they will have an

attempt to read the word. Continue until all of the crumpled papers have been picked & read.

5. *You do:* Teacher will distribute handwriting practice sheets with the words written on them once- students will trace and then write the words atleast twice.
6. *Exit Ticket:* Students will each receive a post it where they will write their name and leave room below it. The teacher should write the word 'say' on the board & read it aloud. On the post-it students will either write the letter 'y' or 'n' if the word the teacher said matches what is written on the board. The teacher will collect the post-its & check to see who answered correctly & who did not. Record any incorrect post-its.

Bathroom Break: (10:15-10:20)

Small Groups/Guided Reading: (10:20-10:45)

Small groups should not be larger than 5 students and smaller than 2.

1. Teacher MUST model and go over small group activities and protocols before you send students in groups! Students must work on the assigned task at their group! Students must ask their group questions first if unclear before asking teacher. Students must remain in their small group space unless they are getting another activity for their group or cleaning up. Bathroom, water, etc is not allowed during groups. Students must use whisper voice when talking in groups. Actual student group time will be shorter the first month or so until students become acclimated to the expectations and routines of small group work.
2. *Small Group 1:* Guided reading. In this group the teacher will begin by first reviewing depending on the level of the students either the alphabets or the sight words introduced earlier that day. For alphabets: on individual white lap boards have students write the letter that you name. You can use magnetic letters so students have a reference to what it looks like if needed. For sight words: using the pre-written index cards with the sight words, show the card and have students state the word on the card. Extensions~ have students write the word on white lap boards or use in sentences. Then move into the text that day. Again depending on the level of the students: choose a text close to their level. Teacher will go over the title of the books and the author. Preview the text by looking through the book and making a prediction what the text may be about based on the pictures, title and cover. Teacher must model to students how to use the sentence frame "I predict __ because __." when making a prediction statement to the group about the text or anything. Next have students make predictions about the book using the sentence frame. Then the teacher will either choose to Echo read (you point and read a page at a time and have them repeat you) or Round Robin read (each student reads a page and you go around the group) and begin reading the text together. Once finished reading, briefly discuss the text, what was it about, who was in it: focus on using the key words beginning, middle and end of the story. After that based on what the focus was before reading the text have the students 'hunt' for the sight words or letters in story. Write down each one found on the white lap boards and then share once the students in the group are finished 'hunting'.
3. Finally have students independently complete a story map.
4. *All Other Small Groups:* Students will use instant learning center kits. Teacher will choose the 2 focused on Ending Sound, Beginning Sounds, Sound Sort & Story Sequencing. Teacher will MODEL/demonstrate how to use any of the new center kits if needed.

Writing Workshop: (10:45- 11:00)

1. *I do:* (6 mins max) The teacher will display the letter, words & sentences from the "Concepts of Print" packet (see appendix) on the board. Next the teacher will ask students to look at what's on the board- how can we sort them? (If that question is too difficult then ask what can they tell you about what they see on the board?) Look for responses that focus on they are words, letters & sentences on the board- or we can sort them that way.
2. The teacher will remind students that letters are the individual letters of the alphabet, words are letters put together to make a word, and sentences are words that are put together.
3. *We do:* The teacher will display the labels "word," "letter," & "sentences" from the "Concepts of Print" packet on the board. Have students assist & come up individually to each move one of the words, letters, or sentences under their correct label. Review once complete.
4. *You do:* The teacher should distribute the 'letter, word, sentences' paper (pg 17 of "Concepts of Print Activities"), pencil & crayons. Explain to students the direction at the top of the activity sheet. Then have students independently complete it.
5. Once completed have students use story writing paper to illustrate and write facts about their favorite animal. Provide the sentence frame: *My favorite animal is __. It ____.* Promote students using invented spelling to complete the sentence frame. For students who need the extra assistance the teacher should write the sentence frame on their paper: for others have them copy & write the sentence frame on their own.
6. The teacher should circulate around to monitor list work and assist those who need it.
7. If time remains the gather students to go over.

Math: (11:00-11:30)
1. The teacher will show large flash cards with the numbers 1-30 on them and begin counting aloud. Encourage students to join in. Today we'll focus on our shapes!
2. *I/We do:* The teacher will draw a hexagon, triangle, square and rectangle on the board. Engage students in reviewing the names of the shapes, how many sides & corners each have.
3. Next, gather students together to complete the "Shapes Tree Map" activity (see appendix- includes directions & picture of activity).
4. *You do:* Distribute shapes tracing activity sheet (see appendix) which will allow students to practice drawing their shapes. There are some shapes that we did not name during the tree activity but please name them for students, pentagon, octagon, diamond & heart.
5. *Exit Ticket:* Teacher will distribute post-it or index cards say a shape aloud. Have student draw the shape on the post-it or card along with their name. Collect and go through noting down any students who did not get it correct.

Closing Activity: (11:30-11:45)
1. Gather students together for a closing activity game on the projector & computer. Choices include Reading Eggs (if accessible) or an ABC game on Starfall.com. Shapes Bingo is an option as well. Review the sight words we've done so far this year is another option (boys vs girls or any variation).

DEAR (Drop Everything And Read) (11:45-11:57)

Week 26 (9:00-12:00)

ELA Focus/Skill: Classifying Nonfiction vs Fiction
Phonics (letter/word family): digraph /th/ & -uck word family
Sound Words: they, there, this
Sight Words: then, them, those
Big Book: "Click Clack Moo, Cows that Type" by Doreen Cronin & "Baby Animals" by Sue Davis
Writing Focus: 1-1 Correspondence
Math Focus: Shapes All Around Us

Objectives: Students will be able to:
- repeat and identify the day, weather and season
- place the letters of the alphabet sequentially
- identify the digraph /th/, it's sound and words that begin with /th/
- sort and identify words within the –uck word family
- to identify & describe the difference between fiction & nonfiction texts
- to identify & show one on one correspondence
- orally identify the sound words and speak phonetically
- identify sight words & use in context
- use word family knowledge, letter, blends & digraph knowledge in inventive spelling while writing
- identify, name and draw the shapes that are in common objects around us

Materials:
"All About Today" pocket chart, "Click Clack Moo Cows that Type" & "Baby Animals" Big books, ABC flash cards, white lap boards, dry erase markers, board erasers, 2 chart paper with a top-hat organizer drawn on it, post-its, pictures of someone thin, a duck, something lucky, something stuck, & the Mr. Yuck face, post-its, chart paper with sight words pre-written, post-its with sight words written on them & bawled up for sight word basketball, container to throw the words in, -ug word family worksheet see appendix, handwriting sheets with the sight words written twice (www.handwritingworksheets.com), Instant Learning Centers: Rhyming Sounds, Ending Sounds, Middle Sounds Building Words, Simple Sentences & Story Sequencing & for math: Making Tens, Counting, Shapes, Patterns, story map organizer for small groups, crayons, pencils, erasers, story writing paper, number flash cards (1-30), computer & projector, Shape Bingo or Chart Paper with old sight words on it for review

ELA
Whole Group: Morning Meeting/Shared Read: (9:00- 9:15)
1. Students will gather together for Morning Meeting where the teacher will model how to use the "All About Today" pocket chart. The teacher will read the information on the pocket chart, using a pointer, starting with the month, date and year using the sentence frame "Today is __." Next have the students repeat the sentence. After that the teacher will continue on with the pocket chart moving to "Yesterday was __." Students will repeat each section after the teacher has pointed and read it aloud. Then teacher will read aloud the objectives for the day, briefly explaining that this is what the goal is by the end of their time together (Use academic language). If extra time, have 1-2 students share something exciting or important news about themselves.

2. *(9:15-9:45) I do:* Teacher will begin with ABC flash cards and distribute the flash cards to students to put them in order on the floor or desks as a whole group from a given letter (for example- sort the letters beginning from E to T in order). Next the teacher will point and read aloud the title "Click Clack Moo Cows that Type," the author Doreen Cronin & the book "Baby Animals" by Sue Davis. The teacher will explain to students that *today we are not going to re-read the stories but we are going to use the Top Hat organizer to compare and contrast them.* One of the Top Hat organizers should be displayed to allow writing.
3. *We do:* Review with students the purpose of the top hat (to organize thoughts related to how two things are similar and different from each other).
4. *Mini-lesson:* Compare and Contrast Fiction vs Nonfiction texts. Have students look at or through the two big books displayed. Instruct them to begin thinking how the two books are different from each other. Provide a few minutes to look and brainstorm differences. After 2-3 minutes gather students together and have a few students share their thoughts. The teacher should record accurate/acceptable responses on the organizer. After a minimum of 4 differences- read the responses aloud to students. If it was not already mentioned, ask students to think about the information in each book, are they real? made-up? What are those texts called? (fiction and non-fiction). If students have difficulty recalling the terms but understand the concept, then the teacher should provide them with the accurate terms. If not, then have students think about which book they would use if they wanted to get information on polar bears? Why would they use the text "Baby Animals"? On the Top Hat be sure to write that one is a fiction & the other a non-fiction.
5. Then ask students what do we write on the bottom of the organizer? If students provide the correct response of how the two things are the same then continue on with the lesson. If not guide students to recall that the top hat organizer looks at how two things are different and the __.
6. After that have students think quietly how the two books are same. Allow students 1-2 minutes to brainstorm ways that the two texts are the same. Gather students together & have a few students share. Record accurate responses on the organizer. If answers are beginning to repeat themselves then end the share. Read aloud the responses once completed writing.
7. If time allows: <u>(if not, then complete this during the beginning of Writing Workshop).</u> Display the 2nd Top Hat organizer & label one side Fiction & the second side Non-fiction. Have students begin to think about how the two are different and the same. Begin with differences and have student share response while the teacher records. At minimum there should be 3 differences. (Possible responses: one gives real information and one is made-up, one has drawings, the other has photos, fiction stories have animals that may talk, non-fiction may have bold words or real people). Switch to similarities once 3 has been reached and have students share at least 2 similarities.
8. (5-7 mins max) Write the letter /th/ on the board (write clearly so students can see how to write both type of letters. Next the teacher will ask if students if they know what sound this letter makes. The teacher should use words such as they, thin, there & this to assist with the sound recognition. The teacher will then correct or reiterate the sound that digraph /th/ makes (focus on the shape your mouth makes, where your tongue goes and how to breath to create the /th/ sound). Have students identify where they hear the /th/. Explain to students that we are going to look at the beginning sound that /th/ makes. Display or draw the picture of something or someone thin. Next to the picture write the word thin,

underlining the /th/. The teacher should then point to and phonetically sound out the word thin, modeling how words are sounded out when they begin with a digraph. Have students repeat after you as you point to each word part. Challenge students to think of other words that begin with the /th/ digraph. Record 3-4 words on the board.

9. Then the teacher will write word family –uck on the board and display a picture of a duck, something lucky, something stuck and Mr. Yuck. Underneath or next of the pictures write the name of each word. The teacher will then read aloud each word and ask what do they hear when all the words are said? Next the teacher should guide students to identify that each word has –uck at the end. Also that each word rhyme & are a part of the –uck word family. Distribute writing paper to students and have students listen to the teacher say the word duck aloud & phonetically. The teacher should also cover, erase or take down the –uck words displayed. Students will then try to sound out and & spell out the word on the writing paper. After 35 seconds have students raise their hands to be checked & one student spells the word aloud. The teacher should write the word down on the board. Have students check their spelling. Is it spelled correctly? If no, then correct spelling underneath or next to the original word.
10. Try again with the word luck, yuck & stuck (which may be a challenge to some). Briefly re-explain to students that one strategy when sounding out new words is to say the word slowly and listen for any letter or word family they already know. Like in the word bin we hear it and know that word family & how to spell it. So I just need to listen to what the beginning/first letter/sound is & write it down. That is how we sound out new words or words we're unsure of.
11. *You do:* Teacher will then guide students to complete –uck work sort (see appendix).
12. *Exit Ticket:* The teacher will write the word family -uck on the board and point to it. Have the student think of and write a word in that word family on index cards. At the count of 3 all the students should raise their cards up so that the teacher will collect them, scan the deck, note & record student responses.

Sight & Sound Words: (9:45-10:15)
1. Have students gather together. The teacher will display the chart paper with the sight words & sound word pre-written on it.
2. *I do:* Teacher will lead a call and response where the teacher will repeat the first word, a student name, while pointing to it and students will repeat it. Continue down the list one time.
3. Next repeat down the list but challenge students to move faster with the teacher still speaking the word first and students repeating clearly. Repeat once more but this time the students will say the words and the teacher will not lead.
4. *We do:* Basketball Word Game- Teacher will have the sight words (new & some old ones) written on strips of paper, next ball up the papers with the words. After that scatter the balled up papers around the room on the floor. Students will each have a turn to pick up a balled up paper. Once they unfold the paper, the student will have to say the word written; if the word is said correctly then students will have the opportunity to 'shoot' the balled up paper into the trash basket. If the word is said incorrectly then the student must ball up the paper and put it down on the same spot on the ground. It is the next persons turn.
5. The teacher should mix up the remaining words once everyone has gone once before beginning a second round.
6. Students and teachers will play until no other papers remain on the floor. If time, play again.

7. *You do:* Teacher will distribute handwriting practice sheets with the words written on them once- students will trace and then write the words atleast twice.
8. *Exit Ticket:* Students will each receive a post it where they will write their name and leave room below it. The teacher should write the word 'those' on the board & read it aloud. On the post-it students will either write the letter 'y' or 'n' if the word the teacher said matches what is written on the board. The teacher will collect the post-its & check to see who answered correctly & who did not. Record any incorrect post-its.

Bathroom Break: (10:15-10:20)
Small Groups/Guided Reading: (10:20-10:45)
Small groups should not be larger than 5 students and smaller than 2.
1. Teacher MUST model and go over small group activities and protocols before you send students in groups! Students must work on the assigned task at their group! Students must ask their group questions first if unclear before asking teacher. Students must remain in their small group space unless they are getting another activity for their group or cleaning up. Bathroom, water, etc is not allowed during groups. Students must use whisper voice when talking in groups. Actual student group time will be shorter the first month or so until students become acclimated to the expectations and routines of small group work.
5. *Small Group 1:* Guided reading. In this group the teacher will begin by first reviewing depending on the level of the students either the alphabets or the sight words introduced earlier that day. For alphabets: on individual white lap boards have students write the letter that you name. You can use magnetic letters so students have a reference to what it looks like if needed. For sight words: using the pre-written index cards with the sight words, show the card and have students state the word on the card. Extensions~ have students write the word on white lap boards or use in sentences. Then move into the text that day. Again depending on the level of the students: choose a text close to their level. Teacher will go over the title of the books and the author. Preview the text by looking through the book and making a prediction what the text may be about based on the pictures, title and cover. Teacher must model to students how to use the sentence frame "I predict __ because __." when making a prediction statement to the group about the text or anything. Next have students make predictions about the book using the sentence frame. Then the teacher will either choose to Echo read (you point and read a page at a time and have them repeat you) or Round Robin read (each student reads a page and you go around the group) and begin reading the text together. Once finished reading, briefly discuss the text, what was it about, who was in it: focus on using the key words beginning, middle and end of the story. After that based on what the focus was before reading the text have the students 'hunt' for the sight words or letters in story. Write down each one found on the white lap boards and then share once the students in the group are finished 'hunting'.
6. Finally have students independently complete a story map.
7. *All Other Small Groups:* Students will use instant learning center kits. Teacher will choose the 2 focused on Ending Sound, Middle Sounds, Sound Sort, Story Sequencing & Simple Sentences. Teacher will MODEL/demonstrate how to use any of the new center kits if needed.

Writing Workshop: (10:45- 11:00)
1. *I do:* (7 mins max) (If not completed during the ELA time) Display the 2nd Top Hat organizer & label one side Fiction & the second side Non-fiction. Have students begin to think about how the two are different and the same. Begin with

differences and have student share response while the teacher records. At minimum there should be 3 differences. (Possible responses: one gives real information and one is made-up, one has drawings, the other has photos, fiction stories have animals that may talk, non-fiction may have bold words or real people). Switch to similarities once 3 has been reached and have students share atleast 2 similarities.
2. (6 mins max) The teacher will display the upper case letters from A-E on the left side of the board in order vertically. On the right side display the lower case letters vertically and mixed up. Explain to students that we are going to work on matching and building our 1 on 1 correspondence. Each letter has a matching uppercase and lower case letter.
3. *We do:* The teacher will call on students to come up and draw lines to match an upper case letter to its lower case. When completed the teacher can display another set of letters.
4. *You do:* Once completed have students use story writing paper to illustrate and write facts about their favorite animal. Provide the sentence frame: *The best food for dinner is ___.* Promote students using invented spelling to complete the sentence frame. For students who need the extra assistance the teacher should write the sentence frame on their paper: for others have them copy & write the sentence frame on their own.
5. The teacher should circulate around to monitor list work and assist those who need it.
6. If time remains the gather students to go over.

Math: (11:00-11:30)
1. The teacher will show large flash cards with the numbers 1-30 on them and begin counting aloud. Encourage students to join in. Today we'll focus on our shapes!
2. *I/We do:* The teacher will draw a hexagon, triangle, square and rectangle on the board. Engage students in reviewing the names of the shapes.
3. Next, gather students to take a look/walk around the classroom, what shapes do they see? Allow students about 1 minute to look/walk around. Then gather students together again and have students share the shapes they see by telling what the object is, *I see a book*. Students should then identify the shape. *It is a square/rectangle*. Have each student share and do not accept more than 2 repeats of the same object.
4. *You do:* Stations with Instant Learning Centers: Making Ten, Shapes, Counting & Pattern.
5. *Exit Ticket:* Teacher will distribute post-it or index cards say a shape aloud. Have student draw the shape on the post-it or card along with their name. Collect and go through noting down any students who did not get it correct.

Closing Activity: (11:30-11:45)
1. Gather students together for a closing activity game on the projector & computer. Choices include Reading Eggs (if accessible) or an ABC game on Starfall.com. Shapes Bingo is an option as well. Review the sight words we've done so far this year is another option (boys vs girls or any variation).

DEAR (Drop Everything And Read) (11:45-11:57)

Week 27 (9:00-12:00)

ELA Focus/Skill: Analyzing Text
Phonics (letter/word family): digraph /ch/ & short vowel /u/ review
Sound Words: cheese, chick, children
Sight Words: soon, of
Big Book: "Chicka Chicka Boom Boom" by Doreen Cronin
Writing Focus: Capital First Names
Math Focus: Shapes All Around Us

Objectives: Students will be able to:
- repeat and identify the day, weather and season
- place the letters of the alphabet sequentially
- identify the digraph /ch/, it's sound and words that begin with /ch/
- sort and classify short vowel /u/ words
- to analyze texts using HOT
- to capitalize the first letter in name
- orally identify the sound words and speak phonetically
- identify sight words & use in context
- use word family knowledge, letter, blends & digraph knowledge in inventive spelling while writing
- identify, name and draw the shapes that are in common objects around us

Materials:
"All About Today" pocket chart, "Click Clack Moo Cows that Type" & "Baby Animals" Big books, ABC flash cards, white lap boards, dry erase markers, board erasers, 2 chart paper with a top-hat organizer drawn on it, picture of a bun, bug, scissors cutting, & duck, post-its, chart paper with sight words pre-written, post-its with sight words written on them & bawled up for sight word basketball, container to throw the words in, short vowel review pg 6 (see appendix), handwriting sheets with the sight words written twice (www.handwritingworksheets.com), Instant Learning Centers: Rhyming Sounds, Ending Sounds, Middle Sounds Building Words, Simple Sentences & Story Sequencing & for math: Making Tens, Counting, Shapes, Patterns, story map & top hat organizers for small groups, crayons, pencils, erasers, story writing paper, number flash cards (1-30), computer & projector, Shape Bingo or Chart Paper with old sight words on it for review

ELA
Whole Group: Morning Meeting/Shared Read: (9:00- 9:15)
1. Students will gather together for Morning Meeting where the teacher will model how to use the "All About Today" pocket chart. The teacher will read the information on the pocket chart, using a pointer, starting with the month, date and year using the sentence frame "Today is __." Next have the students repeat the sentence. After that the teacher will continue on with the pocket chart moving to "Yesterday was __." Students will repeat each section after the teacher has pointed and read it aloud. Then teacher will read aloud the objectives for the day, briefly explaining that this is what the goal is by the end of their time together (Use academic language). If extra time, have 1-2 students share something exciting or important news about themselves.
2. (9:15-9:45) *I do:* Teacher will begin with ABC flash cards and distribute the flash cards to students to put them in order on the floor or desks as a whole group

from a given letter (for example- sort the letters beginning from B to U in order). Next the teacher will point and read aloud the title "Chicka Chicka Boom Boom" by Bill Martin Jr. The teacher will explain to students that while we are re-reading this story I want you to focus and listen for two things….what sound do you hear when you hear chicka? And what causes the coconut tree to fall over? Begin reading the story.

3. *We do:* Half-way through the read aloud stop and check-in with the first question- have students figured out what sound chicka makes? Also, as a review with last week's lesson, what type of story is this, fiction or non-fiction? What evidence from the text supports that?

4. *Mini-lesson:* The teacher will write the following question on the board & read it aloud: What causes the coconut tree to fall over? "Turn and talk" with a neighbor- share possible responses from the text. Allow students 2 mins max to share with their partner. Gather students back together and have 2-3 students share responses to the question. (Responses you are looking forward lead to the idea that the tree falls over because it is too heavy with all of the letters at the top. We know because the tree is leaning as the letters go up the coconut tree.) If needed- guide students to refer back to the pictures within the story and/or re-read certain pages with a focus on the details.

5. Then after the discussion to respond to the question- explain to students that our answer now needs to be in a sentence or sentences that can be written on the board. Who can help with that? Remember that a sentence is a complete thought.

6. Allow students a few moments to think of a sentence in their mind before raising their hand to share. Together as a group think of one-two complete sentences that answers Why the coconut tree falls over? Once a response has been reached the teacher should write the sentence(s) on the board below the question & read it aloud to the students. Check with a thumb up or down if majority agree with the response.

7. (5-7 mins max) Write the letter /ch/ on the board (write clearly so students can see how to write both type of letters. Next the teacher will ask if students if they know what sound this letter makes. The teacher should use words such as chick, cheese & children to assist with the sound recognition. The teacher will then correct or reiterate the sound that digraph /ch/ makes (focus on the shape your mouth makes, where your teeth go and how to breath to create the /ch/ sound). Have students identify where they hear the /th/. Explain to students that we are going to look at the beginning sound that /ch/ makes. Display or draw the picture of a piece of cheese. Next to the picture write the word cheese, underlining the /ch/. The teacher should then point to and phonetically sound out the word cheese, modeling how words are sounded out when they begin with a digraph. Have students repeat after you as you point to each word part. Challenge students to think of other words that begin with the /ch/ digraph. Record 3-4 words on the board.

8. Then the teacher will write short vowel /u/ on the board and display a picture of a bun, bug, cut and duck. Underneath or next of the pictures write the name of each word. The teacher will then read aloud each word and ask what do they hear when all the words are said? The teacher should guide students to identify that each word has a /u/ in it, in the middle. Write the word slug on the board & have students identify in which group would that word belong in. The teacher should also try with the words shut, fun, stuck and hug.

9. *You do:* Teacher will then guide students to complete short vowel /u/ worksheet (see appendix). The teacher will assist in reading the sentences on the pages in the book as well as the word bank to fill in the blanks.
10. *Exit Ticket:* The teacher will write the word family -ug on the board and point to it. Have the student think of and write a word in that word family on index cards. At the count of 3 all the students should raise their cards up so that the teacher will collect them, scan the deck, note & record student responses.

Sight & Sound Words: (9:45-10:15)
1. Have students gather together. The teacher will display the chart paper with the sight words & sound word pre-written on it.
2. *I do:* Teacher will lead a call and response where the teacher will repeat the first word, a student name, while pointing to it and students will repeat it. Continue down the list one time.
3. Next repeat down the list but challenge students to move faster with the teacher still speaking the word first and students repeating clearly. Repeat once more but this time the students will say the words and the teacher will not lead.
4. *We do:* Sight word Tic Tac Toe- Teacher will draw the tic tac toe board on the board. Then inside each box the teacher will write the new sight words just introduced and in the extra boxes the sight words from the previous weeks (said, say, then, those, under, until, came, & run). The teacher will explain the game's rules briefly. There are 2 teams, the X and the O team. 1 player will get picked and they will pick where they want their letter (X or O) to go on the board. To get their spot the player must say the word in the box first. If the word is said correctly then the teacher or player will draw the letter in the box. If the word is incorrect then the next team goes. The first team to 3 in a row wins. The teacher will need to split the class into two teams.
5. Students and teachers will play for 2-3 rounds depending on time.
6. *You do:* Teacher will distribute handwriting practice sheets with the words written on them once- students will trace and then write the words atleast twice.
7. *Exit Ticket:* Students will each receive a post it where they will write their name and leave room below it. The teacher should write the word 'soon' on the board & read it aloud. On the post-it students will either write the letter 'y' or 'n' if the word the teacher said matches what is written on the board. The teacher will collect the post-its & check to see who answered correctly & who did not. Record any incorrect post-its.

Bathroom Break: (10:15-10:20)

Small Groups/Guided Reading: (10:20-10:45)
Small groups should not be larger than 5 students and smaller than 2.
1. Teacher MUST model and go over small group activities and protocols before you send students in groups! Students must work on the assigned task at their group! Students must ask their group questions first if unclear before asking teacher. Students must remain in their small group space unless they are getting another activity for their group or cleaning up. Bathroom, water, etc is not allowed during groups. Students must use whisper voice when talking in groups. Actual student group time will be shorter the first month or so until students become acclimated to the expectations and routines of small group work.
2. *Small Group 1:* Guided reading. In this group the teacher will begin by first reviewing depending on the level of the students either the alphabets or the sight words introduced earlier that day. For alphabets: on individual white lap boards have students write the letter that you name. You can use magnetic letters so students have a reference to what it looks like if needed. For sight words: using

the pre-written index cards with the sight words, show the card and have students state the word on the card. Extensions~ have students write the word on white lap boards or use in sentences. Then move into the text that day. Again depending on the level of the students: choose a text close to their level. Teacher will go over the title of the books and the author. Preview the text by looking through the book and making a prediction what the text may be about based on the pictures, title and cover. Teacher must model to students how to use the sentence frame "I predict __ because __." when making a prediction statement to the group about the text or anything. Next have students make predictions about the book using the sentence frame. Then the teacher will either choose to Echo read (you point and read a page at a time and have them repeat you) or Round Robin read (each student reads a page and you go around the group) and begin reading the text together. Once finished reading, briefly discuss the text, what was it about, who was in it: focus on using the key words beginning, middle and end of the story. After that based on what the focus was before reading the text have the students 'hunt' for the sight words or letters in story. Write down each one found on the white lap boards and then share once the students in the group are finished 'hunting'.
3. Finally have students independently complete a story map or top hat depending on the text used during small groups.
4. *All Other Small Groups:* Students will use instant learning center kits. Teacher will choose the 2 focused on Ending Sound, Middle Sounds, Sound Sort, Story Sequencing & Simple Sentences. Teacher will MODEL/demonstrate how to use any of the new center kits if needed.

Writing Workshop: (10:45- 11:00)
1. *I do:* (6 mins max) The teacher will write their name on the board for students to see. Next ask students what type of letter does the name start with? (Upper/Capital). Then write a students' name on the board- what type of letter does this start with? (Again upper case/capital). One final name should be written on the board & again have students identify the letter it begins with. Ask students if they identify a pattern with names? (All names begin with upper case letters). Explain to students that all names begin with capital letters with we write them down. It does not matter whose name it is.
2. *We do:* The teacher should white lap boards, markers & erasers. Have students practice writing their name & underline the capital letter each time they write it. It should fit at least twice on their lap boards. Once completed have students raise their hands so that the teacher can check that each time the name was written it began with a capital letter.
3. *You do:* Once completed have students use story writing paper to illustrate and write an opinion piece sharing some things that can be done in the winter outside. Provide the sentence frame: *The best food for dinner is ___.* Promote students using invented spelling to complete the sentence frame. For students who need the extra assistance the teacher should write the sentence frame on their paper: for others have them copy & write the sentence frame on their own.
4. The teacher should circulate around to monitor list work and assist those who need it.
5. If time remains the gather students to go over.

Math: (11:00-11:30)
1. The teacher will show large flash cards with the numbers 1-30 on them and begin counting aloud. Encourage students to join in. Today we'll focus on our shapes!

2. *I/We do:* The teacher will draw a hexagon, triangle, square and rectangle on the board. Engage students in reviewing the names of the shapes.
3. Next, gather students to take a look/walk around the classroom, what shapes do they see? Allow students about 1 minute to look/walk around. Then gather students together again and have students share the shapes they see by telling what the object is, *I see a book*. Students should then identify the shape. *It is a square/rectangle.* Have each student share and do not accept more than 2 repeats of the same object.
4. *You do:* Stations with Instant Learning Centers: Making Ten, Shapes, Counting & Pattern.
5. *Exit Ticket:* Teacher will distribute post-it or index cards say a shape aloud. Have student draw the shape on the post-it or card along with their name. Collect and go through noting down any students who did not get it correct.

Closing Activity: (11:30-11:45)
1. Gather students together for a closing activity game on the projector & computer. Choices include Reading Eggs (if accessible) or an ABC game on Starfall.com. Shapes Bingo is an option as well. Review the sight words we've done so far this year is another option (boys vs girls or any variation).

DEAR (Drop Everything And Read) (11:45-11:57)

Week 28 (9:00-12:00)

ELA Focus/Skill: Asking & Answering Questions & Text to Self Connections
Phonics (letter/word family): digraph /wh/ & -et word family
Sound Words: where, why, when, whale
Sight Words: white, what, who
Big Book: "Mrs. Wishy Washy's Farm" by Joy Cowley
Writing Focus: Word Order
Math Focus: Skip counting (10's & 5's)

Objectives: Students will be able to:
- repeat and identify the day, weather and season
- place the letters of the alphabet sequentially
- identify the digraph /wh/, it's sound and words that begin with /wh/
- sort and classify words in the –et word family
- to ask and answer questions in a text
- to identify & place words in order to create sentences
- orally identify the sound words and speak phonetically
- identify sight words & use in context
- use word family knowledge, letter, blends & digraph knowledge in inventive spelling while writing
- identify the pattern of skip counting by 10's & 5's
- skip count by 10's & 5's

Materials:
"All About Today" pocket chart, "Mrs. Wishy Washy's Farm" Big books, ABC flash cards, white lap boards, dry erase markers, board erasers, chart paper with question words (who, what, where, when why) written on it & space between to write 1-2 question using each question stem, post-its, pictures of a whale, a jet, net, wet, & a vet, post-its, chart paper with sight words pre-written, index card with the sight words written on it for 4 corners & small groups, -et word family picture book pgs 14-15 (see appendix), handwriting sheets with the sight words written twice (www.handwritingworksheets.com), Instant Learning Centers: Rhyming Sounds, Ending Sounds, Middle Sounds Building Words, Simple Sentences & Story Sequencing & for math: Making Tens, Counting, Shapes, Patterns, story map & top hat organizers for small groups, crayons, pencils, erasers, Word Order activity (see appendix), number flash cards (1-40), lined paper with the traceable skip counting patterns for 10's & 5's, computer & projector, Shape Bingo or Chart Paper with old sight words on it for review

ELA
Whole Group: Morning Meeting/Shared Read: (9:00- 9:15)
1. Students will gather together for Morning Meeting where the teacher will model how to use the "All About Today" pocket chart. The teacher will read the information on the pocket chart, using a pointer, starting with the month, date and year using the sentence frame "Today is __." Next have the students repeat the sentence. After that the teacher will continue on with the pocket chart moving to "Yesterday was __." Students will repeat each section after the teacher has pointed and read it aloud. Then teacher will read aloud the objectives for the day, briefly explaining that this is what the goal is by the end of their time

together (Use academic language). If extra time, have 1-2 students share something exciting or important news about themselves.

2. (9:15-9:45) *I do:* Teacher will begin with ABC flash cards and distribute the flash cards to students to put them in order on the floor or desks as a whole group from a given letter (for example- sort the letters beginning from E to P in order). Next the teacher will point and read aloud the title "Mrs. Wishy Washy's Farm" by Joy Cowley. The teacher will explain to students that while we are re-reading this story I want you to focus and listen for two things....what does the story remind you of? What things are your wondering or questioning about in the story? Begin reading the story.
3. *We do:* Half-way through the read aloud stop and check-in with the first question- what does the story remind you of? (text to self connections) Also, as a review with previous week's lesson, what type of story is this, fiction or non-fiction? What evidence from the text supports that? Complete reading the story.
4. *Mini-lesson:* The teacher will write the following question words on the board & read it aloud: Who, what, where, when & why. Ask students if they recall when these words are used or for what purpose? Guide student responses if needed with having them recall how we find out answers to questions? What do we do, especially if we are curious? Otherwise- the teacher will re-explain briefly that *these are question words- used when we are asking something. It was just used when I asked when these words are used for? A good reader asks questions as they are reading. Just like we might ask questions as we are watching a movie- why did so and so do this? Or what happened? Maybe even where are they? These same questions and many others could be asked while you are reading a book.*
5. The teacher will display the chart paper with the question words written on it. Read aloud each question word. Remind *students that they were asked to think about what things are you wondering about as they hear the story. We're going to write down those things that you wondered about on this question organizer. We're also going to see if the story answered any of your questions or if someone else knows the answer.*
6. Have students take a moment and try to mentally/quietly turn what they wondered about into a question starting with either who, what, where, when why. After 1-2 of quiet thinking have students share their questions & the teacher will record their responses on the chart paper.
7. Once each person has had an opportunity to share- the teacher should read over the questions asked. Ask students if we know the answer to any of the questions that were asked- take no more than 3-4 minutes to discuss the answers to any of the questions or places to look for/ how to find the answers.
8. (5-7 mins max) Write the letter /wh/ on the board (write clearly so students can see how to write both type of letters. Next the teacher will ask if students if they know what sound this letter makes. The teacher should use words such as whale, where, when & why to assist with the sound recognition. The teacher will then correct or reiterate the sound that digraph /wh/ makes (focus on the shape your mouth makes and how to breath to create the /wh/ sound). Have students identify where they hear the /wh/. Explain to students that we are going to look at the beginning sound that /wh/ makes. Display or draw the picture of a whale. Next to the picture write the word whale, underlining the /wh/. The teacher should then point to and phonetically sound out the word whale, modeling how words are sounded out when they begin with a digraph. Have students repeat

after you as you point to each word part. Challenge students to think of other words that begin with the /wh/ digraph. Record 3-4 words on the board.

9. Then the teacher will write –et word family on the board and display a picture of a jet, wet, net & vet. Underneath or next of the pictures write the name of each word. The teacher will then read aloud each word and ask what do they hear when all the words are said? The teacher should guide students to identify that each word has an -et in it, at the end. Have students brainstorm other –et words & the teacher will write the word to the list.
10. *You do:* Teacher will then guide students to complete the –et picture book (see word family picture book pgs 14-15 in the appendix). The teacher will assist in identifying the pictures on the pages in the book as well as creating a word bank to assist in writing the words on the blanks.
11. *Exit Ticket:* The teacher will write the word family -et on the board and point to it. Have the student think of and write a word in that word family on index cards. At the count of 3 all the students should raise their cards up so that the teacher will collect them, scan the deck, note & record student responses.

Sight & Sound Words: (9:45-10:15)
1. Have students gather together. The teacher will display the chart paper with the sight words & sound word pre-written on it.
2. *I do:* Teacher will lead a call and response where the teacher will repeat the first word, a student name, while pointing to it and students will repeat it. Continue down the list one time.
3. Next repeat down the list but challenge students to move faster with the teacher still speaking the word first and students repeating clearly. Repeat once more but this time the students will say the words and the teacher will not lead.
4. *We do:* 4 Corners Game- Teacher will place the index cards with the 4 sight words other than the student's names in 4 different corners of the room. Rules of the game: the teacher or leader of the game will say one of the words on the index cards. The players will have 10 seconds to go over to that 'corner' that has the word. Anyone who is at the wrong 'corner' is out.
5. Students and teachers will play 4-5 rounds.
6. *You do:* Teacher will distribute handwriting practice sheets with the words written on them once- students will trace and then write the words at least twice.
7. *Exit Ticket:* Students will each receive a post it where they will write their name and leave room below it. The teacher should write the word 'who' on the board & read it aloud. On the post-it students will either write the letter 'y' or 'n' if the word the teacher said matches what is written on the board. The teacher will collect the post-its & check to see who answered correctly & who did not. Record any incorrect post-its.

Bathroom Break: (10:15-10:20)

Small Groups/Guided Reading: (10:20-10:45)
Small groups should not be larger than 5 students and smaller than 2.
1. Teacher MUST model and go over small group activities and protocols before you send students in groups! Students must work on the assigned task at their group! Students must ask their group questions first if unclear before asking teacher. Students must remain in their small group space unless they are getting another activity for their group or cleaning up. Bathroom, water, etc is not allowed during groups. Students must use whisper voice when talking in groups.
Actual student group time will be shorter the first month or so until students become acclimated to the expectations and routines of small group work.

2. *Small Group 1:* Guided reading. In this group the teacher will begin by first reviewing depending on the level of the students either the alphabets or the sight words introduced earlier that day. For alphabets: on individual white lap boards have students write the letter that you name. You can use magnetic letters so students have a reference to what it looks like if needed. For sight words: using the pre-written index cards with the sight words, show the card and have students state the word on the card. Extensions~ have students write the word on white lap boards or use in sentences. Then move into the text that day. Again depending on the level of the students: choose a text close to their level. Teacher will go over the title of the books and the author. Preview the text by looking through the book and making a prediction what the text may be about based on the pictures, title and cover. Teacher must model to students how to use the sentence frame "I predict __ because __." when making a prediction statement to the group about the text or anything. Next have students make predictions about the book using the sentence frame. Then the teacher will either choose to Echo read (you point and read a page at a time and have them repeat you) or Round Robin read (each student reads a page and you go around the group) and begin reading the text together. Once finished reading, briefly discuss the text, what was it about, who was in it: focus on using the key words beginning, middle and end of the story. After that based on what the focus was before reading the text have the students 'hunt' for the sight words or letters in story. Write down each one found on the white lap boards and then share once the students in the group are finished 'hunting'.
3. Finally have students independently complete a story map or top hat depending on the text used during small groups.
4. *All Other Small Groups*: Students will use instant learning center kits. Teacher will choose the 2 focused on Ending Sound, Middle Sounds, Sound Sort, Story Sequencing & Simple Sentences. Teacher will MODEL/demonstrate how to use any of the new center kits if needed.

Writing Workshop: (10:45- 11:00)
1. *I do:* (6 mins max) The teacher will write the words: *see I dog big* on the board & then read it aloud. Ask students if they think that makes sense & then have students think about what can we do to make these words make sense. Allow students 1-2 minutes to think and discuss with a partner.
2. *We do:* Have students share their opinions. If word order is brought up- stay focused on that. If not- suggest to students –what if we change the order of the words, they seem all mixed up? Call on a few students to assist in changing the order to help put the sentence together. It should say "I see a big dog."
3. Once the sentence is completed write the words "Word Order" above the sentence. The teacher should explain to students that *the order of words in a sentence is very important; it helps the sentence make sense and helps us understand what it is telling us. I see a big dog- what is this sentence telling us?* Call on 1-2 students to respond. Then continue- *when I first read the words before we rearranged them could anyone understand or know what the sentence was telling us?* The teacher should look for any hands & confirm that it was not easy to know what the sentence was trying to tell us. *We call this "word order." The order of words in a sentence help the sentence make sense and understand.*
4. *You do:* Students & teachers will complete the Word order activity together. Have the students cut the first set of words: jump Pam can. Together read the three words aloud. With a partner work to re-order the words so that the sentence make sense. When a partner group is ready, raise their hands & say their

response aloud. If the response is correct, everyone will order their words that way & glue them on the separate sheet, in the boxes in order.
5. Complete about 2-3 more together, or as needed & allow partners to complete the activity on their own.
6. The teacher should circulate around to monitor list work and assist those who need it.
7. If time remains the gather students to go over.

Math: (11:00-11:30)
1. The teacher will show large flash cards with the numbers 1-30 on them and begin counting aloud. Encourage students to join in. Today we'll focus on skip counting!
2. *I/We do:* The teacher will display a number chart or line from 1-30. Then explain to students that *there are different ways to count numbers, we've been practicing counting by 1's when we say 1, 2, 3, 4, 5, 6, 7, 8, 9, 10. But there's also counting by 10'a. Here's how it sounds.* The teacher will begin counting by 10 beginning at 10 and going to 50.
3. Next, the teacher will re-count by 10's but as each number is said, point to them on the number line or chart. Ask the students how many numbers is in between 1 and 10. Allow students a few seconds to count & then call on a few until the answer is said. The teacher should model how the answer 10 is reached by pointing to each number in between 1 and 10. Then have students identify how many numbers are in between 10 and 20. Explain to students that we say we're skip counting because we are skipping some numbers as we count. We start at 10 when we skip count by 10 so we skipped 1-9. Next we say 20 so we skipped 11-19. What do we skip when say 30? Call on students to respond- Guide them to use the number line/chart.
4. Gather students together and have them echo count by 10's up to 50. Then introduce them to skip counting by 5's the same way as we did 10. Explain to students that there is another common way to skip count and that is by 5's. Here's how it sounds. The teacher should skip count by 5's up to 50. Prior knowledge- is anyone familiar with hearing this or knows how to count by 5's?
5. Re-count by 5's but this time point to each number said on the number line/chart. Those that may know can join you. Have students then identify how many numbers are skipped when you count by 5's. Again have students reference the number line/chart. Then have students echo the teacher counting by 5's.
6. *You do:* The teacher will write on the lined paper the numbers to skip count by 10's for students to trace as well as the numbers used by 5's. Students will practice writing the numbers before moving into stations with Instant Learning Centers: Making Ten, Shapes, Counting & Pattern.
7. *Exit Ticket:* Teacher will distribute post-it or index cards say the number 30 aloud. Have student write the next number counting by 10 on the post-it or card along with their name. Collect and go through noting down any students who did not get it correct.

Closing Activity: (11:30-11:45)
1. Gather students together for a closing activity game on the projector & computer. Choices include Reading Eggs (if accessible) or an ABC game on Starfall.com. Shapes Bingo is an option as well. Review the sight words we've done so far this year is another option (boys vs girls or any variation).

DEAR (Drop Everything And Read) (11:45-11:57)

Week 29 (9:00-12:00)

ELA Focus/Skill: Pictures & Illustrations
Phonics (letter/word family): 's' blends & -en word family
Sound Words: sleep, stop, snake, smell
Sight Words: slip, skunk
Big Book: "Jen the Hen" by Colin Hawkins
Writing Focus: Naming Sentences
Math Focus: Skip counting (10's)

Objectives: Students will be able to:
- repeat and identify the day, weather and season
- place the letters of the alphabet sequentially
- identify 's' blends, it's sound and words that begin with the 's' blends
- sort and classify words in the –en word family
- to use the pictures & illustrations to analyze texts
- to identify the 'naming' part of a sentence
- orally identify the sound words and speak phonetically
- identify sight words & use in context
- use word family knowledge, letter, blends & digraph knowledge in inventive spelling while writing
- identify the pattern of skip counting by 10's & place numbers in order

Materials:
"All About Today" pocket chart, "Jen the Hen" Big books, ABC flash cards, white lap boards, dry erase markers, board erasers, post-its, pictures of a pen, the number ten, a group of men, & a hen, post-its, chart paper with sight words pre-written, /s/ Blend S'mores activity, -en word family flip book pg 11 & Naming Parts activity (see appendix), handwriting sheets with the sight words written twice (www.handwritingworksheets.com), Instant Learning Centers: Rhyming Sounds, Ending Sounds, Middle Sounds Building Words, Simple Sentences & Story Sequencing & for math: Making Tens, Counting, Shapes, Patterns, crayons, pencils, erasers, blank sheets of papers with the number 10, 20, 30, 40 up to100 written on it, 100 chart to display (even if projected), number flash cards (1-40), computer & projector, Shape Bingo or Chart Paper with old sight words on it for review

ELA

Whole Group: Morning Meeting/Shared Read: (9:00- 9:15)
1. Students will gather together for Morning Meeting where the teacher will model how to use the "All About Today" pocket chart. The teacher will read the information on the pocket chart, using a pointer, starting with the month, date and year using the sentence frame "Today is __." Next have the students repeat the sentence. After that the teacher will continue on with the pocket chart moving to "Yesterday was __." Students will repeat each section after the teacher has pointed and read it aloud. Then teacher will read aloud the objectives for the day, briefly explaining that this is what the goal is by the end of their time together (Use academic language). If extra time, have 1-2 students share something exciting or important news about themselves.
2. (9:15-9:45) *I do:* Teacher will begin with ABC flash cards and distribute the flash cards to students recite the letters them in order as a whole group from a given

letter (for example- sort the letters beginning from E to P in order). Next the teacher will point and read aloud the title "Jen the Hen" by Colin Hawkins & the illustrator Jaqui Hawkins. The teacher will explain to students that while reading this story focus on what ending sound they hear in the words in the title and throughout the book? Begin reading the story.

3. *We do:* Half-way through the read aloud stop and check-in with question- what ending sound do they hear in many of the words throughout the book & in the title? (-en). Also, as a review with previous week's lesson, what type of story is this, fiction or non-fiction? What evidence from the text supports that? Complete reading the story.

4. *Mini-lesson:* The teacher will write the following question words on the board & read it aloud: Who, what, where, when & why. *Ask students who recalls these question words from last week?* Next explain that *we are going to use our memory of the story as well as the illustrations to answer some questions about the story. First, who is in the story? The characters?* The teacher should go turn the pages of the pictures to allow students an opportunity to use the pics respond. Have students' volunteer responses. *Where are they?* Again have students' respond. *What are they doing?* After the responses & a why question based on the text.

5. Briefly discuss how *using pictures and illustration can be helpful and can even tell us some things that the story may not have mentioned. It is important to pay close attention to the pictures in books as well as listen to/read the story.*

6. (5-7 mins max) Write "'s' blends" on the board & underneath write 'st' 'sp' 'sl' 'sw' 'sn' & 'sc.' The teacher will explain to students that when the letter s is partnered with another letter it is called a blend because the two sounds blend together to make one sound but you can still here each sound if you listen carefully (picture a blender). Let me show you. The teacher will make each s blend sound so that the students can hear. Have students think of a word they ma know that begins with each sound. Compile a list of 1 word for each blend. The teacher should guide students in echo reading the list.

7. *You do:* Have students move into partners or groups and the teacher will distribute the marshmallows from the "S blend S'mores" activity (see appendix). With their partner/groups students will work on sounding out/identifying the words they see on the marshmallow (even the non-sense words since they focus on the s-blend). Remind students to look at the first two letters, identify the s-blend & its sound. This will help in the 'sounding out' process. Allow students 4-5 minutes to work.

8. Once the time is up, distribute the t-chart that goes with this activity and provide students with the instructions: sort the words on the marshmallows into two piles real words and nonsense words. Then glue them in their corresponding locations on the t-chart. Allow students a minimum of 6 minutes to work on it. Go over once completed.

9. Then the teacher will write –en word family on the board and display a picture of a pen, number ten, group of men & a hen. Underneath or next of the pictures write the name of each word. The teacher will then read aloud each word and ask what do they hear when all the words are said? The teacher should guide students to identify that each word has an -en in it, at the end. Have students brainstorm other –en words & the teacher will write the word to the list.

10. *You do:* Teacher will then guide students to complete the –en word family book (see word family flip book pg 11 in the appendix). The teacher will assist in

identifying the words/pictures on the pages in the book as well as putting it together to staple.

11. *Exit Ticket:* The teacher will write the word family -en on the board and point to it. Have the student think of and write a word in that word family on index cards. At the count of 3 all the students should raise their cards up so that the teacher will collect them, scan the deck, note & record student responses.

Sight & Sound Words: (9:45-10:15)
1. Have students gather together. The teacher will display the chart paper with the sight words & sound word pre-written on it.
2. *I do:* Teacher will lead a call and response where the teacher will repeat the first word, a student name, while pointing to it and students will repeat it. Continue down the list one time.
3. Next repeat down the list but challenge students to move faster with the teacher still speaking the word first and students repeating clearly. Repeat once more but this time the students will say the words and the teacher will not lead.
4. *We do:* Play doh Words: The teacher will distribute play doh to each student. Students will reference the chart paper for spelling and will 'spell out' each sight word with the play doh and practice saying it. The teacher should check each word spelled and listen to students say the words.
5. *You do:* Teacher will distribute handwriting practice sheets with the words written on them once- students will trace and then write the words at least twice.
6. *Exit Ticket:* Students will each receive a post it where they will write their name and leave room below it. The teacher should write the word 'slip' on the board & read it aloud. On the post-it students will either write the letter 'y' or 'n' if the word the teacher said matches what is written on the board. The teacher will collect the post-its & check to see who answered correctly & who did not. Record any incorrect post-its.

Bathroom Break: (10:15-10:20)

Small Groups/Guided Reading: (10:20-10:45)
Small groups should not be larger than 5 students and smaller than 2.
1. Teacher MUST model and go over small group activities and protocols before you send students in groups! Students must work on the assigned task at their group! Students must ask their group questions first if unclear before asking teacher. Students must remain in their small group space unless they are getting another activity for their group or cleaning up. Bathroom, water, etc is not allowed during groups. Students must use whisper voice when talking in groups. Actual student group time will be shorter the first month or so until students become acclimated to the expectations and routines of small group work.
2. *All Small Groups:* Students will use instant learning center kits. Teacher will choose the 2 focused on Ending Sound, Middle Sounds, Sound Sort, Story Sequencing, Sight Words & Simple Sentences. Teacher will MODEL/demonstrate how to use any of the new center kits if needed.

Writing Workshop: (10:45- 11:00)
1. *I do:* (6 mins max) The teacher will write the sentence *I go home after school.* on the board & reads it aloud to students. Next ask students to identify who is the sentence about, re-read it if necessary. Once students identify the sentence is about me then have students identify how they knew? What word(s) in the sentence tell you that or names me? Again once students identify the word I the teacher should circle the word in the sentence. Above the sentence the teacher should write the words "*Naming Part*". The teacher should explain that *the*

naming part identify or tells who the sentence is about. Most sentences tell something about someone or a group of people. Let's try some more.

2. *We do:* The teacher should write and read aloud the sentence: *She is eating.* Have students identify who the sentence about here. One student's identify a girl and the key word is 'she' then the teacher should circle it. Next write & read aloud the sentence *We are going to the park.* Again have students identify who the sentence is about and once identified the teacher should circle the word. Then write and read aloud the sentence: *My dog is running.* Have students indentify the naming part, my dog, and the teacher should circle it once identified.
3. *You do:* Students & teachers will complete the Naming Parts of a sentence worksheet (see appendix). Teacher will read aloud the sentences for students and students will independently circle the naming parts.
4. The teacher should circulate around to monitor list work and assist those who need it.
5. If time remains the gather students to go over and collect it.

Math: (11:00-11:30)
1. The teacher will show large flash cards with the numbers 1-40 on them and begin counting aloud. Encourage students to join in. Today we'll focus on skip counting!
2. *I/We do:* The teacher will display a number chart or line from 1-100. Then the teacher will lead students in rote counting from 1-70. Students should be familiar up to 30 or possibly 40. Practice counting at minimum twice with students as a whole.
3. Next, the teacher will display a 100 chart for students to reference to when skip counting. The teacher will lead a review in skip counting first by 10's from 10-100 & point to each number on the 100 chart. Students should either echo count or count along. Have students identify if they just counted by 5's or 10's. Repeat the count a second time for reinforcement & add body movements to have students moving and help them recall the pattern.
4. Gather students together on the rug & choose 10 volunteers. Each volunteers should receive one of the numbers written on the blank papers- be sure the numbers are mixed up. Have the remaining students assist in putting the students back in order counting by 10's from 10-100. Once completed the teacher should lead students in skip counting by 10's with the students that are holding the numbers raising their paper up as their number is said.
5. If time, choose 10 new students to repeat the activity.
6. *You do:* The teacher will distribute scissors, glue and the 'skip counting by 10's activity (see appendix). Have students stop at 100, do not have them skip count up to 120 unless you feel a scholar is ready for the challenge. Provide students with clear directions that they will cut out the suns' put them in order & glue them on the blank sun shines to display skip counting by 10's. If completed early, students should practice skip counting.
7. *Exit Ticket:* Teacher will distribute post-it or index cards say the number 50 aloud. Have student write the next number counting by 10 on the post-it or card along with their name. Collect and go through noting down any students who did not get it correct.

Closing Activity: (11:30-11:45)
1. Gather students together for a closing activity game on the projector & computer. Choices include Reading Eggs (if accessible) or an ABC game on Starfall.com. Shapes Bingo is an option as well. Review the sight words we've done so far this year is another option (boys vs girls or any variation).

DEAR (Drop Everything And Read) (11:45-11:57)

Week 30 (9:00-12:00)

ELA Focus/Skill: Main Idea
Phonics (letter/word family): 'r' blends & -ell word family
Sound Words: from, grow
Sight Words: Friday, green, brown, crab
Big Book: "What I Like About Myself" by Alia Zobel Nolan
Writing Focus: Telling/Action Parts of a Sentence
Math Focus: Skip counting (5's)

Objectives: Students will be able to:
- repeat and identify the day, weather and season
- place the letters of the alphabet sequentially
- identify 'r' blends, it's sound and words that have 'r' blends
- sort and classify words in the –ell word family
- to identify the main idea of a text
- to identify the 'telling/action' part of a sentence
- orally identify the sound words and speak phonetically
- identify sight words & use in context
- identify the pattern of skip counting by 5's & place numbers in order

Materials:
"All About Today" pocket chart, "What I Like About Myself" Big books, ABC flash cards, white lap boards, dry erase markers, board erasers, post-its, pictures of a well, bell, someone who fell & a cell phone, post-its, chart paper with sight words pre-written, post-its with the sight words written on & then crumbled up for Basketball, r-Blend activity (p 3 & 5) & -ell word family flip book pg 17 (see appendix), handwriting sheets with the sight words written twice (www.handwritingworksheets.com), Instant Learning Centers: Rhyming Sounds, Ending Sounds, Middle Sounds Building Words, Simple Sentences & Story Sequencing & for <u>math</u>: Making Tens, Counting, Shapes, Patterns, crayons, pencils, erasers, Action & Naming Game & Skip counting by 5's (see appendix), blank sheets of papers with the number 5, 10, 15, 20, 25 up to 50 written on it, 100 chart to display (even if projected), number flash cards (1-50), computer & projector, Shape Bingo or Chart Paper with old sight words on it for review

ELA
Whole Group: Morning Meeting/Shared Read: (9:00- 9:15)
1. Students will gather together for Morning Meeting where the teacher will model how to use the "All About Today" pocket chart. The teacher will read the information on the pocket chart, using a pointer, starting with the month, date and year using the sentence frame "Today is __." Next have the students repeat the sentence. After that the teacher will continue on with the pocket chart moving to "Yesterday was __." Students will repeat each section after the teacher has pointed and read it aloud. Then teacher will read aloud the objectives for the day, briefly explaining that this is what the goal is by the end of their time together (Use academic language). If extra time, have 1-2 students share something exciting or important news about themselves.
2. (9:15-9:45) *I do:* Teacher will begin with ABC flash cards and distribute the flash cards to students recite the letters them in order as a whole group from a given letter (for example- sort the letters beginning from F to T in order). Next the

teacher will point and read aloud the title "What I Like About Myself" by Alia Zobel Nolan & the illustrator Miki Sakamoto. The teacher will explain to students that while reading this story focus on what they like about themselves & be prepared to share. Begin reading the story.

3. *We do:* Half-way through the read aloud stop and check-in with question- what do you like about yourself? Also, as a review with previous week's lesson, what type of story is this, fiction or non-fiction? What evidence from the text supports that? Complete reading the story.
4. *Mini-lesson:* The teacher will write the words "Main Idea" on the board & read it aloud to students. Ask students who recalls what the main idea of a story is? Call on no more than 2 students to share responses. If no one responds accurately the teacher should remind students that the main idea is what the story is mostly about or mainly about. Have students think about and share briefly what is the main idea of this story "What I Like About Myself."
5. Briefly share and discuss responses. When a final, collected response has been agreed upon, the teacher should record the main idea on the board for everyone to see. Together both students and teacher should read aloud the main idea.
6. (5-7 mins max) Write "'r' blends" on the board & underneath write 'fr' 'tr' 'gr' 'cr' 'br' 'dr' & 'pr.' The teacher will explain to students that when the letter r is partnered with another letter it is called a blend just like when 's' is partnered with another letter because the two sounds blend together to make one sound but you can still here each sound if you listen carefully (picture a blender). Let me show you. The teacher will make each r blend sound so that the students can hear. Have students think of a word they ma know that begins with each sound. Compile a list of 1 word for each blend. The teacher should guide students in echo reading the list. Then as a group complete pg 3 of the 'r' blend activity sheet (appendix)
7. *You do:* Have students then turn into partners and the teacher will distribute the 'r' blend activity sheet (pg 5). The teacher will read aloud the word bank at the top of the sheet and then instruct students to do their best to match the picture to one of the words in the word bank. The teacher may need to re-read the words in the word bank aloud to students again or in individual pairs.
8. Allow students 6-7 mins to work and collect activity sheets to check student understanding (exit ticket).
9. Then the teacher will write –ell word family on the board and display a picture of a well, bell, someone who fell & a cell phone. Underneath or next of the pictures write the name of each word. The teacher will then read aloud each word and ask what do they hear when all the words are said? The teacher should guide students to identify that each word has an -ell in it, at the end. Have students brainstorm other –ell words & the teacher will write the word to the list.
10. *You do:* Teacher will then guide students to complete the –ell word family book (see word family flip book pg 17 in the appendix). The teacher will assist in identifying the words/pictures on the pages in the book as well as putting it together to staple.
11. *Exit Ticket:* The teacher will write the word family -ell on the board and point to it. Have the student think of and write a word in that word family on index cards. At the count of 3 all the students should raise their cards up so that the teacher will collect them, scan the deck, note & record student responses.

Sight & Sound Words: (9:45-10:15)
1. Have students gather together. The teacher will display the chart paper with the sight words & sound word pre-written on it.

2. *I do:* Teacher will lead a call and response where the teacher will repeat the first word, a student name, while pointing to it and students will repeat it. Continue down the list one time.
3. Next repeat down the list but challenge students to move faster with the teacher still speaking the word first and students repeating clearly. Repeat once more but this time the students will say the words and the teacher will not lead.
4. *We do:* Basketball Word Game- Teacher will have the sight words (new & some old ones) written on strips of paper, next ball up the papers with the words. After that scatter the balled up papers around the room on the floor. Students will each have a turn to pick up a balled up paper. Once they unfold the paper, the student will have to say the word written; if the word is said correctly then students will have the opportunity to 'shoot' the balled up paper into the trash basket. If the word is said incorrectly then the student must ball up the paper and put it down on the same spot on the ground. It is the next persons turn.
5. The teacher should mix up the remaining words once everyone has gone once before beginning a second round.
6. Students and teachers will play until no other papers remain on the floor. If time, play again.
7. *You do:* Teacher will distribute handwriting practice sheets with the words written on them once- students will trace and then write the words at least twice.
8. *Exit Ticket:* Distribute the white lap boards, erasers & markers. The teacher will say the word from and students will write it on their lap boards. At the count of 3 have students raise their boards up to be checked. The teacher will scan the boards & note down anyone that may need assistance with the sight words.

Bathroom Break: (10:15-10:20)
Small Groups/Guided Reading: (10:20-10:45)
Small groups should not be larger than 5 students and smaller than 2.

1. Teacher MUST model and go over small group activities and protocols before you send students in groups! Students must work on the assigned task at their group! Students must ask their group questions first if unclear before asking teacher. Students must remain in their small group space unless they are getting another activity for their group or cleaning up. Bathroom, water, etc is not allowed during groups. Students must use whisper voice when talking in groups. Actual student group time will be shorter the first month or so until students become acclimated to the expectations and routines of small group work.
2. *All Small Groups:* Students will use instant learning center kits. Teacher will choose the 2 focused on Ending Sound, Middle Sounds, Sound Sort, Story Sequencing, Sight Words & Simple Sentences. Teacher will MODEL/demonstrate how to use any of the new center kits if needed.

Writing Workshop: (10:45- 11:00)
1. *I do:* (6 mins max) The teacher will write the sentence *He is sitting on the bus.* on the board & reads it aloud to students. Next ask students to identify what is the boy doing in this sentence, re-read it if necessary. Once students identify the boy is sitting on the bus have students identify how they knew? What words in the sentence tell you the boy is on the bus sitting? Again once students identify the words sitting on the bus the teacher should underline the words/part in the sentence. Above the sentence the teacher should write the words "Action/Telling Part". The teacher should explain that *the telling or action part tells what the person or people are doing. Remember we talked about the naming part last week now we need to know what the naming part is doing. Let's try some more.*

6. *We do:* The teacher should write and read aloud the sentence: *She is eating*. Have students identify the action part. One students identify eating the teacher should underline it. Next write & read aloud the sentence *We are going to the park*. Again have students identify the action part and once identified the teacher should underline the word. Then write and read aloud the sentence: *My dog is running*. Have students identify the action part, running, and the teacher should underline it once identified. If time challenge students to indentify the naming part of each sentence and the teacher should circle it.
7. *You do:* Students & teachers will complete the Action and Naming Game (see appendix). Teacher will probably need to read aloud the sentences for students and students will work with a partner to create a silly sentence & then independently choose their favorite to re-write and illustrate.
8. The teacher should circulate around to monitor list work and assist those who need it.
9. If time remains the gather students to share and then collect it.

Math: (11:00-11:30)
1. The teacher will show large flash cards with the numbers 1-50 on them and begin counting aloud. Encourage students to join in. Today we'll focus on skip counting!
2. *I/We do:* The teacher will display a number chart or line from 1-100. Then the teacher will lead students in rote counting from 1-80. Students should be familiar up to 30 or possibly 40. Practice counting at minimum twice with students as a whole.
3. Next, the teacher will display a 100 chart for students to reference to when skip counting. The teacher will lead a review in skip counting first by 5's from 5- 100 & point to each number on the 100 chart. Students should either echo count or count along. Have students identify if they just counted by 5's or 10's. Repeat the count a second time for reinforcement & make it fun with movement.
4. Gather students together on the rug & choose 10 volunteers. Each volunteers should receive one of the numbers written on the blank papers- be sure the numbers are mixed up. Have the remaining students assist in putting the students back in order counting by 5's from 5-50. Once completed the teacher should lead students in skip counting by 5's with the students that are holding the numbers raising their paper up as their number is said.
5. If time, choose 5 new students to repeat the activity.
6. *You do:* The teacher will distribute 'skip counting by 5's activity (see appendix). Provide students with clear directions that each group of fishies have 5 so students will skip count by 5's to determine how many fishies are in each group. No one should be counting by 1's. If completed early, students should practice skip counting.
7. *Exit Ticket:* Teacher will distribute post-it or index cards say the number 45 aloud. Have student write the next number counting by 5 on the post-it or card along with their name. Collect and go through noting down any students who did not get it correct.

Closing Activity: (11:30-11:45)
1. Gather students together for a closing activity game on the projector & computer. Choices include Reading Eggs (if accessible) or an ABC game on Starfall.com. Shapes Bingo is an option as well. Review the sight words we've done so far this year is another option (boys vs girls or any variation).

DEAR (Drop Everything And Read) (11:45-11:57)

Week 31 (9:00-12:00)

ELA Focus/Skill: Supporting Details
Phonics (letter/word family): 'l' blends & short vowel /e/ review
Sound Words: black, please, blue, play
Sight Words: plant
Big Book: "Growing Frog" by Vivian French
Writing Focus: Punctuations in a Sentence (period & exclamations)
Math Focus: Coin Identification & Counting individually

Objectives: Students will be able to:
- repeat and identify the day, weather and season
- identify 'l' blends, it's sound and words that have 'l' blends
- sort and classify short vowel /e/ words
- to identify the supporting points/details of a text
- to identify and use punctuation at the end of a sentence
- orally identify the sound words and speak phonetically
- identify sight words & use in context
- identify the value of coins and count them individually

Materials:
"All About Today" pocket chart, "Growing Frogs" Big books, white lap boards, dry erase markers, board erasers, post-its, pictures of a net, pen & a bell, post-its, chart paper with sight words pre-written, r-Blend activity (p 3 & 5) & -ell word family flip book pg 17 (see appendix), handwriting sheets with the sight words written twice (www.handwritingworksheets.com), Instant Learning Centers: Rhyming Sounds, Ending Sounds, Middle Sounds Building Words, Simple Sentences & Story Sequencing & for math: Making Tens, Counting, Shapes, Patterns, crayons, pencils, erasers, Action & Naming Game (see appendix), plastic coins (penny, nickel & dime), large coins to display (penny, nickel & dime), number flash cards (1-50), computer & projector, Shape Bingo or Chart Paper with old sight words on it for review

ELA

Whole Group: Morning Meeting/Shared Read: (9:00- 9:15)
1. Students will gather together for Morning Meeting where the teacher will model how to use the "All About Today" pocket chart. The teacher will read the information on the pocket chart, using a pointer, starting with the month, date and year using the sentence frame "Today is __." Next have the students repeat the sentence. After that the teacher will continue on with the pocket chart moving to "Yesterday was __." Students will repeat each section after the teacher has pointed and read it aloud. Then teacher will read aloud the objectives for the day, briefly explaining that this is what the goal is by the end of their time together (Use academic language). If extra time, have 1-2 students share something exciting or important news about themselves.
2. (9:15-9:45) *I do:* The teacher will point and read aloud the title "Growing Frogs" by Vivian French & the illustrator Alison Bartlett. The teacher will explain to students that while re-reading this story focus on identifying the main idea of this text. Begin reading the story.
3. *We do:* Half-way through the read aloud stop and check-in with question- what is the main idea? Also, as a review with previous week's lesson, what type of story

is this, fiction or non-fiction? What evidence from the text supports that? Complete reading the story.

4. *Mini-lesson:* The teacher will write the words "Main Idea" on the board & read it aloud to students, then record on the board student responses from a bit earlier of what the main idea is of this text. Next have students identify how do they know- what information, words or pictures from the text tell us the story is about frogs that grow? Allow students the opportunity to look through the pictures in the book again for reference. Call on students to share response. Create a web around the main idea written on the board so that the responses students provide that are accurate. Focus on responses that share details in the pictures/text – we see the different stages in a frogs' life, how it changes, what it does to change, the names of each stage, etc.
5. Briefly share the responses that are written on the board. Underneath the teacher should write the words 'supporting details' & briefly explain that *the supporting details support or hold up the main idea. Picture a table, how many legs does it have? (4) and what happens to the table when a leg breaks? (it falls). So the legs support the top of the table. Well the details support the main idea- it holds it up and tells others who may read the main idea that it wasn't made up.*
6. (5-7 mins max) Write "'l' blends" on the board & underneath write 'cl' 'fl' & 'bl.' The teacher will explain to students that when the letter l is partnered with another letter it is also called a blend just like when 's' & 'r' are partnered with another letter. The teacher will make each l blend sound so that the students can hear. Have students think of a word they may know that begins with each sound. Compile a list of 1 word for each blend. The teacher should guide students in echo reading the list.
7. *You do:* Have students then turn into partners and the teacher will distribute the 'l' blend activity sheet (see appendix). The teacher will read aloud the name of each picture and clearly explain that students will cut the letters at the bottom of sheet. Then use the letters to make the 'l' blend that is heard at the beginning of each picture/word. Students should work either independently or with a partner.
8. Allow students 6-7 mins to work and collect activity sheets to check student understanding (exit ticket).
9. Then the teacher will write short vowel /e/ on the board and display a picture of a net, pen and bell. Underneath or next of the pictures write the name of each word. The teacher will then read aloud each word and ask what do they hear when all the words are said? The teacher should guide students to identify that each word has a /e/ in it, in the middle. Write the word sell on the board & have students identify in which group would that word belong in. The teacher should also try with the words smell, wet, ben and ten.
10. *You do:* Teacher will then guide students to complete short vowel /e/ worksheet (see appendix). The teacher will assist in reading the sentences on the pages in the book as well as the word bank to fill in the blanks.
11. *Exit Ticket:* The teacher will write the word family -et on the board and point to it. Have the student think of and write a word in that word family on index cards. At the count of 3 all the students should raise their cards up so that the teacher will collect them, scan the deck, note & record student responses.

Sight & Sound Words: (9:45-10:15)
1. Have students gather together. The teacher will display the chart paper with the sight words & sound word pre-written on it.

2. *I do:* Teacher will lead a call and response where the teacher will repeat the first word, a student name, while pointing to it and students will repeat it. Continue down the list one time.
3. Next repeat down the list but challenge students to move faster with the teacher still speaking the word first and students repeating clearly. Repeat once more but this time the students will say the words and the teacher will not lead.
4. *We do:* Sight word Tic Tac Toe- Teacher will draw the tic tac toe board on the board. Then inside each box the teacher will write the new sight words just introduced and in the extra boxes the sight words from the previous weeks (brown, slip, what who & run). The teacher will explain the game's rules briefly. There are 2 teams, the X and the O team. 1 player will get picked and they will pick where they want their letter (X or O) to go on the board. To get their spot the player must say the word in the box first. If the word is said correctly, then the teacher or player will draw the letter in the box. If the word is incorrect then the next team goes. The first team to 3 in a row wins. The teacher will need to split the class into two teams.
5. Students and teachers will play for 2-3 rounds depending on time.
6. *You do:* Teacher will distribute handwriting practice sheets with the words written on them once- students will trace and then write the words at least twice.
7. *Exit Ticket:* Distribute the white lap boards, erasers & markers. The teacher will say the plant and students will draw a plant on their lap boards. At the count of 3 have students raise their boards up to be checked. The teacher will scan the boards & note down anyone that may need assistance with the sight words.

Bathroom Break: (10:15-10:20)
Small Groups/Guided Reading: (10:20-10:45)
Small groups should not be larger than 5 students and smaller than 2.

1. Teacher MUST model and go over small group activities and protocols before you send students in groups! Students must work on the assigned task at their group! Students must ask their group questions first if unclear before asking teacher. Students must remain in their small group space unless they are getting another activity for their group or cleaning up. Bathroom, water, etc is not allowed during groups. Students must use whisper voice when talking in groups. Actual student group time will be shorter the first month or so until students become acclimated to the expectations and routines of small group work.
2. *All Small Groups:* Students will use instant learning center kits. Teacher will choose the 2 focused on Ending Sound, Middle Sounds, Sound Sort, Story Sequencing, Sight Words & Simple Sentences. Teacher will MODEL/demonstrate how to use any of the new center kits if needed.

Writing Workshop: (10:45- 11:00)
1. *I do:* (6 mins max) The teacher will write the sentence *My cat is flying.* on the board & reads it aloud to students. Have students identify what they see at the end of the sentence, a period. The teacher should then ask *what kind of punctuation can I use to show that I am really excited?* Call on 1-2 students to share response. If no one has identified it, the teacher should tell students that I would use something called an exclamation mark; the teacher should then erase the period at the end of the sentence and replace it with an exclamation mark. Next re-read the sentence with the exclamation mark; be aware to elevate your voice to show the excitement. Briefly explain that *when an exclamation mark is used at the end of a sentence it shows and means excitement. The reader who is reading the sentence should read it with a bit*

   of excitement to really understand what the writer is trying to say. Let's try some.
   2. *We do:* The teacher should write and read aloud the sentence: *We won the prize!* The teacher should read aloud first with excitement & have students echo it. (For a brief review have students identify the naming part of the sentence). Next write & read aloud the sentence *He is going to fall!* Again have teacher read aloud first and students echo it. Identify the action/telling part of the sentence for an extra review. Then write and read aloud the sentence: *My bunny loves to hop!* Have students echo read the sentence & identify the action part.
   3. *You do:* The teacher will distribute story writing paper and briefly give the directions: students will think of and tell a time that they were excited to see or do something. Students will write a sentence or two telling about it (Use the sentence frame "I was excited when __.") and challenge them to use an exclamation mark at the end of one of their sentences. After the sentence then the illustration may begin. Encourage inventive spelling.
   4. The teacher should circulate around to monitor list work and assist those who need it. If time remains the gather students to share (2-3 depending on time) and then collect it.

Math: (11:00-11:30)
   1. The teacher will lead a skip counting by 10's with students from 10-100. Then briefly tell students we are going to take our skip counting skills into counting some money!
   2. *I/We do:* The teacher will display a penny, nickel and dime for students to see. Ask students if *anyone can identify the coins seen or know how much they are worth?*
   3. If no one is able to identify or name the coins and/or its values then the teacher will name each coin & underneath write its name and value. Briefly show students the cent sign as well. The teacher should lead a call and response as the teacher points to the coin, names it and then identifies its values.
   4. Gather students together on the rug & lay out 5 pennies. Have students identify the coin & its value again. Next explain and model to students how to use skip counting skills to count the 5 pennies. Be sure to say and use the term cents when the total is reached. Have students call and respond as the teacher recounts them.
   5. Next model the 5 nickels & point out to students that since we practiced counting by 5's this will be a breeze for us. As well as 5 dimes.
   6. *You do:* The teacher will distribute plastic cup or small containers with pennies, nickels & dimes already sorted & white lap boards, erasers and markers. The teacher will instruct students to pick out & lay 6 pennies. Observe students complete this task & assist as needed. Then have students count the coins- refer to the board or chart paper if needed for coins & values. Once students find the value they should write the number on the white lap board with the cent sign & raise their hands for the teacher to check.
   7. Repeat task but have students pick & lay out 6 nickels to complete the task & then repeat with 6 dimes.
   8. *Exit Ticket:* Teacher will distribute post-it or index cards say the nickel aloud. Have student write the value of the nickel on the post-it or card along with their name. Collect and go through noting down any students who did not get it correct.

Closing Activity: (11:30-11:45)
1. Gather students together for a closing activity game on the projector & computer. Choices include Reading Eggs (if accessible) or an ABC game on Starfall.com. Shapes Bingo is an option as well. Review the sight words we've done so far this year is another option (boys vs girls or any variation).

DEAR (Drop Everything And Read) (11:45-11:57)

Week 32 (9:00-12:00)

ELA Focus/Skill: Review Parts of a Book
Phonics (letter/word family): Review digraphs & blends & short vowel review
Sound Words: must
Sight Words: want, so, soon, new, now
Big Book: Big book of choice- you are not reading but investing all the parts of a book
Writing Focus: Question Words
Math Focus: Coin Identification & Value

Objectives: Students will be able to:
- repeat and identify the day, weather and season
- sort and classify digraphs & blends
- sort and classify words short vowel words
- to identify and name the parts of a book
- to identify and create questions using question words
- orally identify the sound words and speak phonetically
- identify sight words & use in context
- identify and count individually sorted groups of coins (penny, nickel & dimes)

Materials:
"All About Today" pocket chart, A Variety of Big books, white lap boards, dry erase markers, board erasers, post-its, Blends & Digraphs Review & Short Vowel Monster 2 (see appendix), post-its, chart paper with sight words pre-written, post-its with the sight words written on & then crumbled up for Basketball, handwriting sheets with the sight words written twice (www.handwritingworksheets.com), Instant Learning Centers: Rhyming Sounds, Ending Sounds, Middle Sounds Building Words, Simple Sentences & Story Sequencing & for math: Making Tens, Counting, Shapes, Patterns, story writing paper with the words 'who,' 'what,' 'where,' 'when' & 'why' written vertically on them, crayons, pencils, erasers, coin manipulative sorted by coin into cups or container, 'counting coins piggy" pgs 2-5 (see appendix), computer & projector, Shape Bingo or Chart Paper with old sight words on it for review

ELA
Whole Group: Morning Meeting/Shared Read: (9:00- 9:15)
1. Students will gather together for Morning Meeting where the teacher will model how to use the "All About Today" pocket chart. The teacher will read the information on the pocket chart, using a pointer, starting with the month, date and year using the sentence frame "Today is __." Next have the students repeat the sentence. After that the teacher will continue on with the pocket chart moving to "Yesterday was __." Students will repeat each section after the teacher has pointed and read it aloud. Then teacher will read aloud the objectives for the day, briefly explaining that this is what the goal is by the end of their time together (Use academic language). If extra time, have 1-2 students share something exciting or important news about themselves.
2. (9:15-9:45) *I do:* The teacher will display a minimum of 5 big books (variety of fiction and non-fiction). The teacher will ask students to list or name the parts of a book. The teacher should record student responses on the board or chart paper labeled "Parts of a Book." Read back the list of responses back to scholars.

3. *We do:* The teacher will then provide students a few minutes to go through the big books displayed with a partner or a group of 3 and investigate the parts of that book, were there any parts missed? Or were all named? Allow about 2 mins for this. Instruct students on how the big books should be handled.
4. Once the time is up the teacher should gather students together, put the big books to the side and have students share the parts they located within the big books that are on our list and any parts that may have been missed. The teacher should add any new parts to the list that the students identify. The teacher should then look over the list, if there were any parts missed and the students have not mentioned (title, picture on the cover, author, illustrator, title page, ending page, back cover) be sure to include them on the list and share them with students.
5. (5-7 mins max) Write blends & digraphs on the board & underneath write s blend, r blend, l blend, sh, ch, wh & th. The teacher will then have students identify which of all the pairs of letters written on the board are digraphs? (ch, wh, th, sh) Next have students identify as a whole the sounds each digraph makes. Assist as needed. Then write the words: church, shut, whip, think on the board. The teacher will then explain that *even though everyone may not be able to read all of the words written on the board, everyone should be able to their beginning sounds to begin to 'sound out' the words.* Point to church and have students identify the beginning /ch/ sound. Next point to shut and have students identify the /sh/ sound, continue with whip and then think. Allow students a few seconds to either sound out the words or identify the words, if unable then the teacher should tell the students the words & have then echo them back.
6. Next the teacher should write st under the s blend label and have students identify its sound & a word that begins with it (stop, still, stay, etc). Then write the word *from* on the board and have students identify under which blend it belongs too (r blend). Repeat with the word *flip*.
7. *You do:* Stations: The teacher will break students into 4 groups (2 focused on review of blends & 2 focused on review of digraphs). The station work is from the Blends & Digraphs Review (see appendix). The teacher should provide students with clear instructions of what each group is to complete. One group will complete pgs 2 & 4. A second group will complete pgs 3 & 5. A third group will complete pgs 6 & 7. The fourth group will complete pgs 8 & 9.
8. Then the teacher will write the short vowels /a/, /e/, /i/, /o/, /u/ on the board. Have students identify each sound the vowels make & then name a word family for each vowel. Record response underneath or next to the matching vowel. The teacher should then draw a baseball bat and have students identify which short vowel is in the word bat & place/draw/write the bat in the short /a/ section. Repeat with pictures/words of a pen, pig, pot and a hut.
9. *You do:* Teacher will then group students in 3's or 4's & distribute the Short Vowel Monster 2 (see appendix) activity with clear instructions laying out the mats, cutting the words, saying them and sorting them on their matching short vowel mat.
10. *Exit Ticket:* The teacher will write the word family sh on the board and point to it. Have the student think of and write a word in that word family on index cards. At the count of 3 all the students should raise their cards up so that the teacher will collect them, scan the deck, note & record student responses.

Sight & Sound Words: (9:45-10:15)
1. Have students gather together. The teacher will display the chart paper with the sight words & sound word pre-written on it.

2. *I do:* Teacher will lead a call and response where the teacher will repeat the first word, a student name, while pointing to it and students will repeat it. Continue down the list one time.
3. Next repeat down the list but challenge students to move faster with the teacher still speaking the word first and students repeating clearly. Repeat once more but this time the students will say the words and the teacher will not lead.
4. *We do:* Popcorn Word Game- Teacher will have the sight words (new & some old ones) written on strips of paper, next ball up the papers with the words. After that scatter the balled up papers around the room on the floor. Students will each have a turn to pick up a balled up paper. Once they unfold the paper, the student will have to say the word written; if the word is said correctly then students will have the opportunity to 'shoot' the balled up paper into the trash basket. If the word is said incorrectly then the student must ball up the paper and put it down on the same spot on the ground. It is the next persons turn.
5. The teacher should mix up the remaining words once everyone has gone once before beginning a second round.
6. Students and teachers will play until no other papers remain on the floor. If time, play again.
7. *You do:* Teacher will distribute handwriting practice sheets with the words written on them once- students will trace and then write the words at least twice.

Bathroom Break: (10:15-10:20)

Small Groups/Guided Reading: (10:20-10:45)

Small groups should not be larger than 5 students and smaller than 2.

1. Teacher MUST model and go over small group activities and protocols before you send students in groups! Students must work on the assigned task at their group! Students must ask their group questions first if unclear before asking teacher. Students must remain in their small group space unless they are getting another activity for their group or cleaning up. Bathroom, water, etc is not allowed during groups. Students must use whisper voice when talking in groups. Actual student group time will be shorter the first month or so until students become acclimated to the expectations and routines of small group work.
2. *All Small Groups:* Students will use instant learning center kits. Teacher will choose the 2 focused on Ending Sound, Middle Sounds, Sound Sort, Story Sequencing, Sight Words & Simple Sentences. Teacher will MODEL/demonstrate how to use any of the new center kits if needed.

Writing Workshop: (10:45- 11:00)

1. *I do:* (6 mins max) The teacher will write the question words who, what, where, when, why on the board & have students identify the purpose of these words. Next explain that we have used these words to ask and answer questions about the books we read but we can also use them to ask and answer questions about each other.
2. *We/You do:* The teacher will distribute the writing paper with the question words pre-written on them. Next pair students up. Then have students think of and write down one question to ask their partner that begins with the question word. Promote inventive spelling. Allow students 7-10 mins for writing, depending on their needs.
3. Students should then share their questions with their partner and their partner should respond to answer the question. The teacher should circulate around to monitor list work and assist those who need it.
4. If time remains the gather students to share and then collect it.

Math: (11:00-11:30)

1. The teacher will show large flash cards with the numbers 1-50 on them and begin counting aloud. Encourage students to join in. Today we'll continue our focus on skip counting with money!
2. *I/We do:* The teacher will display a penny and have students identify the name of the coin & its value. Next display a nickel & have students identify that coin & its value as well as which skip counting pattern would be needed to count a set of nickels. Then display the dime & have students identify that coin & its value as well as which skip counting pattern would be needed to count a set of dimes.
3. Next, the teacher will have students sit in groups of 3 or 4 & will distribute a container/cups of each to each group of student & white lap board with eraser & marker to each student. On the board draw or display 7 dimes. Without naming the coin have students locate, take out and count the coins at their desk. The total value of coins should be written on the white boards. Observe students to see how this task is handled.
4. The teacher will call on a volunteer to share the total and orally explain how the value was found. Have a different scholar show how to write the number 70 on the board. Students should check their answer- both total and how the number is written.
5. Repeat the activity with dimes but have students take out 4 dimes this time. The teacher should be mindful that students are not using nickels accidentally instead of dimes (common error). Remind students to refer to the number line or 100 chart if their having challenges remembering how to write the number.
6. To build a connection with the outside world the teacher should display a bag of chips (with the projector or a picture or a real bag if available). Ask students to think about if they can buy this bag of chips that cost 50 cents with their 40 cents in front of them? Why or why not? Allow students a few seconds to process the questions before calling on students to respond. If needed the teacher should guide students to think about which number is larger or more than the other.
7. Have 2-3 students share their thoughts about the question. If no one answers correctly the teacher should display 5 dimes & explain that this is what is needed to buy this bag of chips. Then display 4 dimes and explain that this what you currently have- is it enough? Have a brief discussion and guide students to observe the importance of money & being able to count it to buy what we may need or want.
8. If time: have students take out and display 10 nickels. Repeat activity from step '5' with the nickels. Remind students to switch how they are skip counting.
9. *You do:* The teacher will distribute the "counting coin piggy's" pgs 2 & 3 (4 &5 if needed to challenge) to each group. Provide students with clear instructions that with a partner (groups can break into partners) they will use pennies to show the amount indicated on the piggy. The teacher should check the piggy before students switch or move on to a new piggy.
10. *Exit Ticket:* Teacher will distribute post-it or index cards say the 5 nickels aloud. Have students use the coins to find the value & write it on the post-it or card along with their name. Collect and go through noting down any students who did not get it correct.

Closing Activity: (11:30-11:45)
2. Gather students together for a closing activity game on the projector & computer. Choices include Reading Eggs (if accessible) or an ABC game on Starfall.com. Shapes Bingo is an option as well. Review the sight words we've done so far this year is another option (boys vs girls or any variation).

DEAR (Drop Everything And Read) (11:45-11:57)

Week 33 (9:00-12:00)

ELA Focus/Skill: Review Parts of a Story
Phonics (letter/word family): Plural "s" & short vowel review
Sound Words:
Sight Words: find, people
Big Book: Big book of choice- you are not reading but investing all the parts of a book
Writing Focus: Adjectives/Describing words- size, color, feel
Math Focus: Coin Identification & Value & Intro Quarter

Objectives: Students will be able to:
- repeat and identify the day, weather and season
- pluralize nouns by adding 's'
- sort and classify words short vowel words
- to identify and name the parts of a story
- to identify words that describe color, size & feel
- identify sight words & use in context
- identify and count individually sorted groups of coins (penny, nickel & dimes)
- identify the quarter and name its value

Materials:
"All About Today" pocket chart, A Variety of Big books, white lap boards, dry erase markers, board erasers, post-its, blank chart paper, "Plurals on a Farm" activity, 'short vowel activity pack' & "coin identification" (see appendix), chart paper with sight words pre-written, play doh, handwriting sheets with the sight words written twice (www.handwritingworksheets.com), Instant Learning Centers: Rhyming Sounds, Ending Sounds, Middle Sounds Building Words, Simple Sentences & Story Sequencing & for math: Making Tens, Counting, Shapes, Patterns, story writing paper, crayons, pencils, erasers, coin manipulative sorted by coin into cups or container, computer & projector, Shape Bingo or Chart Paper with old sight words on it for review

ELA
Whole Group: Morning Meeting/Shared Read: (9:00- 9:15)
1. Students will gather together for Morning Meeting where the teacher will model how to use the "All About Today" pocket chart. The teacher will read the information on the pocket chart, using a pointer, starting with the month, date and year using the sentence frame "Today is __." Next have the students repeat the sentence. After that the teacher will continue on with the pocket chart moving to "Yesterday was __." Students will repeat each section after the teacher has pointed and read it aloud. Then teacher will read aloud the objectives for the day, briefly explaining that this is what the goal is by the end of their time together (Use academic language). If extra time, have 1-2 students share something exciting or important news about themselves.
2. (9:15-9:45) *I do:* The teacher will display a minimum of 5 big books (all fiction). The teacher will ask students to list or name the parts of a story. The teacher should record student responses on the board under the label "Parts of a Story." Read back the list of responses back to scholars.
3. *We do:* The teacher will then display the blank chart paper and begin drawing the outline for a story map without the label but do write the title "story map" at the top. Once the drawing is completed ask students to help you label the sections

of the story map. Compare the sections they named to the list written on the board previously. Was there anything missed on either list?

4. Briefly review that all fiction stories have characters, a setting, a beginning, middle and end. The teacher should pick up one of the big books that are displayed & the students are familiar with the story: go through the big book story and have students point out/identify who the character(s) are in, the setting, what happened in the beginning, middle & end. Then have students identify where each of that information would go on the 'story map.' Guide students to make the connection that a story map is literally a map of a story- to help us find important locations/information about the story. One final review of the parts of a fiction story.

5. (5-7 mins max) Write the word "plural" on the board & say it aloud to the students. The teacher should ask students if anyone is familiar with the word? Assess for prior knowledge. Then the teacher should write the word cat on the board and ask students if I had to cat here how do I say to someone that I have two cat? What does the word sound like? Again the teacher should assess if any of the scholars know to add 's' to the word to make cats. If no one responds correctly continue by telling students "I have two cats." Explain that the word cat becomes cats.

6. Next the teacher should write 's' on the board and explain to students that *to show more than one of something like cat, we add the letter 's' to most words. And that is called pluralizing or the plural of the word cat is cats. Lets practice.* The teacher should write the word 'boy' on the board and ask students what would I do to the word boy to show that there are now three boy in the room? Students should respond that an 's' needs to be added to the word & then it is pronounced boys. Continue to practice with the words kids, book, chair, pencil, & girl. Then using the projector open the document "plurals on a farm" and have students practice reading the comparison sentences from pages 11-17 (pick & choose your sentences).

7. *You do:* Teacher will then provide clear instructions for students to match the picture to the words on the 'plurals to farm' activity (pgs 34-39) & pgs 28-33 if you are in need of some challenge work on pluralization.

11. Short Vowel Review station: Then the teacher will write the short vowels /a/, /e/, /i/, /o/, /u/ on the board. Have students identify each sound the vowels make & then name a word family for each vowel.

12. *You do:* Teacher will then break students up into 4 small groups: have one group complete pg 2 in the 'short vowels activity pack,' another group pg 3, pg 4 for another group, pg 5, & pg 6

8. *Exit Ticket:* The teacher will write the word family sit on the board and point to it. Have the student think of and write that word in plural form on index cards. At the count of 3 all the students should raise their cards up so that the teacher will collect them, scan the deck, note & record student responses.

Sight Words: (9:45-10:15)

1. Have students gather together. The teacher will display the chart paper with the sight words & sound word pre-written on it.

2. *I do:* Teacher will lead a call and response where the teacher will repeat the first word, a student name, while pointing to it and students will repeat it. Continue down the list one time.

3. Next repeat down the list but challenge students to move faster with the teacher still speaking the word first and students repeating clearly. Repeat once more but this time the students will say the words and the teacher will not lead.

4. *We do:* Play doh words- Teacher will distribute play doh to the students & have students practice spelling the sight words. Use the chart paper as reference. The teacher should check the spelling of each word before students move to the next word.
5. *You do:* Teacher will distribute handwriting practice sheets with the words written on them once- students will trace and then write the words at least twice.

Bathroom Break: (10:15-10:20)

Small Groups/Guided Reading: (10:20-10:45)

Small groups should not be larger than 5 students and smaller than 2.
1. Teacher MUST model and go over small group activities and protocols before you send students in groups! Students must work on the assigned task at their group! Students must ask their group questions first if unclear before asking teacher. Students must remain in their small group space unless they are getting another activity for their group or cleaning up. Bathroom, water, etc is not allowed during groups. Students must use whisper voice when talking in groups. Actual student group time will be shorter the first month or so until students become acclimated to the expectations and routines of small group work.
2. *All Small Groups:* Students will use instant learning center kits. Teacher will choose the 2 focused on Ending Sound, Middle Sounds, Sound Sort, Story Sequencing, Sight Words & Simple Sentences. Teacher will MODEL/demonstrate how to use any of the new center kits if needed.

Writing Workshop: (10:45- 11:00)
1. *I do:* (6 mins max) The teacher will write the words 'blue, orange, soft, tall, bumpy and short' on the board & read them aloud to the students. Ask students to identify what these words all have in common or how are they the same. Allow 2-3 students to share their responses. Looking for the answer that they are describing words.
2. The teacher will explain that *these are words are describing words & they help readers picture something better. For example, if I say "I see a cat." Then I will probably draw a cat (the teacher should draw a cat on the board). But what if I say "I see a fat cat." My picture is going to look a little different (draw a fat cat). Just because I added the word 'fat' then my picture changed.*
3. *We/You do:* The teacher will distribute the writing paper, pencil and crayons to students. The teacher will then write the sentence "that is a circle" & read it aloud to students. Have students echo read it back & then on their paper have students illustrate the sentence (draw a circle). Raise their papers up when finished. Next the teacher will re-write the sentence to say "that is a blue circle" & read it aloud to students. Again students will echo read it back and on their paper illustrate it (draw a circle & color it blue). Have students identify the difference between the two pictures & sentences. Allow 3-4 students to share.
4. The teacher should then split the class in two: one half of the class will write and illustrate the sentence: I see a dog. The second half of the class will write and illustrate the sentence: The sun is out. Allow students about 4-5 minutes to complete the task.
5. Then gather students together & have them share their pictures. Focus on the first sentence & ask students what size or color word could be added to the sentence to make it more interesting? Allow 3-4 students to respond & then everyone choose 1 word. The teacher should re-write the sentence with the new adjective & that group of students should re-write the sentence on the back of their paper & illustrate the new sentence.
6. Repeat for the second sentence.

7. If time remains the gather students to share and then collect it.

Math: (11:00-11:30)
1. The teacher will show large flash cards with the numbers 1-70 on them and begin counting aloud. Encourage students to join in. Today we'll continue our focus on skip counting with money!
2. *I/We do:* The teacher will display and review the names & values of the penny, nickel & dime. Then introduce the quarter. Display a picture of the quarter (either real or projected) for students to reference. The teacher should name the coin as a quarter and identify its value as 25 cents. Be sure to model to students how to write the 25 with the cent sign.
3. Next, the teacher will have students sit in groups of 3 or 4 & will distribute a container/cups of each coin to each group of student & white lap board with eraser & marker to each student. The teacher will tell the students to find a nickel & raise it up. On their board write the value of the nickel & raise their board up as well. The teacher will need to assess the students responses. Repeat with the penny, dime & quarter.
4. On the board draw or display 7 nickels. Without naming the coin have students locate, take out and count the coins at their desk. The total value of coins should be written on the white boards. Observe students to see how this task is handled.
5. The teacher will call on a volunteer to share the total and orally explain how the value was found. Have a different scholar show how to write the number 35 on the board. Students should check their answer- both total and how the number is written.
6. Repeat the activity with dimes but have students take out 4 nickels this time. The teacher should be mindful that students are not using nickels accidentally instead of dimes (common error). Remind students to refer to the number line or 100 chart if their having challenges remembering how to write the number.
7. If time: have students take out and display 1 quarter. Repeat activity from step '5' with the quarter. Remind students to switch how they are skip counting.
8. *You do:* The teacher will distribute the "coin identification" worksheet to students. Provide students with clear instructions that independently with the teacher reading aloud the directions- students will complete the activity sheet.
9. *Exit Ticket:* Teacher will distribute post-it or index cards say the 3 nickels aloud. Have students use the coins to find the value & write it on the post-it or card along with their name. Collect and go through noting down any students who did not get it correct.

Closing Activity: (11:30-11:45)
1. Gather students together for a closing activity game on the projector & computer. Choices include Reading Eggs (if accessible) or an ABC game on Starfall.com. Shapes Bingo is an option as well. Review the sight words we've done so far this year is another option (boys vs girls or any variation).

DEAR (Drop Everything And Read) (11:45-11:57)

Week 34 (9:00-12:00)

ELA Focus/Skill: End of Year Assessment
Phonics (letter/word family):
Sound Words:
Sight Words:
Big Book: Big book of choice-
Writing Focus:
Math Focus:

Objectives: Students will be able to:
- repeat and identify the day, weather and season
- assess on short vowel words & sounds
- assess sight words & use in context
- assess on number recognition & rote counting to 100

Materials:
"All About Today" pocket chart, A Variety of Big books, white lap boards, dry erase markers, board erasers, post-its, blank chart paper, chart paper with previous sight words written, handwriting sheets with the sight words written twice (www.handwritingworksheets.com), Instant Learning Centers: Rhyming Sounds, Ending Sounds, Middle Sounds Building Words, Simple Sentences & Story Sequencing & for <u>math</u>: Making Tens, Counting, Shapes, Patterns, story writing paper, crayons, pencils, erasers, computer & projector, Shape Bingo or Chart Paper with old sight words on it for review

ELA
Whole Group: Morning Meeting/Shared Read: (9:00- 9:15)
1. Students will gather together for Morning Meeting where the teacher will model how to use the "All About Today" pocket chart. The teacher will read the information on the pocket chart, using a pointer, starting with the month, date and year using the sentence frame "Today is __." Next have the students repeat the sentence. After that the teacher will continue on with the pocket chart moving to "Yesterday was __." Students will repeat each section after the teacher has pointed and read it aloud. Then teacher will read aloud the objectives for the day, briefly explaining that this is what the goal is by the end of their time together (Use academic language). If extra time, have 1-2 students share something exciting or important news about themselves.
2. (9:15-9:45) *I do:* The teacher will begin the end of the year assessment to determine student progress.
3. Students will work in groups on instant learning centers (no more than 3 per group): Beginning Sound, Ending Sound, Middle Sounds, Sound Sort, Story Sequencing, Sight Words, Syllable Count, Sound Switch & Simple Sentences

Sight Words: (9:45-10:15)
1. Have students gather together. The teacher will display the chart papers with the previous sight words pre-written on it.
2. *I do:* Teacher will point to a word & students will sound them aloud.
3. Next repeat down the lists but challenge students to move faster with the teacher still speaking the word first and students repeating clearly. Repeat once more but this time the students will say the words and the teacher will not lead.

4. *We do:* Play doh words- Teacher will distribute play doh to the students & have students practice spelling the sight words (minimum of 5). Use the chart paper as reference. The teacher should check the spelling of each word before students move to the next word.

Bathroom Break: (10:15-10:20)

Small Groups/Guided Reading: (10:20-10:45)

Small groups should not be larger than 5 students and smaller than 2.

1. Teacher MUST model and go over small group activities and protocols before you send students in groups! Students must work on the assigned task at their group! Students must ask their group questions first if unclear before asking teacher. Students must remain in their small group space unless they are getting another activity for their group or cleaning up. Bathroom, water, etc is not allowed during groups. Students must use whisper voice when talking in groups. Actual student group time will be shorter the first month or so until students become acclimated to the expectations and routines of small group work.
2. *All Small Groups:* Students will use instant learning center kits. Teacher will choose the 2 focused on Ending Sound, Middle Sounds, Sound Sort, Story Sequencing, Sight Words & Simple Sentences. Teacher will MODEL/demonstrate how to use any of the new center kits if needed.

Writing Workshop: (10:45- 11:00)

1. *I do:* (6 mins max) The teacher will write story writing paper and pencil to students. On the board the teacher will write the sentence frame: I wish to ___. & read it aloud to students.
2. Students will copy the sentence frame & then using the skills practiced throughout the program & inventive spelling; complete the frame with more than one sentence. An illustration must be included.
3. If time remains the gather students to share and then collect it.

Math: (11:00-11:30)

1. The teacher will show large flash cards with the numbers 1-90 on them and begin counting aloud. Encourage students to join in.
2. The teacher will administer the end of the year assessment.
3. Students will work on instant learning centers in groups of no more than 3: Counting, Making Ten, Shapes, Comparing Numbers & Patterning.

Closing Activity: (11:30-11:45)

1. Gather students together for a closing activity game on the projector & computer. Choices include Reading Eggs (if accessible) or an ABC game on Starfall.com. Shapes Bingo is an option as well. Review the sight words we've done so far this year is another option (boys vs girls or any variation).

DEAR (Drop Everything And Read) (11:45-11:57)

www.ingramcontent.com/pod-product-compliance
Lightning Source LLC
Chambersburg PA
CBHW060315240426
43661CB00059B/2771